Doing Justice, Doing Gender

Women and the
Criminal Justice System

Eve S. Buzawa, Series Editor
University of Massachusetts, Lowell

In this series . . .

DOING JUSTICE, DOING GENDER
by Susan Ehrlich Martin and Nancy C. Jurik

WOMEN AS OFFENDERS
by Meda Chesney-Lind

WOMEN AS VICTIMS
by Eve S. Buzawa

Doing Justice, Doing Gender

Susan Ehrlich Martin
Nancy C. Jurik

WOMEN AND THE CRIMINAL JUSTICE SYSTEM

SAGE Publications
International Educational and Professional Publisher
Thousand Oaks London New Delhi

For information address:

SAGE Publications, Inc.
2455 Teller Road
Thousand Oaks, California 91320
E-mail: order@sagepub.com

SAGE Publications Ltd.
6 Bonhill Street
London EC2A 4PU
United Kingdom

SAGE Publications India Pvt. Ltd.
M-32 Market
Greater Kailash I
New Delhi 110 048 India

Printed in the United States of America

Library of Congress Cataloging-in-Publication Data

Martin, Susan Ehrlich.
  Doing justice, doing gender / authors, Susan Ehrlich Martin,
Nancy C. Jurik.
    p. cm. — (Women and the criminal justice system ; v. 1)
  Includes bibliographical references and index.
  ISBN 0-8039-5197-3 (acid-free paper). — ISBN 0-8039-5198-1
(pbk. : acid-free paper)
  1. Sex discrimination in criminal justice administration—
United States. 2. Policewomen—United States.
  3. Women correctional personnel—United States. 4. Women lawyers—
United States. I. Jurik, Nancy C. II. Title. III. Series.
  HV9950.M3 1996
  364'.082—dc20   95-41817

96 97 98 99 10 9 8 7 6 5 4 3 2 1

This book is printed on acid-free paper.

Sage Typesetter: Danielle Dillahunt

Contents

List of Tables

Acknowledgments

This book is the outcome of the equal collaboration of the authors. We are indebted to the work of Candace West and Don Zimmerman (1987) for inspiring the "doing gender" portion of our title, as well as for their part, and that of their coauthor Sarah Fenstermaker, in informing the conceptual framework used in our book. The work of Joan Acker, James Messerschmidt, Robert Connell, and Iris Young also was important in developing our approach to the material.

Our efforts would not have been possible without the initiative of Eve Buzawa, the Sage series editor, and Sage editor Terry Hendrix. We also wish to thank Sage's three reviewers, Peter K. Manning, Donna Hale, and an anonymous individual. They plowed through a significantly longer earlier draft of the manuscript and made numerous constructive suggestions for focusing and tightening our work.

In addition, several colleagues shared their ideas, criticisms, and editorial suggestions and provided much support and encouragement. James Messerschmidt read and commented on the entire manuscript. Candace West, Marjorie Zatz, Sam Walker, Natalie Sokoloff, Julie Cowgill, Jane Aiken, Phoebe Stambaugh, John Hepburn, Susan Miller, and Nancy Hogan read and gave many helpful comments on specific chapters. Gray Cavender reviewed and edited numerous chapters and helped develop solutions to several intellectual problems that arose in the writing process. Malcolm Martin provided strong support from initiation to completion of the undertaking.

Susan Martin dedicates this book to the late
Muriel Cantor, her intellectual guide and "mother."

Nancy Jurik dedicates this book to her mother,
Carolyn Nekuza Jurik.

1

Introduction

Changes in Criminal Justice Organizations, Occupations, and Women's Work

Before 1972, the number of women employed in the justice system as police officers, lawyers, judges, and correctional officers (COs) was minuscule; those women were excluded from most jobs that entailed the exercise of authority over men. Women worked only as "specialists," drawing on qualities and skills associated with their gender. Policewomen supervised women arrestees and dealt with women, children, and typewriters (Milton, 1972). Women probation and parole officers usually supervised women and juvenile offenders. Women lawyers were concentrated in specialties deemed appropriate for women, such as domestic relations; they rarely litigated cases and were virtually excluded from the judiciary. Women COs worked in prisons for women or in juvenile institutions, where their capacity for "mothering" was considered beneficial for rehabilitating delinquent youth (Morton, 1992).

As part of a larger societal trend in which women have entered occupations traditionally held by men, a growing number of women

1

now work in all parts of the justice system. In the criminal justice system (CJS), large police agencies hire women as patrol officers, and probation and parole departments assign mixed-gender caseloads to women (Martin, 1980; Schoonmaker & Brooks, 1975). Most state prison systems and the Federal Bureau of Prisons hire women to guard men inmates (Morton, 1991b). Women lawyers handle civil and criminal cases as private or government attorneys and, to a limited extent, serve as judges and magistrates (Curran, 1986). As professors in law schools and departments of criminal justice, criminology, and sociology, women also make up a growing proportion of academicians who educate CJS personnel.

Despite progress, the resistance to women in justice agencies has been zealous, and they have not been completely integrated into the station house, courtroom, or prison. What appears to be an open door to occupations dominated by men is actually a revolving door: More women enter than in the past, but many of them quickly exit (Jacobs, 1989). Those who remain encounter obstacles that limit their advancement opportunities and confine them to gender-stereotyped tasks.

The obstacles faced by women justice workers are part of larger organizational and social patterns that construct and support women's subordination to men. Women in fields numerically dominated by men face many barriers: exclusion from informal work cultures, hostility expressed at the interactional level, organizational policies that promote gender segregation, differential assignments, and sexual harassment. The confluence of these barriers produces lower pay and slower advancement for women in these fields.

Resistance to women may be associated with the social control functions of justice occupations. Criminologist Frances Heidensohn (1992) has argued that social control is a "profoundly gender-linked concept" (p. 99). Women have always helped to maintain social order; initially, this was accomplished only informally, in the family. Later, women were given institutional authority over children and other women, but they had to operate within control systems dominated by men. They rarely were granted formal authority over men: "The view that men 'own' order and have sole rights to preserve it seems to be at the core of much of the equality debates" (Heidensohn, 1992, p. 215).

This book examines the organization of justice occupations along gender lines. In examining these fields, we must remember that an occupation is more than a set of tasks or the source of a paycheck. It provides social and emotional rewards and affects many aspects of life and identity. One's occupation affects the manner in which a person is treated by others, even outside of work. It defines social status and shapes income, lifestyle, and children's life chances. In industrial societies, what one does is a primary source of who one is (Hall, 1994, pp. 6-9).

We examine the justice system occupations of policing, law, and corrections. We focus broadly on the field of law, both civil and criminal, and more narrowly on municipal policing and correctional security in men's prisons. Our choices reflect both the limited literature available on other aspects of justice work and the intense gender-based resistance to women who enter these three fields.[1] This book addresses the following questions:

1. Historically, what have been the roles of women working in the justice system?
2. How and why have women's assignments and contributions expanded over the past 20 years?
3. What barriers have women in justice occupations encountered at the interpersonal, organizational, occupational, and societal levels?
4. How have women performed in their expanded duties, and how have they responded to workplace barriers?
5. What effects have women had on the justice system, victims, offenders, coworkers, and the public?

The answers to these questions combine three divergent areas of inquiry: the changing justice system, work and occupations, and gender studies, particularly how gender differences are constructed, maintained, challenged, and reconstructed.

The gender division of labor in the justice system is part of larger ongoing processes of differentiation in society. Social differentiation, or the practice of distinguishing categories based on some attribute or set of attributes, is a fundamental social process and the basis for differential evaluations and unequal rewards. Differentiation assumes, magnifies, and even creates behavioral and psychological differences to ensure that the subordinate group differs from the dominant one. It presumes that differences are "natural" and desirable. Social differentiation based on gender is found in virtually every society (West & Zimmerman, 1987).

The next section of this chapter provides a brief overview of the CJS mission. It is followed by discussions of the history of women in justice occupations and of socioeconomic conditions that led to expanding opportunities for women workers.

The CJS:
Mission, Processes, and Workforce

The mission of the CJS is to control conduct that violates the criminal laws of the state. The components of the CJS include law enforcement, courts, and corrections; they are responsible for the prevention and detection of crime and the apprehension, adjudication, sentencing, punishment, and rehabilitation of criminals.

The CJS components have separate tasks but are linked in the processing of criminal offenders. In actual operation, the coordination across agencies often is lacking. CJS agencies are characterized by internal and interorganizational conflicts over goals, resources, and authority that are complicated because these agencies work at different levels of government and often have overlapping jurisdictions.

The CJS in the United States is large and costly. In 1990, its total expenditures were more than $74 billion, about half of which was spent on salaries for more than 1.7 million employees. More than 800,000 persons (or about 46% of CJS employees) work for law enforcement agencies, mostly in 17,000 local police and sheriff's departments. Some 20% of CJS employees work for local, state, and federal courts. This includes about 225,000 judicial employees, most of whom work in local courts, more than 100,000 people who work for prosecution and legal services, and 15,000 in public defenders' offices (Maguire, Pastore, & Flanagan, 1993).

Corrections has several subsystems: local jails; state and federal prisons; community corrections including probation, parole, and community residential centers; and juvenile corrections. These agencies employ about 550,000 people, including about 300,000 workers in prisons and jails (Maguire et al., 1993).

Since 1970, there has been an enormous increase in CJS expenditures and personnel. Between 1971 and 1990, total expenditures grew 606%. This figure includes increases of 416% for police, 737% for judicial-legal services, and 990% for corrections (Maguire et al., 1993).

Historical Context of
Women in Justice Occupations

The ratio of men to women in occupations, in the justice system and elsewhere, is seldom static. Internal pressures within work organizations and in larger social and economic arenas produce changes. To understand women's situation, we must consider their CJS work history and changes in the CJS mission.

Throughout the 19th century, U.S. justice and crime control were inefficient and corrupt; reforms were sporadic and ineffectual. In both the United States and the United Kingdom, women entered the public sector through participation in moral improvement campaigns to end slavery, adopt prohibition, and establish social welfare institutions such as the juvenile court. Women's efforts addressed economic deprivation and men's moral depravity as the causes of "fallen women." Reformers attacked public indifference to the poor and to moral double standards for men and women. By caring for fallen women, they hoped to bring about a moral reordering of society (Heidensohn, 1992).

At first, women worked as volunteers in social services. However, as they succeeded in getting the state to assist and extend social control over the poor, many women sought formal positions in public institutions. They presented themselves as specialists to work with women and children (Rafter, 1990). They argued for police matrons to "save wayward youth and helpless women from the evils of industrialism, alcohol, and other abuses" (Martin, 1980, p. 22). They demanded the hiring of prison matrons to work with incarcerated women and children in facilities separate from men's prisons (Freedman, 1981).

In their efforts to protect women from men and from their own worst instincts, reformers became part of social control systems dominated by men. Ironically, as reformers tried to curb vice and crime, they simultaneously participated in the oppressive protection of their own sex, especially regarding impoverished or working-class women and girls (Odem & Schlossman, 1991). Although they carved out new forms of women's work, early CJS professionals reinforced gender stereotypes that limited women's career possibilities.

Early in the 20th century, immigration, urban migration, the failure of Prohibition, and the rise of organized crime compounded CJS problems and made periodic reform efforts short-lived. In 1931, the National Commission on Law Observance and Enforcement (the Wickersham Commission) detailed the crime problem and shortcomings of the U.S. justice system. The reforms suggested by the commission were impeded by the Depression and World War II. During this period, women's CJS work opportunities stagnated. From the 1930s to the 1970s, women's numbers diminished, and restrictions on their duties continued.

Economic prosperity after World War II obscured the seeds of disaffection and rebellion that exploded in the 1960s and 1970s. Precipitating conditions included the middle-class exodus to the suburbs, cultural values focused on consumption, deteriorating inner cities, rising urban crime rates, political corruption, racism, poverty, and gender subordination (Friedan, 1963; Miller & Nowak, 1977). These social tensions converged with CJS problems that had been ignored since the 1920s. The result was a turbulent decade that included the civil rights and antiwar movements, urban riots, political assassinations, the women's movement, and lesbian and gay rights movements.

A second wave of feminism was stimulated by women's participation in civil rights and antiwar activities; women were denied leadership positions in those movements (Freeman, 1989; Ryan, 1992).[2] Once set in motion, the women's movement created a dynamic pattern in which legal changes altered social attitudes and led to further demands for change.

The women's movement was fueled by increases in women's education and their massive entry into paid work, increases that were largely unnoticed in the 1950s and 1960s. These changes stimulated middle-class women's frustration with the "feminine mystique" (Friedan, 1963) and contributed to the formation of groups such as the National Organization for Women (NOW). NOW supported the anti-sex-discrimination provisions of the 1964 Civil Rights Act and Equal Pay Act of 1963, the Equal Rights Amendment (ERA), and the expansion of abortion rights (Cott, 1987).

Much of the energy of the women's movement was dissipated by the mid-1970s because of factionalism and the unsuccessful battle over the ERA. Nevertheless, feminism was taken more seriously after congressional passage of the ERA and the 1973 Supreme Court decision in *Roe v. Wade*, which made abortion a legal option for women. Feminist goals, such as women's rights to paid employment, to equal pay for equal work, and to jobs in all occupations without limitations imposed by sex discrimination, became more socially accepted. As the movement matured during the 1980s, it overcame factionalism and sharpened its focus (Ryan, 1992). Despite social acceptance of these goals and passage of legislation supporting them, their implementation has been slow.

The social activism of the civil rights and women's movements, as well as other other social change efforts, stimulated a variety of changes in the legal system and in the CJS. These changes converged with changing economic conditions to increase the demand for women workers in justice occupations.

Legal Changes

During the 1960s and 1970s, legislation extended civil rights and equal employment opportunities to formerly excluded social groups, including women. Interpretation of these laws by courts has shaped both the implementation and effectiveness of this legislation in three areas critical to working women: equal employment opportunity, sexual harassment, and the treatment of pregnancy and maternity leave.

Equal employment opportunity law rests on Title VII of the Civil Rights Act of 1964 and the Equal Employment Opportunity (EEO) Act of 1972, which expanded coverage of Title VII to most private and public employers, including state and local governments. Title VII prohibits discrimination on the basis of race, religion, creed, color, sex, or national origin with regard to hiring, compensation, terms, conditions, and privileges of employment. Employers may not segregate, classify, or refuse to hire employees so as to deprive them of employment opportunities because of sex. An exception is permitted only if it can be proven that sex is "a *bona fide* occupational qualification (BFOQ) reasonably necessary for the normal operation of that particular business or enterprise" (Civil Rights Act of 1964, § 2000e[2][e]). This interpretation is warranted only "where it is necessary for the purpose of authenticity or genuineness," such as in hiring an actor or actress (Civil Rights Act of 1964, § 2000e[2][e]). The law prohibits an employer from refusing to hire a woman because of assumptions about the comparative employment characteristics of women in general (e.g., they are not as strong as men) or because of gender stereotypes (e.g., that women are less capable of aggressive salesmanship), or because of the preferences of coworkers, employers, clients, or customers (Equal Employment Opportunity Commision) [EEOC] Guidelines on Discrimination Because of Sex § 1604.2). Title VII also established the Equal Employment Opportunity Commission to enforce its provisions.

In the early 1970s, several cases challenged sex-based classifications that had limited women's work opportunities. In *Griggs v. Duke Power Co.* (1971), the U.S. Supreme Court made it easier to win discrimination cases by ruling that the plaintiff does not have to prove that the employer intended to discriminate. Once a plaintiff shows that job qualifications disproportionately exclude a group or class, the burden falls on the employer to prove that the requirements are BFOQs and that no other selection mechanisms can be substituted. Application of this standard (i.e., discriminatory impact regardless of intent) invalidated minimum height and weight requirements that had excluded women from police and corrections work.

However, courts permitted exceptions. In *Dothard v. Rawlinson* (1977), the Court agreed that height and weight requirements for COs in Alabama's maximum security prisons violated Title VII, but it still ruled that the ban on women working in contact positions was justifiable given the "jungle-like" atmosphere that made these prisons unsafe for women.

During the 1970s, courts and the EEOC gradually interpreted *Griggs* as requiring employers to establish equal employment opportunity (EEO) plans, such as numerical goals for the hiring and promotion of protected race and sex groups. In the 1980s, the Court limited affirmative action programs and narrowed the grounds on which plaintiffs could win discrimination suits, but many employers have continued to implement affirmative action policies.

Sexual harassment is another important legal issue affecting working women. Sexual harassment, a term that came into use in 1976 (MacKinnon, 1978), is recognized as a form of sex discrimination prohibited under Title VII of the Civil Rights Act of 1964. Two general types of sexual harassment have been addressed by the courts: *quid pro quo* and the hostile work environment. Quid pro quo harassment involves an explicit exchange: There is a sexual advance or proposition with which the woman must comply or forfeit an employment or educational benefit. Hostile environment sexual harassment does not necessarily involve sexual demands. This type of harassment creates a hostile environment as a condition of work. It includes a variety of overtly sexual behaviors such as touching, teasing, and making comments about a woman's appearance or sexuality, behaviors that require no response on the woman's part but make her work environment unpleasant or hostile.

The courts first recognized hostile environment harassment in *Bundy v. Jackson* (1981), a case involving a woman prison counselor. Bundy claimed that she had been harassed by several supervisors and that her rejection of their overtures had blocked and delayed her job advancement. The court reasoned that whether or not the complaining employee lost tangible benefits (i.e., quid pro quo harassment), the employer had condoned a hostile and discriminatory work environment that violated Title VII. Unless employers are prohibited from maintaining a "discriminatory environment," a woman employee could be sexually harassed with impunity as long as the action stopped short of firing or taking other formal action against her if she resisted.

In *Meritor Savings Bank FSB v. Vinson* (1986), the U.S. Supreme Court unanimously affirmed that both quid pro quo and hostile environment sexual harassment are prohibited by Title VII. It held that in hostile environment cases, the victim does not necessarily have to demonstrate economic harm, but for sexual harassment to be actionable, it must be so severe or pervasive that it alters the conditions of the victim's employment.[3]

In *Harris v. Forklift Systems, Inc.* (1993), the Court clarified this standard, ruling that for a work environment to be abusive, the harassing conduct does not have to "seriously affect [an employee's] psychological well being" or cause her to "suffer injury" (S.C. 92-1168, p. 4) The Court adopted what it termed "a middle path" between conduct that is "merely offensive" and that which causes psychological injury. Determination of what is sufficiently severe and pervasive to be actionable is based on the totality of the circumstances and depends on such factors as its frequency, severity, and whether it physically threatens or humiliates or unreasonably interferes with the employee's work.

Another area of law that affects women workers is maternity leave. In two decisions, *Geduldig v. Aiello* (1974) and *General Electric Company v. Gilbert* (1976), the U.S. Supreme Court held that exclusion of pregnancy-related disabilities from an insurance plan was not sex discrimination. When existing benefits or opportunities are offered equally to men and women, it is not discrimination to withhold additional benefits that might be particularly valuable to one sex, the Court said.

In 1978, Congress rejected the Court's view and amended Title VII with the Pregnancy Discrimination Act (PDA). The PDA prohibits discrimination on the basis of pregnancy, childbirth, or related medical conditions; it requires employers who provide employment benefits to treat pregnancy like any other temporary disability. The law assures women of at least the same minimum benefits offered men; it permits but does not require an employer to provide additional protection for pregnant workers.

Reforms and Expanding Opportunities for Women

As civil rights law and related court interpretations opened many educational and employment opportunities previously closed to people of color and white women, the CJS was expanding and facing pressures to reform. During the 1960s, discontent with the CJS and its inability to respond to growing urban problems led to an emphasis on "law and order." This was a shorthand expression for a general fear not only of street crime, but of the violence and demonstrations surrounding civil rights and antiwar activities. In 1965, President Johnson expanded the federal government's role in criminal justice processes. He appointed the President's Commission on Law Enforcement and the Administration of Justice (also called the President's Crime Commission) to analyze the nature and origins of crime in the United States and to make policy recommendations. The commission recommended that criminal justice agencies be shaped to form an integrated "system," with better coordination among police, courts, and corrections. It called for upgrading CJS personnel by recruiting white women and people of color, widening women's assignments, raising selection standards, and providing more rigorous training to all system personnel.

To implement these recommendations, Congress passed the Omnibus Crime Control and Safe Streets Act of 1968. The act created the Law Enforcement Assistance Administration (LEAA), which supplied funds to states for criminal justice planning, innovative programs, and personnel training.

LEAA funds and higher educational qualifications expanded community college and university programs in criminology and criminal justice in the 1970s. This program growth, combined with EEO regulations, generated increasing numbers of women graduates from associate's and bachelor's degree programs in criminal justice and related fields. These trends produced a growing pool of white women and people of color to fill CJS demands for more highly educated workers.

Many women earned graduate degrees and have become the researchers and professors who educate future CJS practitioners (Pearson et al., 1980). The majority of graduate students in criminology and criminal justice, as well as sociology and related fields, are now women (Roos & Jones, 1993). Social activism also contributed to the creation of new law schools and their burgeoning enrollments. Breakdowns in gender barriers surrounding legal education facilitated a shift in law school enrollments so that women now make up a majority of the students in a number of law schools and a growing proportion of lawyers working in the CJS.

Feminist academicians have directed more attention to gender and racial equality and ethical issues in the CJS (Daly & Chesney-Lind, 1988). They have affected law school curricula and challenged accepted legal canon across a range of legal specialties (Frug, 1992).

As further impetus for expansion and reform, prison riots during the 1970s and 1980s forced federal and state officials to address crowded and squalid living conditions in prisons, racial tensions, and inmates' rights issues. These riots occurred in a context of expanding legal services for the poor and growing civil rights for racial and ethnic minority groups, who were disproportionately incarcerated (Hawkins & Alpert, 1989). Court-ordered racial integration of prisons heightened tensions in overcrowded facilities (Irwin, 1980). Courts intervened to protect inmates' constitutional rights. Commissions formed to deal with the prison-riot crisis recommended solutions similar to those of the President's Crime Commission: increased rationalization, centralization, and staff professionalization (Jurik & Musheno, 1986; Task Force on Corrections, 1973).

These factors alone might not have been sufficient to create more CJS jobs for women had it not been for the 1973 Crime Control Act, which amended the 1968 Omnibus Crime Control and Safe Streets Act. It prohibited discrimination against women in the employment practices of any agencies that received LEAA funds. LEAA Equal Employment Opportunity guidelines required agencies to assess their recruiting and hiring practices, analyze promotion and training procedures, formulate an equal employment opportunity program, and file it with the state planning agency through which most of their funds were disbursed. Other guidelines prohibited hiring standards (e.g., minimum-height requirements) that discriminated against women and were not associated with successful police job performance. LEAA threatened to withhold payments to grant recipients who failed to comply with these regulations. Loss of LEAA monies was a serious threat to law enforcement agencies (Feinman, 1986). Gradual enforcement of the EEOC guidelines caused a ripple effect throughout the CJS, so that by the late 1970s, departments had begun to hire more white women and people of color (U.S. Department of Justice, 1981; Walker, 1985).

The shift to law and order and a tougher approach to crime during the 1970s led to further CJS expansion. Ronald Reagan's election to the presidency in 1980 accelerated the political shift to the right that had begun in the 1970s. Conservative laws and judicial interpretations eroded defendants' rights and moved the nation toward more severe punishment for criminals. Together with the War on Drugs, these trends prompted increases in the number of people arrested, tried, convicted, and incarcerated, stimulating further increases in the demand for CJS personnel.

Demographic factors in the 1970s and 1980s led to a shortage of qualified white men willing to work for CJS wages. EEO legislation and the extension of higher education opportunities to white women and people of color provided new pools of college and law school graduates to fill these gaps.

Economic recession and industrial restructuring in the 1970s and 1980s strained middle- and working-class families, forcing many married women, including those with young children, into the paid workforce. Rising divorce rates increased the number of single mothers in search of jobs that paid decent wages. These conditions, along with increased educational opportunities, produced a labor pool of high school- and college-educated women available for the growing number of CJS jobs (Jurik, 1985).

Women and Justice
Professionalization/Deprofessionalization

Changes in justice occupations have important implications for the acceptance of or resistance to women. Reform, professionalization, and deprofessionalization processes affect the integration, barriers, and advancement of women in policing, law, and corrections.

In our society, some occupations are accepted as professions (e.g., lawyers, doctors); others want to be so regarded (e.g., police, librarians). Definitions of *profession* vary, but the recognition of any occupation as a profession depends on the power of its members to persuade lawmakers and the public that they are a profession (Hall, 1994, pp. 44-53) and deserve that status. Often, a group seeks such recognition to gain the higher salaries, greater social standing, and increased autonomy associated with the label (Seron & Ferris, 1995).[4]

In the past three decades, police and corrections administrators have tried to professionalize personnel, primarily by raising training and educational requirements. Their efforts were inspired by chief administrators' desire to protect their agencies from external control and to enhance their power in governmental lobbying. CJS line staff have neither initiated nor been primary beneficiaries of increased professionalism (Jurik & Musheno, 1986). In fact, most professionalization programs have done little to enhance the autonomy or control of line staff over their jobs. Correctional administrators actually sought greater control over line officers, and COs continue to be ranked among the lowest-status occupations (Zimmer, 1986).

In contrast, law, which has traditionally been seen as a model profession, appears to be deprofessionalizing. The proportion of lawyers in solo practice has dropped, and the proportion of salaried employees in large firms and other organizations has increased (Curran, 1986). Such trends hold for many lawyers working in the CJS, including public defenders and prosecutors, who work in large bureaucratic organizations. Work in large organizations is accompanied by a significant loss of autonomy. Lawyers are also now a steady target of increasing public attempts to regulate their behavior (Rothman, 1984).

These changes make it useful to treat the three occupations discussed in this book as being arrayed along a continuum of professionalization. We then compare the extent to which each occupational group and the individuals within it meet professional characteristics or criteria.

Justice system reform and professionalization efforts have important implications for women working in the system. Attempts to transform CJS agencies into rational, efficient, bureaucratic organizations challenged informal, particularistic, and arbitrary practices and instead mandated universal rules that can be applied evenhandedly in all situations.

Changes in CJS personnel practices, combined with EEO regulations, challenged arbitrary and culturally biased personnel practices, such as selection criteria and assignments based on friendship or on attributes unrelated to job performance. Administrators' control over officers' personal lives, from hair length to living arrangements, has been increasingly challenged by a new generation of officers. Universalistic standards have produced more opportunities for people with particular skills, regardless of how well they "fit" into the informal group, and thus have created more heterogeneous CJS staffs. Heterogeneity has facilitated the acceptance of women and men of color and white women who meet established, formal hiring criteria.

CJS reforms also challenged the arbitrary use of force in policing and corrections. Detailed rules were written to govern the use of force by professionalized police and correctional officers, making it a means of last resort. The well-trained professional officer relies on interpersonal skills, exercises restraint, and does not rely on brute force. Because women are not generally associated with or reliant on physical strength to attain their ends, this attempt to undermine the centrality of force in police and corrections served to bolster the position of women workers (Britton, 1995).

Bureaucratization and professionalization of policing and corrections did not end the salience of force or the discrimination against white women and people of color in the CJS. However, these trends contributed to an ethos that was more conducive to the inclusion and advancement of these groups. Many reform advocates hoped that professionalization would promote gender neutrality, fairness, efficiency, and respect for the CJS and its workers. Despite significant improvements, problems remain. Because efforts to professionalize police and corrections often were aimed at individuals rather than at organizations, they often have worsened rather than improved the working environment (Marquart & Crouch, 1985).

Other factors have undermined CJS reform efforts and the integration of women into justice occupations. These include high rates of unemployment and underemployment, decreases in spending for social services, and public demands for law and order. Together these factors have increased social unrest and arrest rates, particularly for drug offenses. They also have overcrowded courts and correctional systems and overwhelmed the CJS reform agenda, especially efforts to decrease the emphasis on physical force among line staff (Jurik & Musheno, 1986; Marquart & Crouch, 1985). Thus, to the disadvantage of women workers, force continues to be a salient feature of work in the CJS.

Finally, the image of professionalized police and correctional officers may not so easily benefit women. Images of the professional are linked closely with images of masculinity, such as objectivity and universalism in making decisions; women are viewed as too emotional and attached to others to make impartial judgements.

In sum, this book examines the organization of justice occupations along gender lines. Women entered justice fields as reformers and then assumed the role of specialists who worked with women and children. As a result of the social activism of the 1960s, the CJS and women's roles in it changed dramatically.

Growing public fear of crime and changing economic conditions have increased demands for CJS workers and created new opportunities for white women and persons of color. These groups changed the gender and race-ethnic ratios of justice occupations. However, as we will see in the following chapters, barriers remain, and seemingly gender-neutral organizational dynamics differentiate and subordinate women who work in these fields.

Contents of This Book

The following chapters provide a conceptual framework for understanding gender differentiation in the workplace, look more closely at women's experiences and contributions in our three focal justice occupations, and then synthesize themes across these occupations. Chapter 2 begins with a review of alternative perspectives on the barriers to women in occupations traditionally held by men. It elaborates our framework for examining the social production of gender differences and subordination of women in policing, law, and corrections work. Chapters 3 through 8 form the heart of our analysis. We divide the discussion of each occupation into two chapters. Policing is discussed in Chapters in 3 and 4; law in Chapters 5 and 6; and corrections in Chapters 7 and 8. For each occupation, the initial chapter deals with the historical and contemporary situation of women and the barriers that women face in everyday work situations. The second chapter for each occupation connects these everyday barriers to their larger organizational and societal milieu. Chapter 9 integrates these issues by comparing barriers, problems, and achievements of women across justice occupations. It examines women's effects on the occupation, work organization, and clients by addressing the question, Do women make a difference?

The analysis illuminates the gendering of justice organizations and occupations. It demonstrates that these jobs are not gender-neutral, empty positions waiting to be filled by the best qualified candidate (Acker, 1990). It reveals how these work organizations operate according to ideologies, customs, and practices that produce and reproduce gender inequality (P. Martin, 1991, p. 208). Labor markets, occupations, organizational hierarchies, supervisory practices, procedures for hiring and advancement, work groups, and work activities—all are infused with gendered images and consequences.

A Note on Perspective and Terminology

Recent scholarship about gender and racial equality has criticized traditional social science notions of objectivity and universality, claiming that what one writes or chooses to study is influenced by the writer's social location. Critics assert that claims of objective knowledge are based on an elite, white, heterosexual, Eurocentric, man-centered perspective (e.g., P. Collins, 1991; Smith, 1979). The critics suggest that writers identify themselves in terms of gender, race, sexual orientation, social class, and any other relevant biographical information to enable readers to better evaluate the truth claims attached to the knowledge that is being presented (P. Collins, 1991).

With this in mind, we state that both authors are white, heterosexual, and middle class. Susan Ehrlich Martin grew up in suburbia and has lived with her husband in the Washington, D.C., area for 30 years. Nancy C. Jurik was raised on a small farm in the southwestern United States during the 1950s and 1960s and now lives in the Phoenix area.

Our book follows a feminist approach: It places women at the center of inquiry in building a base of knowledge and an understanding of gender as a feature of all aspects of human culture and relationships (Stacey & Thorne, 1985, p. 305). Feminism is not treated as a single theory; it embraces a worldview and movement for social change; it includes a diverse set of perspectives identifying and representing women's interests; it holds distinct agendas for ending women's oppression.

One aspect of our feminist commitment is to avoid sexism and racism in language. This is no easy matter; it has resulted in phrases that sound awkward because they do not conform to customary language usage (e.g., men-dominated occupations).

Historically, the term *sex* referred to biological categories of individuals—men or women—determined by hormones, anatomy, and physiology. Since the 1960s, the term *gender* has come to refer to the aspect of human identity that is socially learned—masculinity or femininity. With the gradual recognition that biological and cultural processes are more interrelated than previously assumed, conceptualizations of sex or gender as unchanging attributes of individuals have yielded to recognition of the importance of interaction in constructing each. We follow the usage and definitions of Candace West and Don Zimmerman (1987), who distinguish among three separate concepts: sex, sex category, and gender. Sex is the application of socially agreed on biological criteria for classifying people as men or women, usually based on chromosomal typing or genitalia. In everyday life, people are placed or proclaim their membership in a sex category based upon visible indicators such as clothing and hair style. Gender refers not simply to what one *is* but also to something one *does* or enacts on an ongoing basis. Hence, the book's title includes the phrase "doing gender," which will be more fully explained in Chapter 2 (West & Zimmerman, 1987).

We use the terms *women of color, men of color,* or *people of color* to refer collectively to racial-ethnic groups that are not of white European origin. The terms *African American* and *black* are used interchangeably to refer to Americans with African heritage. In the absence of more detailed racial-ethnic breakdowns, the undifferentiated term *Hispanic* refers to individuals who are of Puerto Rican, Mexican American, or other Latin American heritage. For the same reasons, the undifferentiated terms *Asian Americans* and *American Indians* are employed.

Despite our determination to present data addressing both gender and race-ethnicity, this was often impossible because data on CJS workers rarely are compiled along both gender and racial-ethnic lines, and there are very limited data about variations in the CJS work experiences of women from different racial-ethnic groups.

Even when race-gender breakdowns exist, they often are grouped into distinctions of "white" and the undifferentiated category, "nonwhite." Nevertheless, whenever possible, we describe the experiences of women justice workers from various racial-ethnic groups. Likewise, the presumption of heterosexuality has led to the virtual absence of data detailing lesbian perspectives; we discuss the ways in which this presumption is used to control women justice workers.

Notes

1. We would have liked to focus on women's activities in the practice of criminal law. Apart from several studies comparing sentencing by men and women judges, there simply are no studies available on women in criminal law per se. The activities of Los Angeles County prosecutor Marcia Clark in the O. J. Simpson trial may inspire research on women prosecutors.

2. The "first wave" of feminism emerged in the late 1800s and ended with women's suffrage in 1920 (see Freeman, 1989).

3. According to the facts presented, the plaintiff, Michelle Vinson, had acquiesced to sexual relations with her immediate superior out of fear of losing her job, but she neither reported the problem nor used the bank's complaint procedure. The alleged harasser denied all allegations of sexual misbehavior; the bank claimed that, because it did not know of the situation, it could not be held responsible.

4. Most definitions of *profession* include (a) a theoretical body of knowledge based on lengthy study and not possessed by outsiders; (b) formal organization of members; (c) occupational self-regulation through control of recruitment and training, and performance standards based on a code of ethics; (d) a service orientation toward clients and the community; and (e) a distinctive occupational culture (Trice, 1993). Seron and Ferris (1995) emphasize autonomy or authority to control their work as the key element.

2
☐

Explanations for Gender Inequality in the Workplace

The history of women's work needs to be retold . . . as part of the story of the creation of a gendered workforce. In the 19th century, . . . certain conceptualizations of male skill rested on a contrast with female labor (by definition unskilled).

Scott, 1990, p. 144

The subordination of women in justice occupations reflects larger inequalities that permeate social life. Jobs and tasks are assigned according to the worker's sex category. Women's paid work is usually accompanied by lower levels of income and status than men's. The segregation of occupations according to sex category and the devaluing of women's work explain much of the wage differential between men and women (Reskin & Roos, 1990).

Paid work is also divided along lines of race and class. In the Western world, whites tend to hold better paying and higher status jobs (Amott & Matthaei, 1991). More advantaged socioeconomic groups gain access to more desirable jobs. Social relations of race, class, and gender converge to shape the nature and distribution of work. Historically, African American women have performed low-

paid domestic work, and elite white men have headed major institutions (Amott & Matthaei, 1991).

When women enter occupations numerically dominated by men,
they have encountered much resistance from clients, coworkers,
and supervisors. The women who remain in these occupations
often are restricted to assignments and tasks designated for women.

Gender-differentiation processes highlight presumed natural differences between men and women and create them where no real
differences exist (Reskin, 1988; West & Zimmerman, 1987, p. 137).
Such differentiation "justifies" the unequal treatment of women
and men workers. Social scientists have begun to use *gender* as a
verb to describe the process of differentiating between men and
women (Acker, 1990, p. 146). For example, they describe how
different cultural and organizational practices *gender* work. This
usage emphasizes the socially constructed nature of gender differences and gender subordination. Society is also differentiated along
dimensions of race-ethnicity, class, and sexual orientation.

This chapter reviews some traditional explanations for gender
differentiation and women's subordination. Then it details a social
construction approach for studying the struggles of women working
in justice agencies (Lorber & Farrell, 1991).

Past Analyses of
Gender Inequality at Work

A variety of approaches have been used to explain gender inequality in the workplace. We discuss several approaches to women's
workplace subordination: *liberal feminist* with *gender role* and
gender-neutral organization/perspectives; radical-cultural feminist;
and *socialist feminist* theories. Each includes a theoretical explana-
tion of subordination and a policy prescription for change.

LIBERAL FEMINIST PERSPECTIVES

Liberal feminist perspectives argue that women's subordination
to men emanates from the creation of separate spheres of activity

and influence for men and women. Women traditionally have been relegated to the private sphere of home and family and excluded from the public domains of politics and paid work. Liberal feminists' goals focus on policies that include women in the public sphere of social life and permit women to attain the same work-related skills and traits as men (Freeman, 1989; Friedan, 1963).

Gender Role Theory

Gender role theory posits that childhood learning processes (i.e., gender role socialization) instill different occupational aspirations and capabilities in men and women. Boys are encouraged to develop traits associated with competence, instrumentality, and achievement. Girls' socialization emphasizes their future family roles and encourages the development of nurturance, emotional expressiveness, and physical attractiveness (Nieva & Gutek, 1981; Parsons & Bales, 1955). This perspective complements microeconomic human capital theory, which argues that women's wages are lower because, relative to men, they invest less time and money in their education, job training, and continuous labor force participation (Mincer & Polachek, 1974).

Men coworkers and managers also may be socialized to resent women's encroachment into "their" spheres. They learn to prefer working with men as peers or supervisors (Nieva & Gutek, 1981).

Gender-Neutral Organization Theory

Some sociologists argue that job and organizational characteristics, not gender-role learning, cause gender subordination at work. Rosabeth Moss Kanter (1977) identifies opportunity, distribution of power, and proportional representation as key organizational determinants of workers' experiences, attitudes, and job performance. *Power* consists of the resources to get things done, the formal and informal ability to make and enforce decisions. *Opportunity* means the chance for upward mobility; only upper-echelon jobs offer the real power to make decisions that affect organizational policies. *Proportional representation* refers to the organizational representation of individuals from various social groups (e.g., gender, race-ethnic, class, physical disability, and sexual orientation).

Those whose social type constitutes a numerical minority (less than 15%) in their job or work organization are more visible, experience performance pressure, and often are excluded by dominant social groups. These "tokens" are pressured to conform to stereotyped images of their social type (Kanter, 1977).

LIBERAL FEMINIST POLICY— EQUALITY AS SAMENESS

Gender-role theory and gender-neutral organization theory converge in a liberal feminist policy approach for achieving gender equality that emphasizes the same treatment for women and men (i.e., a "sameness" approach). This includes gender-neutral socialization practices for children and the elimination of discrimination in education and jobs through equal employment opportunity laws (Bird & Briller, 1969; Friedan, 1963). Affirmative action policies will increase the numbers of women and other minority social types and reduce resistance to these organizational newcomers. Gender-neutral organization approaches suggest policies to flatten organizational hierarchies and extend greater opportunity and power to all workers (Kanter, 1977).

A recurrent theme in liberal feminist perspectives is that women's essential nature is the same as men's. Gender-role theory suggests that gender-neutral socialization practices will make women's behavior more like men's. Gender-neutral organization theory emphasizes that women and men behave similarly *when* they have equal power, opportunity, and numbers.

These theories view behavior that corresponds to feminine gender roles as problematic in the workplace. Women should behave in ways that correspond to images of men workers, that is, aggressive, confident, and dispassionate. Work organizations are viewed as essentially gender-neutral (Acker, 1992). Liberal feminists advocate policies that provide women access to a full range of jobs and treat them in the same way as men.

RADICAL-CULTURAL FEMINIST PERSPECTIVE— EQUALITY AS DIFFERENCE

Some feminists criticize the sameness approach for using men's behavior as the standard for evaluating women. They argue that inclusion in men-dominated institutions and the right to work on the same terms as men will not end gender subordination.

Radical feminists view masculine power and privilege as the root cause of all forms of inequality (MacKinnon, 1989; Waters, 1989). Some argue that women's physiology produces a culture that is different from and superior to men's (Daly, 1984); others attribute differences to childhood socialization (Chodorow, 1978). Cultural feminists have reassessed the value of so-called feminine traits (e.g., Daly, 1984). Carol Gilligan's (1982) research on moral development suggests that men focus on abstract concepts of rules and rights, an abstract ethic of justice, while women are concerned with relationship and responsibility, an ethic of care.

Whether they locate the root of these differences in physiology or in cultural learning, of radical-cultural feminism proponents emphasize the value of feminine characteristics to public life. Gilligan (1982) argues that the moral domain should include both care and justice. In the past, because caring is associated with femininity, it has been defined as morally immature. Gilligan's "different voice" construct stresses the value of both feminine and masculine ethical voices. Her analysis has led feminist legal scholars and social scientists (e.g., Brush, 1992; Menkel-Meadow, 1986) to conclude that guiding images in law and the workplace have been masculine. They predict that replacing masculine with feminine culture could reduce workplace hierarchy, increase concern for clients and consensual decision making, decrease violence, and make better accommodations to the conflicting demands of family and work life.

SOCIALIST FEMINISM

Socialist feminism has emphasized the importance of both capitalism and patriarchy in producing women's subordination (Young, 1981). Although there are competing approaches, most socialist feminists stress the economic dimensions of men's resistance to women workers. Sexist ideology binds women to the home and legitimates their exclusion from higher-paying men's jobs. Patriarchal ideologies and exclusionary practices produce pools of women who provide cheap, flexible labor (Hartmann, 1979).

Socialist feminists have identified historical economic conditions that change labor market demands for women (Milkman, 1976). Management has used gender and race-ethnic antagonisms to divide workers struggling for better wages and working conditions (Hossfeld, 1990).

Socialist feminists advocate widespread economic and cultural changes to dismantle both capitalism and patriarchy. They would extend equal work opportunities to men and women workers and also institute policies to alleviate women's double workday by increasing child care/family leave programs and increasing men's involvement in domestic work. Their analyses have begun to incorporate a critique of other forms of exploitation such as racism, imperialism, ageism, and heterosexism (Walby, 1986).

CRITIQUES OF GENDER DICHOTOMIES:
POSTMODERNISTS AND WOMEN OF COLOR

Postmodernists (Cixous, 1971; Scott, 1990), feminists of color (P. Collins, 1991; Davis, 1981; Hurtado, 1989), and others (Connell, 1987; Messerschmidt, 1993; West & Fenstermaker, 1995) have criticized extant feminist theories as static, ethnocentric, and ahistorical. They challenge notions of equality that focus on whether women as a group are the same as or different from men as a group, and they argue that differences may be a by-product of centuries of domination by men (Acker, 1992; Connell, 1987; MacKinnon, 1989; Messerschmidt, 1993). Postmodernists criticize tendencies to universalize women's experience and to view sex categories as natural dichotomies (Cixous, 1971; Scott, 1990).

Empirical research reveals important racial-ethnic differences in women's oppression. Women's experiences of social class, work, and family vary across racial-ethnic and other groups (P. Collins, 1991; Davis, 1981; Glenn, 1992). Lesbians and women of color object to generalizations about women that are based on the experiences of white, heterosexual, middle-class women (e.g., P. Collins, 1991; Hurtado, 1989).

Socialist feminists have begun to consider racial-ethnic exploitation, but they do not capture the simultaneity of various forms of oppression in social life (Acker, 1989; Sokoloff, 1988). They also neglect the importance of culture and interpretation and the dynamic quality of gender production in daily work life.

Socialist, liberal, and radical feminist approaches converge in a view of gender as a static, individual trait (Messerschmidt, 1993). They portray gender as learned in early childhood and largely solidified by the time a man or woman takes a job (West & Fenstermaker, 1993). The pervasiveness of gender as an organizing feature of economies and workplaces is ignored (Acker, 1989).

In each perspective, men and women have essential natures; women are either essentially the same as or different from men. Historical, individual, and situational variations of masculinity and femininity are ignored (Scott, 1990).

Such theoretical treatment of gender reflects general societal practices of categorizing and dichotomizing social phenomena (Young, 1990). Western cultures commonly construct femininity and masculinity in opposition to each other: Femininity represents what masculinity is not (de Beauvoir, 1974). Race-ethnicity, sexual orientation, and class are also viewed categorically. This cultural habit stems from a general tendency in Western philosophical thought to conceptualize reality in terms of sets of mutually exclusive and opposing categories (Cixous, 1971; Scott, 1990; Young, 1990).[1]

Historical and cross-cultural research has indicated significant variations in the conceptions of masculinity and femininity over time and across cultures (Kessler & McKenna, 1978). Even within one society, individuals hold different and sometimes conflicting notions of what behavior constitutes socially appropriate masculinity and femininity. Gender-appropriate behavior varies from one situation to the next. Conceptualizations of gender as an individual attribute do not adequately convey the fluidity of gender across social contexts. Therefore, in our analysis of women working in justice occupations, we conceptualize gender as a social process.

A Social Construction
of Gender Perspective

We analyze gender in the justice workplace as an ongoing social production. Gender subordination is interwoven with race and class domination, as well as with domination in other social institutions and sites (e.g., the state, family).

Gender is not a fixed attribute of individuals but an emergent property of social practice. Social practice refers to interactions and their larger social structural and institutional contexts (Giddens, 1976). We draw on analyses of gender and other forms of social differentiation (e.g., race-ethnicity, sexual orientation) as interactional accomplishments (West & Fenstermaker, 1993, 1995; West & Zimmerman, 1987) that occur within the context of larger social structures (Connell, 1987; Messerschmidt, 1993; Simpson & Elis, 1995; Young, 1990) and institutions (e.g., gendered work organizations) (Acker, 1990, 1992; Kelly, 1991).

DOING GENDER: GENDER
AS A ROUTINE ACCOMPLISHMENT[2]

Sociologists Candace West and Don Zimmerman (1987) have argued that although gender is presumed to reflect natural differences rooted in biology, these differences are accomplished by individuals in routine interactions with others. In Western industrialized societies, infants are assigned to one of two sex categories based on chromosome type before birth or genitalia after birth. Throughout life, we identify and categorize people according to their sex category and categorize ourselves in relating to others (West & Zimmerman, 1987).

However, in most daily social interactions, people are unable to observe these physiological criteria. They must rely on social signs of sex category, such as hairstyle, dress, and physical appearance (Goffman, 1976). In addition to such social signs, the production of gender involves the activity of managing conduct in light of social perceptions regarding "conceptions, attitudes, and activities appropriate to one's sex category" (West & Zimmerman, 1987, p. 127).

Once individuals are categorized, their behavior is viewed through the lens of the sex category to which they "naturally" belong; this behavior also serves as evidence of the natural differences between men and women, or boys and girls. The observer's role in defining the behavior as masculine or feminine is forgotten (West & Zimmerman, 1987).

GENDER AS STRUCTURED INTERACTION

The accomplishment of gender does not occur in a vacuum. Individuals realize that others may call them to account for their behavior, so they configure and orchestrate their actions in anticipation of others' interpretation in that situation:

> Marking or displaying gender must be finely fitted to situations and modified or transformed as the occasion demands. Doing gender consists of managing such occasions so that . . . the outcome is seen and seeable in context as gender-appropriate or purposefully gender-inappropriate. (West & Zimmerman, 1987, p. 132)

Thus, femininity and masculinity are neither settled beforehand nor fixed for life. They are *accomplished* in everyday social interactions shaped by larger social structural patterns. The expression "doing gender" refers to the situated accomplishment of gender difference (West & Zimmerman, 1987).

Social structures underlie interactions and locate individuals along the lines of race, class, and sexual orientation, as well as gender. Social structures are regular patterns of interactions that emerge over time; they constrain and channel behavior (Giddens, 1976, p. 127; Messerschmidt, 1993, p. 63). Social interactions presuppose social structure because making sense of them requires a knowledge of these patterns of social rules and resources (Connell, 1987, p. 94). Robert Connell (1987), Iris Young (1990), and James Messerschmidt (1993) have described interconnected social structures: gendered divisions of labor, power, and culture/sexuality.[3]

The division of labor includes the distribution of tasks, occupations, and working conditions. Fundamental to the division of labor in Western industrialized society are separations between the planning of work and task execution and between paid and unpaid labor (Braverman, 1974; Hochschild, 1989; Young, 1990). Historically, elite white men have been associated with planning and conceptualizing work. Working- and lower-class white men and men of color have been associated with task execution or manual labor. Women have been associated with the unpaid planning and execution of domestic work for their families. Women's family responsibilities are replicated in the paid workplace, where they are responsible for paid execution and support of men's plans or for tending to the bodily needs of others (Anderson, 1988). Women of color have often been relegated to paid domestic labor for white families or to other forms of paid manual labor (e.g., factory work) (Amott & Matthaei, 1991).

Associated with the division of labor are corresponding levels of power, a second dimension of social structure. Power refers to the ability to set up the rules and procedures whereby decisions will be made, as well as to the access to material resources and decision-making positions (Young, 1990, pp. 22-23). The gendered division of labor means that women are typically located in jobs with less decision-making power than those occupied by men (Connell, 1987; P. Martin, 1991). Men control the large-scale economic, religious, political, and military institutions of authority in society. They also tend to control other smaller groups and institutions, including the family and peer groups.

Culture refers to recurrent social practices, including "symbols, images, meanings, habitual comportment, stories, and so on through which people express their experience and communicate" (Young, 1990, p. 23). Within any society, there are varied, competing, and conflicting cultural views, but some cultural notions usually predominate over others. Sexuality, which includes sexual desire, behavior, and identity, also is socially constructed (Burrell & Hearn, 1989, p. 18). Cultural images define a hierarchy of more or less acceptable forms of sexuality, with married heterosexual parents at the top (Messerschmidt, 1993).[4]

Social structures are neither absolute determinants of nor external to social interactions. They are realized only through social action, but actions are always shaped by structures (Messerschmidt, 1993, p. 63; also see Giddens, 1976, p. 127).

The Production of Gender in Work Organizations

Men and women do gender in social interactions in the workplace. Interactions simultaneously arise from, reproduce, and sometimes challenge existing social structural divisions of labor, power, and culture hierarchies. Social structures constitute durable but historically variable social relations, including those of gender, race, and class (Messerschmidt, 1993).

Joan Acker (1992) stresses the importance of the production of gender in concrete social institutions such as work organizations. Gender is a pervasive feature of every aspect of organizational life. Acker (1992) examines the creations of gendered divisions of labor and power in work organizations. She identifies cultural images, interactions, identities, and policies that produce gendered divisions of labor and power. Other social institutions—family, state, and labor markets—impinge on the production of gender in work organizations.

LINKS BETWEEN THE FAMILY AND THE WORKPLACE

Western industrial societies treat home and work as naturally separate spheres, but this arrangement has not always prevailed. In preindustrial, agrarian societies, the household was the center of economic production. Beginning in England in the mid-1800s, industrialization moved production out of the home. Men, women, and children went to work in factories, where men assumed the highest skilled, best paying jobs (Hartmann, 1979). In the 1840s, upper-class reformers and men's labor unions called for restrictions on the labor of children and women. Women were accused of deserting their children to steal men's jobs (Seccombe, 1986). Eventually a "family wage" was developed, which paid the upper layers of working-class men enough so that their wives could stay at home. A similar system for "preserving the family" developed in the United States (Messerschmidt, 1993; Zaretsky, 1978). Although many families, especially families of color, did not receive the family wage, it had the symbolic effect of designating men as breadwinners and women as homemakers, or as working for pin money, at the margins of economic activity (Young, 1981).

Today, more than half of mothers of infants (and more than 65% of all mothers) are in the paid labor force. Yet, women still bear a disproportionate share of unpaid domestic responsibilities (U.S. Department of Labor, 1990, p. 132). After their first shift of paid work, women perform a second shift of child care and housework; thus, they work about 15 hours more than men work per week (Hochschild, 1989, p. 254). Women's domestic and paid work responsibilities also overlap more than men's in both time and space (e.g., getting calls from sick children at work, leaving work to take a child to an after-school program). These disproportionate domestic responsibilities foster cultural images that devalue women's worth in the workplace.

There is a dialectical relationship between gender subordination in domestic life and gender subordination in the paid workplace. A woman's domestic identity makes her a less desirable worker to employers. Her low income and subordination in the paid work world diminish her power in the family and increase her economic dependence on a man or on state welfare (Walby, 1986). Women's historical relegation to criminal justice jobs that provided clerical support or specialized in the needs of women and children illustrates the spillover of domestic responsibilities into justice work organizations.

Labor is simultaneously divided according to class, race, and gender. Evelyn Glenn (1992) describes historical divisions of domestic labor along these lines. In the 19th century, middle-class white women accepted gender-based divisions of labor and the "domestic code," but, they sloughed off more burdensome domestic tasks onto women of color. This freed white women for more supervisory tasks in the home and for cultural and volunteer activities. Racial division of domestic labor benefits white men by insulating them from dirty work and from those who do it at home and in the workplace (Glenn, 1992).

In this century, much domestic work formerly done in the home has become paid work in public settings, but gender and racial divisions of labor persist. Women of color still are disproportionately employed in dirty work (e.g., cooking food, cleaning or caring for the elderly and ill), whereas white women in the same settings are disproportionately employed as lower level professionals (e.g., receptionists, nurses) or supervisors (Amott & Matthaei, 1991).

Accordingly, divisions of labor simultaneously construct race and gender and overlap both paid and unpaid worlds of work. White women hold the preferred jobs. Initially, women workers in policing and corrections were overwhelmingly white, but today increasing percentages of women of color, especially African American women, are assuming posts in both occupations.

THE GENDERED STATE

Historically, the state, which includes both political and legal institutions, has facilitated domination by white men workers in many ways (Connell, 1987; Messerschmidt, 1993). Despite struggles to increase their representation in law-making and regulatory bodies, women are a small minority in these realms.

Until 1971, a woman's rights and responsibilities were essentially determined by her position in the family, and laws that classified according to sex were constitutional (Rhode, 1989; Schultz, 1991). Laws have limited women's access to paid employment, upheld racially and sexually discriminatory hiring practices, criminalized forms of fertility control (e.g., abortion and some contraceptive devices), regulated marriage and divorce, prohibited women's ownership of property or businesses, supported unequal education, and restricted women's immigration from some countries (Amott & Matthaei, 1991).

In the past quarter-century, political struggles challenged sex, race, and other forms of discrimination in the workplace. Civil rights and women's movements questioned white men's birthright to the most desirable jobs. Demonstrations by various disadvantaged groups (e.g., African Americans, American Indians, Asian Americans, Chicanos/as, senior citizens, gay and lesbian coalitions, the physically challenged) stimulated legislative attempts to eliminate discrimination in many areas of social life. In the 1970s, mounting public opposition led some employers to end overt discriminatory hiring and promotional preferences for young, white, nondisabled men (Reskin & Roos, 1990).

Although the legal situation has improved, most laws continue to be rooted in the experiences of heterosexual, white, and nondisabled men workers. Those whose situations are not similiar to that of this ideal worker may be disadvantaged (MacKinnon, 1989; Minow, 1988). For example, maternity leave policies and practices in many justice work organizations continue to significantly disadvantage women. Within law firms, women are often penalized informally when they take maternity leave.

Of course, state policies are neither unified nor consistent. State actions regarding the extension of employment opportunities to women and other disadvantaged groups are often contradictory. Some actions may increase opportunities for women workers; others may diminish them (Walby, 1986).

We will observe many such inconsistencies in the experiences of women workers in justice occupations. For example, federal laws requiring equal employment opportunity helped advance the position of women in corrections, but, during the same period, federal court rulings regarding inmate privacy restricted women's work assignments in men's prisons (Jurik, 1985).

GENDERED LABOR MARKETS

Barbara Reskin and Patricia Roos (1990) have conceptualized the gender and race-ethnic composition of occupations as a queueing process: There are gendered and racialized *labor queues* in which employers rank waiting workers, and *job queues* in which workers rank job opportunities. Changes in the gender (or race) composition of occupations occur when employers change their ordering of workers in the labor queue, or alternatively, when workers reorder their valuations of jobs.

Various social forces, including political, legal, economic, and demographic changes, shape employer and worker preferences, and accordingly, job and labor queues. For example, social policies (e.g., hospital policies requiring that all nurses be RNs) may increase the educational requirements for an occupation. Social and economic factors also may increase the proportions of college-educated workers for existing labor queues. If educational requirements increase but salary levels do not, a shortage of qualified white men applicants may develop. Qualified white women and both men and women of color may then be hired to make up the deficit of workers of the desired social type. This pattern has been one of several forces behind the entry of women into men's justice system jobs.

Political and legal struggles may also alter employers' hiring practices. Legal changes, such as affirmative action hiring and the prohibition of discriminatory educational admission practices, can change employment opportunities for women workers (Kelly, 1991, pp. 10-12). Other political changes, such as war, can result in shortages of men workers and an increase in the hiring of women workers (e.g., as in World Wars I and II).

Virtually all changes in the social, political, and economic spheres of society affect the demand for workers and for jobs. Labor market queueing processes reveal the gendered consequences of ostensibly gender-neutral macrosocial and economic changes.

In Chapter 1, we discussed some of the historical conditions that increased the demand for women workers in the criminal justice system (CJS). Perceived increases in crime rates, social movements, and state legislative and policy directives increased the size of the CJS and pressures for agency reforms. Reforms converged with demographic changes, economic forces, and equal employment and educational opportunity laws to increase the demand for and availability of women workers for men's justice occupations.

GENDERED WORK ORGANIZATIONS

Gender relations in the family, state, and labor market are inextricably connected to the production of gender in work organizations. Analysis of gendered work organizations considers how "advantage and disadvantage, exploitation and control, action and emotion, meaning and identity are patterned in terms of a distinction between male and female, masculine and feminine" (Acker, 1990, p. 140). The analytically distinct but inherently connected dimensions of the gendered organization are discussed in the following sections.

Division of Labor in Work Organizations

Organizations include interactions that control, segregate, exclude, and construct hierarchies of workers based on gender, race, and class (Acker, 1992). Throughout work organizations, jobs are segregated along these lines.

In recent decades, women have made disproportionate gains in some men-dominated fields, but most occupations have shown little change in the segregation level (Reskin & Roos, 1990). In 1980, almost half of all employed women worked in occupations that were filled by at least 80% women, and more than two thirds of men worked in occupations that were at least 80% men (Reskin & Hartmann, 1986). Women's movement into men's occupations during the 1970s appears to be progress, but these figures mask a trend toward ghettoization. Within occupations and firms, there is pervasive internal stratification: Men and women perform different tasks (Reskin & Roos, 1990).[5] Jobs become informally identified as "men's" or "women's" work.

Men gatekeepers (owners, managers) often seek to exclude women from occupations, organizations, or jobs if they perceive women as a threat to men's material or symbolic status (Cockburn, 1991). Supervisors hinder women's advancement by reserving better assignments for men. Higher pay, greater social status, and more power accompany men's jobs. Differences apply even when women and men perform the same tasks (Acker, 1989; Bielby & Baron,

1986). In the CJS, work assignments of women and men often result in disparate access to power structures. Higher profile work assignments are more often given to men (Jurik, 1988).

Culture and Sexuality in Work Organizations

Gendered organizations are also sites for the construction and display of cultural images, symbols, and ideologies that legitimate and, on occasion, challenge divisions of labor and power hierarchies. Workers develop informal occupational and organizational cultures. They make sense of the world by creating shared meanings and frameworks to understand life (Trice, 1993). Cultures create a sense of "we-ness" by drawing boundaries between members and others. They are constructed through verbal and nonverbal communication, including dress and demeanor.

Work cultures are informal because they do not always correspond to the formal rules of the work organization. Informal work cultures may also operate outside of organized occupational groups such as professional associations and unions. Yet, work cultures are influenced by mandates of formal work organizations and occupational associations. Work cultures also are shaped by cultural hierarchies outside work organizations.

The term *work culture* is not monolithic. There may be multiple or competing work cultures within a work organization or occupation. Researchers have described competing occupational cultures within policing, with "management cops" and "street cops" each having its own distinctive ideology and cultural form (Reuss-Ianni, 1983). Within one occupation, work cultures also may converge with the organizational climate of particular work settings. Correctional officer cultures are shaped by the distinctive character of the prison in which they are located (e.g., minimum- versus maximum-security prison).

Work cultures draw on larger cultural ideals to develop their own versions of masculinity and femininity. Robert Connell (1987, 1993) has used the terms *hegemonic masculinity* and *emphasized femininity* to designate culturally idealized forms of gender in given historical settings. These forms are honored, glorified, and extolled in the media.

Connell (1987) recognizes the existence of multiple cultural images of masculinity and femininity, but he emphasizes that some are more dominant than others. Images of masculinity and femininity associated with white, middle-class, and heterosexual men and women are more likely to be ideologically dominant.

In Western industrialized societies, hegemonic masculinity is characterized by paid employment, subordination of women and girls, heterosexism, uncontrollable sexuality, authority, control, and aggressiveness. Emphasized femininity complements hegemonic masculinity and is defined through it: sociability, fragility, compliance with men's desire for ego stroking, sexual receptivity, marriage, housework, and child care (Connell, 1987).

Behavior interpreted as conforming to hegemonic masculinity, emphasized femininity, or any other vision of gender is open to reinterpretation in each new social situation. Although ideals of masculinity as aggressive, dispassionate, and competitive and of femininity as passive, nurturing, and emotional may be culturally dominant, opposing visions of masculinity and femininity may coexist in the same society.

In occupations held mostly by men, dominant work-culture images often associate effective job performance with culturally dominant ideals of masculinity for the sex category and social class of job incumbents. Although its exact forms vary, the suppression of emotions appears to characterize masculinity across social classes. Physicians and lawyers are expected to conform to dominant notions of middle-class masculinity that include the rational manipulation and control of ideas. Men's working-class occupations often expose workers to physical demands, fear, and danger. Consequently, in these occupations, competence becomes associated with culturally dominant notions of working-class masculinity that call for displays of physical strength, courage, and aggressiveness (see Skolnick, 1966; Williams, 1989). For example, men in occupations such as mining and policing often equate fearlessness with masculinity (Fitzpatrick, 1980; Hunt, 1984). Such masculine images are constructed as opposites of culturally emphasized femininity, which is weak, emotional, and incompetent. Accordingly, jobs become resources for doing masculinity (Messerschmidt, 1993, pp. 174-185).

Work cultures may advance unsavory images of women and other cultural subordinates (e.g., men of color, gays, lesbians). Workers who are members of culturally dominant groups respond to subordinates' behavior accordingly. Cultural images construct and justify existing gendered divisions of labor (Acker, 1990), but these images vary across race-ethnic and class groups.

Kanter (1977) identifies four subordinating cultural images of femininity:

The *little sister* is dependent and incompetent.

The *seductress* is incompetent and flirts with men at work.

The *iron maiden* is competent but cold and harsh.

The *mother* takes care of men's emotions but is sometimes "nagging."[6]

These images are applied to women workers in the justice system.

Angela Davis (1981) and Patricia Hill Collins (1991) discuss subordinating images of black women:

Mules do the dirty work for which white women are too delicate.

Jezebels are sexually promiscuous and aggressive.

Mammies are deferential and "know their place."

Matriarchs are aggressive and controlling

Uppity black women do not "know their place" and expect to be treated as though they were equal to white women or to white men.

Sexuality is a significant component of the cultural meanings and practices of gender subordination in the workplace. Enforced heterosexuality is a primary mechanism for subordinating women at home and on the job (Cockburn, 1991; Rich, 1980). As in other occupations, heterosexuality is a central aspect of masculinity

among CJS workers. Questioning sexual orientation is a tactic used
to devalue both men and women workers.

Workplace Interactions and Identities

Men and women workers actively produce gender differences in
social interactions within the workplace. These interactions simultaneously produce and stem from other aspects of the work organization and other institutions in society. There is considerable
interplay between wider cultural imagery and competing constructions of masculinity and femininity in the workplace. Workers'
everyday practices are accountable to these cultural images but may
not necessarily correspond to them. In this way, workers construct
varieties of femininity and masculinity through specific practices
(Messerschmidt, 1995).

In occupations traditionally held by men, interactions between
men and women are gendered and sexualized (Williams, 1989).
Men coworkers and superiors sometimes demonstrate overt hostility, but they also use more subtle interactional techniques to
undermine women workers. They can exert performance pressure
by constantly questioning or scrutinizing women's performance.
They also use boundary maintenance techniques to separate
women from men socially or physically (Kanter, 1977). Superiors
may give women different assignments (e.g., clerical chores). Managers in corrections assign women to areas that are physically
isolated from men coworkers and inmates (Jurik, 1985).

Boundary maintenance techniques include verbal cues such as
commenting on women's appearance, performance, or sexual relationships, as well as nonverbal cues such as stares or "playful"
touching (Kanter, 1977; Martin, 1978). Men can also emphasize
their difference from women by exaggerated displays of masculinity
(e.g., sexual jokes or telling of sexual exploits).

Exclusionary tactics help maintain boundaries. Historically,
women were not admitted to law schools, a necessary prerequisite
for practice. In occupations such as policing and corrections, where
essential training is conducted informally on the job, coworkers

often exclude women from training interactions or sabotage them, even to the point of jeopardizing women's physical safety.

Friendships off the job are important sources of information and informal influence. In some occupations (e.g., banking, law), the golf course or social club may be as important as the office or the courtroom for making influential contacts and trading information. If women are excluded from these organizations, they are deprived of the benefits of informal information exchange and lose opportunities for mentoring.

Paternalism refers to situations in which men extract submission and even gratitude from women in exchange for excusing them from difficult jobs. In occupations such as policing and corrections, paternalism is an effective interactional mechanism for doing masculinity and dominance. Because men's protection of women appears to be helpful, women may welcome relief from hard assignments, but paternalism denies women the chance to demonstrate their abilities and creates resentment among other workers (Reskin, 1988; Swerdlow, 1989).

Other interactional devices for constructing men's dominance include undermining and invalidating. Men invalidate women by refusing to accept their authority, denigrating their work products, and magnifying their failures. When women complain about discrimination, men may respond that women's disadvantage is simply a handicap that nature imposed on them. Men's achievements are attributed to skill, but they often imply that a woman's promotion or other accomplishments are the result of sexual favors or reverse discrimination, and they may even seek legal redress by making such claims (Cockburn, 1991).

The production and reproduction of work organizations is inextricably associated with sexuality, as well as with gender (Burrell & Hearn, 1989, p. 2). Sexualization may occur through subtle avenues of dress, demeanor, and behavior. Sexualization also includes sexual harassment—overtly sexual talk, unwanted contact, and physical advances (Cockburn, 1991).

Sexual harassment reinforces gender, race, and class subordination. Power differentials, gender ratios, race, ethnicity, and age significantly affect the likelihood of being sexually harassed (MacKinnon, 1978; Schneider, 1991). Nonetheless, even women in supervisory positions are harassed by men subordinates (Stambaugh, 1995).

Organizational policies toward sexuality are often inconsistent within and across work organizations: Employers use women's sexuality in advertising and client relations to increase profits, but they try to limit its expression in employee interactions. Waitresses may be expected to wear short skirts and to flirt with men customers (Hall, 1993). In contrast, women correctional and police officers may be expected to wear uniforms that disguise breasts or other physiological signs of sex category (Martin, 1980; Zimmer, 1986). Finally, although managers may regard relationships among workers as problematic for the organization, men managers' exercise of the "sexual prerogative" with women subordinates is informally condoned.

Responsibility for sexualization is usually attributed to women. Men's heterosexuality is not problematic in the workplace, but women must be asexual. If women return men's sexual humor or "flirt," they are labeled negatively: "What is funny coming from a man is obscene coming from a woman" (Cockburn, 1991, p. 156). It is usually women who are blamed, demoted, transferred, or fired for "sexuality problems" arising at work.

Women who ignore or reject men's advances are labeled prudes or lesbians. This "lesbian threat" enforces heterosexual dominance and undermines women's efforts to bond with each other for political and friendship purposes (Cockburn, 1991).

The construction of gender is not solely a reflection of culturally dominant images of masculinity, femininity, and competence. Individual workers may seek to construct gender identities that oppose or conflict with dominant cultural and organizational images of femininity or masculinity.

Despite the widespread resistance to women in fields that were traditionally associated with men, men's responses are not uniform. Some men in corrections have supported women's entry into what used to be men's jobs and allied themselves more closely with women coworkers than with sexist men coworkers and superiors (Jurik, 1985; Jurik & Halemba, 1984). Other men denigrate supportive men as "mama's boys" or "women," and question their masculinity (Cockburn, 1991).

There are significant differences in the experiences and behavior of women workers according to race-ethnicity and sexual orientation. Women of color sometimes feel that white women coworkers are no more sensitive to issues of racism than are white men. They sometimes bond more closely with men of their own race than with white women coworkers (Owen, 1988). They also tend to be less willing than are white women to file claims of sexual harassment. If the harasser is a white man, they fear that they will not be believed; if he is a man of their own race, they feel disloyal (Belknap, 1991; Martin, 1994). In contrast, lesbians appear more willing than are straight women to use the term *sexual harassment* to describe unwanted sexual approaches from men in the workplace (Schneider, 1982).

Research indicates that women's work styles vary according to age, education, rank, and tenure. Sometimes, women succumb to the pressures of men-dominated work cultures. They acquiesce to men's protection and accept restricted work assignments. They reproduce cultural notions of emphasized femininity as passive, supportive, and emotional (Martin, 1980; Zimmer, 1986).

In other cases, women emulate culturally dominant forms of masculine work behavior. They refuse protection or special duties and struggle to demonstrate their equality to men coworkers by engaging in "masculine" behavior (Martin, 1980; Zimmer, 1986). Women who display qualities associated with masculinity are criticized even when they exercise appropriately assertive behavior: Coworkers describe them as "mannish." This label becomes "a stick with which to threaten other women" (Cockburn, 1991, p. 69). Women who adopt less authoritarian approaches meet resistance because they are seen as "weak" leaders.

Some women have challenged work-culture imagery that equates competence with dominant notions of masculinity. They claim that "feminine qualities" such as caring, communication, and conflict diffusion skills enhance work performance, and they argue that femininity and competence are not mutually exclusive categories. Other women have tried to substitute more androgynous or gender-neutral professional images that emphasize rational-formal, rule-oriented behavior and oppose aggressive, macho behavior (Brush, 1992; Jurik, 1988).

However, the professional ideal still fails to challenge institutionalized images of workers as men devoid of family responsibilities. Iris Young (1990) describes other cultural biases in the professional ideal:

> Professional behavior . . . signifies rationality and authoritativeness, [and] requires specific ways of sitting, standing, walking and speaking, namely without undue expression. . . . One should speak firmly, without hesitation or ambiguity, and slang, dialect, and accent should be absent from one's speech. (pp. 139-140)

The model of "the professional" is another version of masculinity, one associated with elite white men. Connell (1993) suggests that culturally dominant forms of masculinity are changing from an interpersonally and physically aggressive (read: working-class) style to one that is more technocratic. The professional now is a detached manager, an expert, and bureaucrat. These managers and technocrats are not openly hostile toward women; they "do not directly confront feminist programs, but instead, under-fund or shrink them in the name of efficiency and voluntarism" (Connell, 1993, p. 615; see also Cockburn, 1991). The ideal professional aims for organizational universalism, rather than "special rights" for women or other social groups.

Gendered Organizational Logic

Organizational rules and regulations often intentionally or unintentionally disadvantage women. Gender is implied in the logic of organizations through written work rules and practices surrounding training, work assignments, and promotions.

Research on women in nontraditional occupations reveals the ways in which organizational logic is gendered. Employers' and employees' devaluing of work characteristically performed by women is institutionalized through formal organizational rules and procedures. Acker's (1990) study of comparable worth describes the gendered character of task valuation:

> Organizational logic assumes a congruence between responsibility, job complexity, and hierarchical position. . . . Lower-level positions, the . . . jobs filled predominantly by women, must have equally low levels of complexity and responsibility. Complexity and responsibility are defined in terms of managerial and professional tasks. (pp. 148-149)

In most work organizations, supervisors rely on ostensibly objective training, assignment, and assessment procedures that are really social constructions of competence. Generally, work qualifications have been developed based on notions of masculine competence, which now frame the assessments of working women (Acker, 1989; Morash & Greene, 1986). For example, training in policing and corrections emphasizes physical criteria that may have little relevance to effective job performance but that disadvantage women. Conversely, qualities such as negotiation and mediation skills typically attributed to women lawyers often are not included among formal evaluation criteria (Menkel-Meadow, 1986). Gendered organizational logic shapes affirmative action, maternity/family leave, and sexual harassment policies, as well as the resources allocated for their enforcement (Cockburn, 1991).

Summary

Many analyses of women's subordination in the workplace have conceptualized gender as an individual attribute that is socially and biologically determined. Gender is viewed as a preemployment attribute of workers who enter ostensibly gender-neutral work organizations. Gender differences at work are regarded either as the

result of inherent worker differences or as not really gender differences at all. These views ignore the changes in gender across history,
cultures, and situations.

We rely instead on a view of gender as a process that emerges
through social practice. Accumulated patterns of social interaction
throughout history generate structured societies—divisions of labor,
power, and culture. These practices simultaneously locate people
according to gender, race, and class. Social constraints shape the
forms of femininity that are available, encouraged, and permitted,
depending on a person's situation, class, race, and sexual orientation. Thus, as individuals do gender, they simultaneously reflect,
reproduce, and sometimes challenge existing social structural arrangements.

Gender is integral to every aspect of life in social institutions. We
have analyzed the social construction of gender in work organizations through divisions of labor, work cultures, interactions, and
organizational logic. The construction of gender within work organizations is also shaped by dynamics in the family, State, and the
labor market. As these institutional processes produce gender, they
produce race, class, and other forms of social differentiation (see
Frankenberg, 1993).

Drawing on the framework outlined here, the following chapters
analyze the social production of gender in justice work organizations. For the occupations of policing, law, and correctional security,
we examine the following:

1. *Changing labor queues* produced by wider changes in institutions such as the State, family, and labor market
2. *Gendered work cultures* and their link to the nature of the
   occupation and wider cultural images
3. *Men doing gender* in their interactions with women entrants
   to justice organizations
4. *The gendered logic* of justice organizations
5. *Women doing gender* in responding to gender subordination

A concluding chapter compares the forms of gender subordination across justice occupations and considers the significance of changing gender ratios for justice fields.

Notes

1. Each category is treated as a distinct and consistent whole: Similarities among members are emphasized. Describing the unified group is easiest when contrasting it with some other opposite group (e.g., man/woman, same/different). Then, individual cases are neatly located in the appropriate category. Overlaps between and differences within categories are deemphasized. The first category is more highly valued than the second, which threatens to disrupt the unity of the first. Historically, men have been viewed as rational and objective; women have been viewed as less than men because they are regarded as emotional and ruled by their bodies (Young, 1990).

2. West and Zimmerman (1987) developed the phrase "doing gender."

3. Connell (1987) defines power, division of labor, and cathexis as key structures of gender subordination. Messerschmidt (1993) uses *sexuality* instead of cathexis. We chose Young's (1990) formulation of culture, which seems to be more inclusive of race-ethnic and class subordination.

4. Less desirable options include married but childless heterosexuals, single heterosexuals, celibates, monogamous homosexuals, and so forth. (see Messerschmidt, 1993, p. 74).

5. *Segregation* and *ghettoization* are commonly used in the literature, but these terms may wrongly equate women's experiences with those of oppressed race-ethnic groups (Reskin & Roos, 1990).

6. We viewed Kanter's (1977) term, *role stereotypes*, as too static for our conceptualization of gender as a process.

3

The Nature of Police Work and Women's Entry Into Law Enforcement

 Before the 1970s, nearly all police officers in the United States were white men; women accounted for less than 2% of sworn personnel and "policewomen" served in specialized positions. Racial-ethnic minorities also were greatly underrepresented in policing. Common language, job titles, and the media presented images of police that were both gendered and linked to white working-class culture. In the past 25 years, the image of a police officer as a white man has been weakened, and both the number and proportion of women in policing have grown. By October 1993, women made up 9.4% of sworn personnel (U.S. Department of Justice, 1994) and could be found in all specialized assignments and ranks, including chief. Nonetheless, women still are underrepresented, regarded with suspicion by many men officers, and confronted with discriminatory practices within the informal police culture and the formal organization.

Legislation, executive action, and judicial decisions have altered eligibility criteria, selection standards, and assignment and promotion practices that discriminated against women. The open and organized harassment encountered by the first women on patrol has largely disappeared. Yet, women officers still must cope with gendered organizational policies and practices, hostile work environments, and an occupational culture whose "cult of masculinity" glamorizes violence and denigrates women (Young, 1991, p. 192).

This chapter explores the history of women in policing, their broadened occupational roles since the 1970s, and the ways the work and police occupational culture contribute to the continuing resistance to women officers.

Historical Overview:
From Matron to Chief

PRELIMINARY PHASE: 1840-1910

Women first entered the criminal justice workplace in the mid-19th century when they became involved in moral reform and rescue activities with "fallen" women and children. Although their employment in the criminal justice system (CJS) was part of the pattern of women's increased employment, it also was unique because the women stressed the moral basis of their work and the ways their activities differed from those of men in the CJS.

Prohibited from becoming sworn police officers, some women gained employment as jail matrons, initially in the New York Police Department and subsequently in other large city agencies. They supervised girls and women who were detained or sentenced to jail, then gradually extended their responsibilities beyond strictly custodial work (Schulz, 1995).

THE SPECIALIST PHASE: 1910 TO 1972

In 1910, Alice Stebbins Wells became the first sworn woman officer. From then until the mid-1970s, policewomen were restricted in number, paid less than men, selected by different criteria from men officers, and assigned to work primarily with women and children. Wells sought an appointment as a sworn officer in the Los Angeles Police Department, convinced she could be more effective in preventive and protective work with women and children if she had police powers.

The early policewomen's movement had several sources. First, women of the "social purity" reform movement in the late 19th and early 20th centuries sought social change and staked out work roles that were extensions of women's domestic roles and their feminine characteristics. Many of the early policewomen were upper-middle-class women eager "to act as municipal mothers to those whose lifestyles they believed needed discipline," namely poor women (Schulz, 1995, p. 374).

Second, women's early successes in establishing a place for themselves in policing stemmed from the confluence of their aims with those of some progressive police reformers. Both sought to free policing from corrupting politics, to upgrade personnel, and to professionalize police work. In the 1920s, reform efforts were characterized by competition between two models of reform: a crime control or efficiency/managerial model and a social service/crime prevention model (Walker, 1977). The latter claimed that scientific police work could prevent crime by discovering and eliminating its causes. Wells and other women reformers espoused "crime prevention . . . as a recognized and growing part of police duty" (Wells, 1932, p. 15). Few reform-oriented men, however, mentioned the association of crime prevention or professionalism with policewomen. Rather, the policewomen's presence caused a dilemma: If preventing crime was the primary duty of the police and if women were better at it than the men, then men would assume second-rate status within police departments.

Many leaders of the policewomen's movement understood the threat they posed to men and sought to reduce it. They created Women's Bureaus that were separated administratively, and sometimes physically, from the rest of the department. They avoided wearing uniforms and carrying guns, often were required to have a college education, and met lower physical standards than the men.

When their upper-middle-class backgrounds, higher level of education, and sense of superiority resulted in tension and opposition from the mostly working-class men, policewomen often sought a peripheral role. Consequently, they were "kept at arm's length from the main organization and, perhaps, a little despised by the remainder of the force" (Hutzel, 1933, p. 3).

Women's inroads into policing came to a halt during the 1930s. The crime control model of police work, which viewed officers primarily as soldiers in a war against crime, almost totally eclipsed the crime prevention model. Although it was less visible, there also was a shift in the actual content of police work toward the order maintenance and service aspects of the role (Walker, 1983).

The crime control model, fostered at the national level by the FBI and its longtime director, J. Edgar Hoover, centralized control and adopted a military-style command structure to address police corruption. The crime control model also firmly reinforced male, working-class culture and values in police departments and reaffirmed the superiority of the masculine virtue of being able to overcome resistance (Bittner, 1967).

For the next 40 years, a few policewomen gained assignments to detective, vice, and crime lab units, but the vast majority were assigned to juvenile work or secretarial duties. Their recruitment, training, salary, and promotion remained limited. In 1960, there were only 5,617 women in policing and security work in the United States (U.S. Census figures cited in Heidensohn, 1992, p. 55), and they made up less than 1% of sworn personnel.

FROM POLICEWOMAN TO CHIEF: CHANGES SINCE 1972

Change for women in policing began in the 1960s and accelerated in the 1970s. In 1961, a policewoman won a lawsuit against New York City and gained the right to compete in a promotional process not previously open to women. Four years later, Felicia Schpritzer became the city's first woman sergeant (Bell, 1982). In 1968, the Indianapolis Police Department assigned two women to patrol duties;

in 1972, the Metropolitan Police Department of Washington, D.C., became the first municipal agency to put a significant number of women on patrol (initially as an "experiment"). Since then, the representation of women in all types of departments has increased, and women have been integrated into patrol and virtually all other police activities.[1]

Women's recent transformation from specialist policewoman to generalist patrol officer is related both to the police crisis of the 1960s and to social and economic changes in the status of women during that decade (discussed more fully in Chapter 1). Each reform movement contributed to the new role for women in policing by changing their place in the labor queues.

Police Crisis of the 1960s

In the 1960s, the police faced a series of challenges. Rates of violent crime rose. Low salaries and the retirement of World War II veterans resulted in "manpower" shortages. There were urban riots stemming from the civil rights movement, rising economic and social expectations, but continuing poverty. The police encountered growing public frustration with what became known as police brutality. Officers had to adapt to new procedures for protecting citizen's rights to due process resulting from several U.S. Supreme Court decisions.

In reviewing CJS problems, two presidential commissions called for sweeping changes, with particular emphasis on the police. Their recommendations included higher personnel standards, improved management, greater use of science and technology, a reexamination of the meaning of police professionalism, and attention to police-community relations. They also called for subordination of strength and aggressiveness to the qualities of emotional stability and intelligence; sensitivity to minority problems in recruitment of personnel; elimination of discriminatory selection criteria; and recruitment of more officers who were college educated, people of color, and women.

The Women's Movement

The women's movement contributed to expanding the recruitment pool of women officers by changing gender stereotypes and values and by altering traditional concepts of masculinity and femininity. Although the women's movement did not assure equal opportunities for female officers, it stimulated a new social climate within police departments. Social norms and practices, ranging from standards of sexual behavior, appearance, and grooming to women's educational options and career choices, were challenged and changed during the 1960s and 1970s, fostered by and supporting challenges to the legal status quo.

Legal Changes: Legislation and Judicial Interpretation

Antidiscrimination laws contributed to the influx of women into police work. Before passage of the Equal Opportunity Act of 1972, many local laws and ordinances barred women from patrol assignments and promotions in rank. The 1972 act extended to local police agencies provisions of the Civil Rights Act of 1964 and expanded the powers of the Equal Employment Opportunity Commission (EEOC) to enforce Title VII. The Crime Control Act of 1973 required police departments with 50 or more employees that received $25,000 or more in federal grants to implement equal employment opportunity programs for women or face withdrawal of funds (Bell, 1982).

In the 1970s, many police agencies were sued for discriminating on the basis of gender, race, or both. Lawsuits contested departmental entrance requirements related to education, age, height, weight, and arrest records; selection criteria, including written examinations, agility tests, and veterans' preference; and discriminatory assignment and promotion procedures (Potts, 1983; Sulton & Townsey, 1981). Many of these cases resulted in court orders or consent decrees that established affirmative action programs, including quotas and timetables for hiring and promoting white women and people of color. Other decisions supported plaintiffs' challenges to height and weight standards and agility tests that were shown to be neither sufficiently job-related nor adequately validated (Hale & Menniti, 1993).

To comply with emerging case law, police agencies modified their recruitment practices, eligibility requirements, and selection criteria. Most agencies eliminated or altered height and weight requirements and physical agility tests that disproportionately eliminated women and Hispanic and Asian men.[2] They also replaced agility tests that emphasized upper body strength with physical performance tests that assessed health and fitness. The new tests measured cardiovascular function, body composition, flexibility, and dynamic and absolute strength, and performance norms were adjusted for age and sex.

Police departments also revised written entrance examinations that adversely affected people of color and standardized oral screening procedures for both selection and promotion. Personal interviews were standardized, with a single set of questions administered by trained interviewers, including white women and men and women of color. These newer procedures leave less room for arbitrary decisions, but candidates still tend to be judged on qualities, standards, or attributes associated with masculinity (e.g., self-confidence and assertiveness).

The affirmative action policies adopted by many police departments have significantly affected the representation of white women and people of color throughout policing and in supervisory positions (S. Martin, 1991). During the 1980s, the U.S. Supreme Court's reinterpretation of Title VII limited the use of affirmative action programs but did not eliminate them. By 1987, more than half of police agencies serving populations larger than 50,000 had implemented affirmative action plans.

Other Supreme Court decisions in the 1960s and early 1970s also radically altered traditional concepts of law enforcement. The "due process revolution" required police agencies to alter street justice practices such as arbitrary arrests, random searches and seizures, and other violations of civil liberties. The "tough cop" tactics characteristic of the control model of policing gave way to more restrained behavior as the pendulum swung back toward a crime prevention model.

The Impact of Research

Because the initial assignment of women to patrol in large numbers in 1972 was regarded as an experiment, nine evaluations of women's performance were conducted to determine whether women could perform adequately on street patrol in diverse jurisdictions. These included Washington, D.C. (Bloch & Anderson, 1974), St. Louis (Sherman, 1975), New York City (Sichel, Friedman, Quint, & Smith, 1977), Denver (Bartlett & Rosenblum, 1977), Newton, Massachusetts (Kizziah & Morris, 1977), Philadelphia (Bartell Associates, 1978), California (California Highway Patrol, 1976), and Pennsylvania (Pennsylvania State Police, 1974).

Although some gender differences were found, all but one of these evaluations (the second phase of the Philadelphia study) concluded that men and women were equally capable of police patrol work. Some of the studies found women to be less proficient in the use of firearms and to have more accidents in comparison to men (St. Louis, Washington, and New York); others reported that women have a "less aggressive" policing style, evidenced by fewer arrests (Washington), and fewer citizen complaints (Denver).

There are several explanations for the finding that women made fewer arrests. Crites (1973, p. 12) suggests that women are less likely than men to provoke a violent reaction and thus are less likely to have to make arrests. The New York City evaluation data suggest that women are less likely than men to work with a steady partner, and thus they are at a disadvantage in negotiation over who gets credit for an arrest (Sichel et al., 1977, p. 51).

Morash and Greene (1986) identified a number of areas in which these evaluations were gender biased.[3] Nevertheless, the evaluation findings meant that sex could no longer be considered a bona fide occupational qualification (BFOQ) for the job of patrol officer and that women had to be given an opportunity to serve on street patrol.

The Increasing Representation
of Women in Police Work

By the end of the 1970s, these changes in policing and in the larger social and legal environment led to women's assignment to patrol duties in most large municipal, state, and federal law enforcement agencies. Since then, women's representation and responsibilities have steadily expanded despite resistance from most of the men. For example, in 1975, women constituted 2.2% of the sworn personnel in municipal departments (Martin, 1980). By 1993, they made up 9% of the officers in those cities and an even greater proportion in the larger departments, as shown in Table 3.1.

Increases in the representation of women in law enforcement have occurred in agencies of differing sizes, types, and regions, and they have included women of color. Comparing 1990 data across agency types, as shown in Table 3.2, the proportion of women is greatest in sheriff's departments, where they constituted 15.4% of all deputies (although some probably were assigned to custodial rather than road patrol duties), followed by municipal agencies and state police agencies, in which they make up only 4.6% of the sworn personnel (U.S. Department of Justice, 1992b). In addition, women have entered the federal law enforcement agencies. For example, in the FBI, which hired no women prior to 1972, 11.3% of the special agents as of March 1, 1992 were women.

Men and women of color make up a substantial proportion of police, particularly in large cities. As indicated in Table 3.2, 10.5% of sworn municipal personnel are black, 5.2% are Hispanic, and 1.3% are American Indians and Asian Americans. In the large cities (populations of 250,000 or more), however, 17.2% are black, 8.7% are Hispanic, and 11.5% are women of all racial-ethnic groups (U.S. Department of Justice, 1992b, p. 3). These data clearly show that law enforcement, particularly urban policing, is no longer an exclusively white men's preserve. The proportion of people of color in policing (17%) approaches their representation in the U.S. population. Women continue to be greatly underrepresented, but one third of the women officers are women of color, and women make up 19%

TABLE 3.1 Women Officers in Municipal Policing by Agency Size: 1980-1993

Year	Large[a]		Medium[b]		Smaller[c]		Small[d]		Total[e]	
	Number	Percentage	Number	Percentage	Number	Percentage	Number	Percentage	Number	Percentage
1980	5,131	4.6	1,242	4.2	1,010	3.1	3,615	3.0	11,179	3.8
1985	10,223	8.6	2,120	6.6	1,468	4.5	5,441	4.2	19,388	6.2
1990	15,673	12.6	2,851	8.2	2,363	6.2	7,494	5.2	28,335	8.3
1993	17,740	13.7	3,277	9.0	2,736	6.8	8,817	5.8	32,592	9.1

Source: U.S. Department of Justice, 1981, 1986, 1991, and 1994.

a. Cities with populations greater than 250,000. In 1985, this included 60 cities; in 1990, 62 cities; and in 1993, 64 cities.
b. Cities with populations between 100,000 and 250,000. In 1985, this included 121 cities; in 1990, 127 cities; in 1993, 133 cities.
c. Cities with populations between 50,000 and 100,000. In 1985, this included 286 cities; in 1990, 321 cities; in 1993, 344 cities.
d. Cities with populations less than 50,000. In 1985, this included 8,761 cities; in 1990, 8,997 cities; in 1993, 9,362 cities.

TABLE 3.2 Full-Time Sworn Local Police, Sheriff's Deputies,
and State Police in 1990 by Gender and
Race-Ethnicity

	Municipal (N = 363,001)		Sheriff's Departments (N = 141,418)		State Police (N = 52,372)	
	% Men	% Women	% Men	% Women	% Men	% Women
White	77.5	5.5	72.6	11.9	83.1	3.9
Black	8.5	2.0	7.2	2.6	7.1	0.4
Hispanic	4.7	0.5	3.9	0.8	4.2	0.2
Other	1.2	0.1	0.9	0.1	1.0	a

Source: U.S. Department of Justice, 1992, page 3, Table 3; page 11, Table 28.
a. Less than 0.05%.

of all black officers. (In contrast, white and Hispanic women account for less than 10% of white and Hispanic officers, respectively.)

Several factors may contribute to the large proportion of black women among women in municipal policing. First, black women may view law enforcement as an attractive option compared to the narrow range of jobs traditionally open to them. Second, black women have long been activists and leaders in the black community. Becoming a police officer enables a black woman to wield authority in the African American community and to work to alter an organization often viewed as oppressive.[4] Third, affirmative action recruiting messages reach both women and men.

Women are slowly being promoted into supervisory ranks. In 1978, women made up less than 1% of the personnel above the officer rank in municipal agencies serving populations over 50,000 (Sulton & Townsey, 1981); by the end of 1986, women still made up only 3.3% of supervisory personnel in those agencies and were found mostly at the lower ranks (e.g., 3.7% of the sergeants but only 1.4% of supervisory personnel of a higher rank (S. Martin, 1990). Although more recent data on all these departments are not available, a 1992 survey of police departments in the 50 largest U.S. cities found that women made up 7% of personnel with the rank of sergeant or above (Walker & Martin, 1994).

In 1990, a breakthrough occurred when Elizabeth Watson was selected as chief of the Houston Police Department, the sixth largest municipal agency in the United States. She served in that position until 1992, when a newly elected mayor selected a new chief; Watson currently is chief in Austin, Texas. A recent informal survey identified more than 60 women who were chiefs of agencies, ranging from local police and sheriff's departments to campus police (Jennings, 1994, p. Md-5).

It is not surprising that the proportion of women supervisors is lower than the proportion of entry-level officers from whom supervisors are chosen after several years of service. However, women have served on patrol for more than 20 years in most large agencies; their underrepresentation among supervisors, particularly in command staff positions, reflects the extent to which police management remains a gendered occupation.

The Nature of Policing: Scope of Work and Occupational Culture

NATURE OF THE WORK

Police officers are the gatekeepers of the criminal justice system, enforcing the law and arresting offenders. In addition, officers are expected to prevent crime, protect life and property, maintain peace and public order, and provide a wide range of services to citizens 24 hours a day. A common thread unifying these diverse activities is the potential for violence and the right to use coercive means to enforce the officer's definition of the situation to establish social control at that moment (Bittner, 1970). Policing has traditionally been regarded as men's work because it is associated with crime, danger, and coercion. Yet, people frequently fail to question the logical shifts in the statement that "*coercion* requires *force* which *implies physique* and hence policing by *men*" (Heidensohn, 1992, p. 73; emphasis in original).

Crime fighting is the aspect of the job that both officers and the public regard as "real" police work. It is visible, publicly valued, and the most satisfying part of the work for most officers. Detectives focus on investigating crimes and making arrests, are relieved of service or order maintenance tasks, and get more pay, prestige, and personal autonomy. The association of catching criminals with danger and bravery marks police work as a man's job.

The daily reality of policing is far less glamorous. Most police calls involve requests for service or order maintenance tasks. One study of police activity in three California departments found that only 31% of all incidents involved officers in crime-related activities (i.e., apprehending felons or investigating and suppressing crime) (Brown, 1981). Violence, even verbal aggression, is a relatively rare occurrence (Bayley & Garofalo, 1989). Rather, policing involves officers with people at their worst—when they have been victimized, are injured or helpless, or are guilty and seeking escape. To be effective, officers must restore order in volatile situations and use interpersonal skills, rather than bravado, to gain compliance.

THE POLICE OFFICER'S "WORKING PERSONALITY"

The combination of danger related to unpredictable physical violence, authority to exercise force, and organizational pressure for efficiency has resulted in a unique set of behaviors and attitudes termed the officers' "working personality" (Skolnick, 1966). Faced with danger, officers become suspicious. Because they have discretion to decide when and whether to use morally dirty means to handle problems, they are feared by and isolated from citizens.

In an effort to inhibit the abuses of power and corruption historically associated with urban policing, administrators have adopted a quasi-military organizational structure and have imposed numerous rules on officers. Despite the elaboration of rule books, discretion is an essential part of the job. Street patrol requires situational decision making; rigid rules have little value in fluid and sometimes volatile situations. Consequently, most officers routinely violate or circumvent rules (Hunt, 1990; Manning, 1977).

To protect themselves from supervisors who may punish these infractions and from a citizenry viewed as hostile, officers have created a unique, cohesive occupational culture. Police rely on fellow officers for physical protection, support, solidarity, and social identity. Their job becomes a way of life, and the occupational culture provides both an alternative morality and an identity (Manning, 1977; Skolnick, 1966; Westley, 1970).

OCCUPATIONAL CULTURE

The informal work culture of street patrol officers has several rules. Officers are expected to remain silent about other officers' illicit behavior, to provide physical backup to fellow officers, and to mete out street justice to people who display disrespect for the police. Officers who fail to do so are not trusted by others and face ostracism, the silent treatment, and outright rejection as partners (Westley, 1970).

For many years, police assured group solidarity by recruiting and selecting a homogeneous group of working-class white men. "Outsiders" were eliminated by physical requirements (women) and written tests and/or educational requirements (blacks and other people of color). Background investigations and personal interviews eliminated the remaining candidates who failed to express "correct" masculine attitudes emphasizing toughness and aggressiveness (David & Brannon, 1976; Gray, 1975).

Much of the foregoing characterization of police culture is more than two decades old. Although there is general agreement that the "street cop" culture that emphasizes toughness and physical prowess still exists, it is much less clear how the culture has changed in response to external demands and internal pressure in the past two decades. Despite many examinations of such reforms as professionalization and community-oriented policing, researchers have largely neglected the effect of increased employment of women and people of color on the police culture (but see Heidensohn, 1992; Hunt, 1990; Walker, 1985).

RECENT TRENDS IN POLICING
AND THEIR IMPLICATIONS FOR WOMEN

For more than half a century, efforts to reform the police have focused on changing street practices to eliminate three categories of recurrent problems: corruption, police brutality, and alienation from the community (Sykes, 1985). In the 1970s, these issues were addressed primarily by "professionalizing" policing in a way that was narrow in scope and conceptually inaccurate. Professionalization included efforts to increase organizational efficiency and productivity by expanding top-down control, improving recruitment and training, hiring more white women and people of color, and adding technology and resources. This contributed to tension between management cop and street cop cultures (Reuss-Ianni, 1983).

In the 1980s, community-based policing became the watchword for gaining public support by linking the officer to the community, neighborhood, and citizens in the "co-production" of crime control and public safety services (Skolnick & Bayley, 1986). Champions of such programs as the return of foot patrol and "problem-oriented policing," in which officers identify and seek to solve recurrent problems, believe that they will improve two-way interaction and communication between police and community (Eck & Spelman, 1987; Pate, Skogan, Wycoff, & Sherman, 1986). Critics suggest that this community-oriented effort deflects community concerns for more police accountability, placates the most vocal citizens, and further mystifies the police role (Klockars, 1988; Manning, 1984).

Community-based policing requires police organizations to reconceptualize what is "real police work," changing the focus from individual "crimes" to recurrent problems affecting order and public services. It also demands officers who are trained in problem identification, analysis, solutions, and interpersonal skills. The grip of traditional control-centered management must be relaxed under community-based policing to allow more officer discretion and autonomy (Greene, 1993).

The extent to which community policing programs go beyond rhetoric and actually redefine the police role, expand reciprocity in police-community relations, and decentralize police services and command still is unclear. The Rodney King incident illustrated that relations between the police and citizens, particularly people of color, remain troubled. In light of the long-standing tension between the service and crime-fighting components of the police role, community policing offers the prospect of a shift toward greater emphasis on and rewards for community service, crime prevention, and problem solving. Officers are expected to rely on interpersonal skills rather than crime fighting, a change that might be regarded as "feminizing" the management of social control. Therefore, despite benefits this reform might bring to street patrol officers, many men are likely to resist or undermine it, either openly or covertly.

The Police Culture and Men's Opposition to Women Officers

Few occupations have been so fully defined as masculine or have resisted integration of women as vigorously as policing. Despite changes in both the nature of policing and the status of women, many men officers continue to believe that women cannot handle the job physically or emotionally and, therefore, should not be allowed to exercise the moral authority of the state or be integrated into policing. This hostile attitude has been characterized as "a huge if shadowy presence which hangs like a miasma" over women officers (Heidensohn, 1992, p. 65). Beyond the attitudes of individual men, the work culture is characterized by drinking, crude jokes, racism, and demands that women who enter it "assume 'male characteristics' to achieve even a limited social acceptability" (Young, 1991, p. 193).

Men's most vocal concerns about women as police usually are stated in terms of physical capabilities, but the scope of opposition to women officers is far broader and deeper. Martin (1980) has argued that "the integration of women into police patrol work as coworkers threatens to compromise the work, the way of life, the social status, and the self-image of the men" (p. 79). Thus, resistance is related to the nature of the work, the occupational culture, and the manner in which these are used as resources for doing gender.

THE LOGIC OF SEXISM AND WOMEN'S THREAT TO POLICE WORK

Police work involves diverse and sometimes conflicting tasks. Jennifer Hunt (1984, p. 294) observed that "the policeman's world constitutes a symbolic universe permeated with gender meanings" that explain much of their behavior. The logic of sexism rests on the dualistic worldview that associates gender-stereotyped opposi- tions (i.e., masculinity/femininity) with various organizational symbols (e.g., street/station house), occupational themes and work activities (e.g., crime fighting/service and order maintenance), and situational meanings (public/domestic; dirty/clean). In each of the gender-stereotyped opposites, the item associated with the feminine is undervalued (Hunt, 1990).

Based on this dualistic view, men create an idealized image of policing as action-oriented, violent, and uncertain. They define themselves through these images, which are closely associated with the masculine side in contrasting pairs of gender-linked symbols. They use their work as a resource for doing masculinity. Thus, officers associate "real police work" with crime fighting. This takes place on the street and often involves collusion in "dirty knowledge" of illicit activity, the celebration of physical prowess and involve- ment in fights, and evasion of the formal rules; all of these are characteristics of street cop culture (see Reuss-Ianni, 1983). In contrast, supervisory, station house, and police academy assign- ments are associated with feminine labor involving "inside work" and women's skills. These are associated with the management cop culture disdained and resisted by street cops (Hunt, 1990).

Women threaten these working-class men's cultural norms, group solidarity, and definition of policing as men's work and police officers as masculine. Thus, the integration of women into street patrol has evoked strong opposition, which men generally explain in terms of the physical differences between themselves and women, who tend to be smaller and weaker. Although men assert that women's physical characteristics are the primary reason that women are less able to perform the job, the assignment of women to patrol poses a dilemma. In one of the few remaining occupations in which strength and physical ability occasionally are useful, women's presence implies either that the men's unique asset— physical strength—is irrelevant or that a man who works with a woman will be at a disadvantage in a confrontation.

Two other less frequently articulated concerns also support men's resistance to women: the belief that women are "mentally weaker" and the view that women are unable to command public respect as officers. Besides providing less "muscle" to a partner, women are seen as mentally weaker and, therefore, unreliable in the face of danger. If women cannot be trusted to aid their partners in physical confrontations, they threaten one of the basic norms of police work. Many men assert that they patrol in a more cautious (and, in their view, less effective) way with a woman partner.

WOMEN'S THREAT TO THE PUBLIC IMAGE AND CITIZEN "RESPECT"

Women officers are perceived to threaten the rule that the police should maintain respect on the street. In some instances, the uniform and badge are insufficient; the officer's personal authority and manner of conveying it are needed to gain citizen compliance. Men in this society are accustomed to viewing women as objects to be dominated rather than authority figures to be feared and obeyed. Conversely, women are unused to exercising authority over men. Men officers, therefore, fear that citizens will deny or resist women officers' efforts to exercise police authority and that this challenge to authority will be generalized to the police. Yet, the alternative scenario, a woman exercising authority over men, is also threatening to men officers' identities (Martin, 1980).

Women also threaten to expose the police myth that hides the demeaning nature of the work and sustains the public image of the police officer as a successful crime fighter. They remind the men that "they can only achieve illusory manhood by denying and repressing the essential feminine dimension of police work which involves social relations, paperwork, and housekeeping in the public domain" (Hunt, 1984, p. 294).

WOMEN'S THREAT TO GROUP SOLIDARITY AND MEN'S IDENTITY

Women's presence also undermines the solidarity of the men's group by changing the informal rules by which officers relate to and compete with each other. The world of the men's locker room is filled with crude (sexual) language and talk focused on sports, women's bodies, and sexuality that fosters men's bonds based on normative heterosexuality. Men officers virulently oppose homosexuality among police as a threat to group solidarity, police control of "deviant" behavior, and the hierarchy of sexualities. As the objects of much of the men's talk, women cannot participate in it on equal terms. Their integration raises the specter of sexual intimacy between officers. Such sexual ties compete with the demands of loyalty to the group that is essential in work involving danger. Despite the possibility of homosexual relationships, when all police were men, the department treated their sexuality as unproblematic as long as it was heterosexual. The fear of heterosexual competition among the men, however, causes organizations to try to eliminate sexuality and emotion from organizational functioning (Acker, 1992).

Women officers also threaten to disturb the informal distribution of rewards because officers no longer compete on equal terms. The "rules of chivalry," (i.e., code of gender interaction by which a "gentleman" relates to a "lady"), as well as the potential for the abuse of power (and violation of the rules of chivalry) to coerce sexual favors, often come into play in a gender-integrated police force. In such cases, gender is invoked as some men offer, and some women accept, exemptions and favorable assignments by taking "unfair advantage" of their sex. Because within the men's status order, sexual dalliances are viewed as power perquisites, women who accept sexual bargains are targets of officers' resentment, but men supervisors who permit such inequality to arise among officers are not.

Men's opposition to the integration of women also reflects a "deeper concern about who has a right to manage law and order" (Heidensohn, 1992, p. 215). In fact, Heidensohn asserts, the view that "men 'own' order and have sole rights to preserve it" is the real but unstated issue underlying their arguments that women are unsuitable and will shatter men's solidarity. Men's resistance to women on patrol is better understood as emanating from a struggle over the ownership of social control.

Women's integration challenges men's use of police work as a means of doing masculinity. Men strengthen their gendered identities through doing work that is labeled "masculine" and by fostering the image of their jobs as men's work. Gender segregation in the workplace, therefore, enables them to heighten the distinction between masculinity and femininity (Williams, 1989, p. 133). Preserving job activities labeled "for men only" simultaneously reinforces the association between masculinity and social control. If a man relies on another man, it is defined as male bonding or camaraderie; his reliance on a woman is viewed as a sign of weakness and, therefore, unmanly. The presence of women poses a bind for a man who wants to depend on his partner but does not want to depend on a woman. For many men, the simplest solution is to exclude women from patrol work. Because that is not possible except in very small departments, the most vigorous opponents of women in patrol work deal with their presence by avoidance; the rest appear to view "good" women cops as exceptions but treat women as a group as outsiders.

In sum, the combination of danger and power over the mechanisms of social control has resulted in a close association between policing and masculinity. The men have opposed women's integration into their ranks as a threat to their definition of the work, occupational culture, social status, and self-image as men's men, which is a psychological fringe benefit of the job.

Barriers to Women Officers: Interaction, Ideology, and Images

Men express their opposition to women officers through interactional patterns that marginalize and exclude them. Women's social isolation denies them mobility opportunities by limiting information, mentors, informal training, and a sense of comfort on the job. Women also face conflicting expectations and double standards regarding their performance. On the one hand, their visibility leads to higher performance standards than men confront; at the same time, they encounter paternalistic treatment in which little is expected of them. Sexual and gender harassment also are common occurrences. Each of these barriers is shaped by race-ethnicity as well as by gender.

The resistance faced by the first women on patrol was blatant, malicious, widespread, organized, and sometimes life-threatening (Bloch & Anderson, 1974; Hunt, 1984; Martin, 1980). Initially, many men refused to teach these women skills routinely imparted to new men; they failed to respond quickly or assist women seeking backup. Often, supervisors assigned women to dangerous foot beats alone (while men worked in pairs), overzealously enforced rules, depressed women's performance evaluations, sexually harassed them, and ignored women's mistreatment by fellow officers.

A few men favored the integration of women into patrol and assisted women. However, they did so at the risk of being ostracized by fellow street cops, and their actions on behalf of women tended to be viewed by other men as directed toward particular individuals rather than efforts to benefit women as a group (Martin, 1980). Today, the proportion of men who are comfortable working with women partners has grown substantially, but such men still rarely overtly resist the dominant attitudes.

Discrimination and hostility are less openly tolerated now, but they continue to permeate police organizations. In the station house, through frequent pranks, jokes, and comments that call attention to women's sexuality, men make clear to women that they are outsiders. By sexualizing the workplace, men superimpose their supposed gender superiority on women's claims to work-based equality.

INTERACTIONAL DILEMMAS

Because women make up only a small proportion of officers, they also suffer the consequences of tokenism (Kanter, 1977). Their visibility as tokens leads to little margin for error. At the same time, women are treated paternalistically, expected to do less than the men, extravagantly praised for doing an average job, denied opportunities to take initiative, and are criticized for doing so (i.e., acting "like a man"). They are also pressured to conform to gendered stereotypes of mother, little sister, or seductress. The errors of an individual woman are exaggerated and generalized to all women as a class. Conversely, positive efforts to organize a women's association or advance an individual woman, regardless of her accomplishments, raise concerns about favored treatment.

Both the physical and social environments provide a variety of cues that reflect and maintain women's subordinate status. Physical arrangements make clear that both the street and police station are "male turf." Locker room and lavatory facilities for women are limited; girlie calendars and pornographic materials "accidentally" left in the station are common sights (Martin, 1978).

Double standards also persist regarding language, sexuality, appearance, and demeanor. Women face language dilemmas in deciding whether to curse (and use "male" language) or not (and give up the opportunity to make "strong" statements), whether to tolerate men's use of gross language, and how to deal with being called "hon" or "sweetheart" by colleagues. Women supervisors also must deal with the refusal of men subordinates to acknowledge their rank. In fact, Morash and Haarr (1995) found that language harassment (defined as offensive use of profanity) was a significant source of stress for women. Describing the work environment and double standards that women encounter, a woman sergeant in Susan Ehrlich Martin's (1990) study summarized the situation this way:

> There's a certain finesse a woman has to have, a certain feminine grace. If you tell it like it is and don't watch your figure or fix yourself up or have what the men expect, you won't be given quite the preference. . . . For example, they let a capable woman go from (a detective assignment) because she's fat . . . yet they'll give breaks to the biggest male toad with a foul mouth. (p. 153)

Off-duty socializing also poses interactional dilemmas for women officers. The men often drink together after work and participate in team sports or other shared recreational activities. Women's limited participation in this informal socializing deprives them of an important source of information and feedback, as well as the opportunity to make contacts, cultivate sponsors, and build alliances that contribute to occupational success (Martin, 1980). Although the "stag party" atmosphere of off-duty partying has diminished, women are only partially integrated into the informal activities and influence structure. Some women choose not to socialize outside of work due to family responsibilities or concern with gossip. Although it protects their reputations, this social withdrawal isolates women. Other women participate in social activities, but at the risk of sexual rumor and innuendo.

THE SEXUALIZED WORKPLACE

Men maintain women's status as outsiders by sexualizing the workplace (Cockburn, 1991; Swerdlow, 1989). Women experience sexual propositions and threats as well as other forms of sexual harassment as a condition of work; this harassment may include unwanted touching, comments that call attention to their sexuality or express antiwoman sentiment, and a variety of pranks and jokes (Hunt, 1984; Martin, 1980; Young, 1991). Women find sex magazines, dildos, and vibrators in their lockers and mailboxes; they encounter betting pools on who will be the first to have sex with a new woman officer.

Most women officers have experienced sexual harassment on the job. In one study, Susan Ehrlich Martin (1990) found that 63% of 72 women officers interviewed in five large urban departments recounted instances of sexual harassment on the job, including 25% who had experienced quid pro quo harassment. According to a 1990 Michigan State University study of 26 urban and rural departments, 12% of the women officers said they had been touched by supervisors in an offensive way in the past year; 4% said their bosses had tried to force them to have intercourse (cited in Cooper, 1992, p. A-10).

Regardless of how they react, such harassment is problematic for women. It is an important source of stress (Morash & Haarr, 1995; Wexler & Logan, 1983), it isolates women from men colleagues, and it divides women. Although many women officers experience sexual harassment, they have not united or taken coordinated action to press for change. Instead, women tend to reproach other women, asserting that those who get sexually harassed "ask for it" through their demeanor or behavior. Such victim blaming makes the woman rather than her harasser the target of criticism.

THE INTERSECTION OF
RACE-ETHNICITY AND GENDER

The simultaneous effects of race-ethnicity and gender for women in policing rarely have been examined. Sociologist Diane Pike (1992) observed that "being black as opposed to being female generates a very different organizational adaptation and response" because "black men do not challenge the quintessential police officer role in the same way women do" (pp. 275-276). However, she ignored the unique situation of black women officers.

Men's initial resistance to the presence of women on patrol led to hostile treatment regardless of race. Nevertheless, reactions to and treatment of black and white women reflect differences in cultural images and attitudes (Belknap & Shelley, 1992; Bloch & Anderson, 1974; Martin, 1994; Price, Sokoloff, & Kuleshnyka, 1992; Worden, 1993). Initially, black men tended to be less hostile than white men to women on patrol, but they also stated a preference for men partners (Bloch & Anderson, 1974). Because cultural images or stereotypes of white and black women differ, black women often are treated according to separate norms and images. They are less frequently put on a pedestal or treated as "ladies" or little sisters to be protected by white men. Rather, they are treated as jezebels (i.e., sexually aggressive women) or welfare mothers (i.e., seen as likely to get pregnant and take advantage of "light duty") (P. Collins, 1991).

Susan Ehrlich Martin (1990) found that white women, particularly those who were physically attractive, were more likely than black women to get inside assignments and protection on street patrol. A number of black women observed that white men backed them up when they had a white partner but not when they had a black one. Belknap and Shelley (1992, p. 63) found that black women were less likely than white women to believe that fellow officers recognized when they had done a good job. Black women also report encountering racist stereotypes (e.g., that they are stupid) and outright racial harassment. As one black women noted in commenting on the combination of race and gender problems, "sometimes I couldn't tell if what I faced was racial or sexual or both. The black female is the last one on the totem pole in the department" (Martin, 1994, p. 393).

Racial concerns also have affected the women's responses to sexual harassment. A black woman in a department with a long history of racial discrimination explained that, although she was sexually harassed by a black man superior, she decided against filing a complaint "'cause he's black." She observed, "I guess that makes me a racist, but I looked at the overall problem it would have caused and how it would be played up in the press and didn't do it" (Martin, 1994, p. 394).

Summary

This chapter has examined the work of patrol officers, the historical and current role of women in police work, and the sources of men's resistance to women's presence. Initially, women entered policing as specialists, doing work that was an extension of their domestic roles. Women's integration into police patrol was fostered by a number of factors related to both changes in the nature and organization of police work following urban unrest and changes in the social status of women, particularly legal changes following the 1972 amendments to the 1964 Civil Rights Act.

The number of women officers has grown in the past two decades; they currently represent nearly 10% of sworn personnel and 3% of supervisors. Despite these changes, policing remains associated with masculinity and the informal work culture continues to be strongly resistant to women because their presence threatens men's definition of their work and themselves. Women are perceived as a threat to the men's physical safety, group solidarity, and occupational identity as macho crime fighters. In addition, women's presence undermines the close association of their work with masculinity and men's control over social order.

Women officers encounter interactional barriers and gendered images that establish them as outsiders, sexual objects, targets of men's resentment, and competitors who threaten to change the rules of officer interaction. Compounding these stresses for black women officers are dilemmas arising from racist stereotypes.

In addition to an informal work culture that marginalizes and excludes them, women enter a police organization with rules, policies, and practices that are far from gender-neutral. These organizational barriers and on-the-street dilemmas for women and the manner in which they have responded to and overcome them are the subject of the next chapter.

Notes

1. For more data on the history of women in policing in the United States, see Horne (1980), Feinman (1986), and Price and Gavin (1982). For studies of women police in Britain, see Lock (1979), Jones (1986), Young (1991), and Heidensohn (1992).

2. Fyfe's (1987) survey found that by 1986, fewer than 4% of municipal agencies still had minimum height and weight standards as entry criteria.

3. Morash and Greene (1986) point out several biases. The evaluations emphasized situations and characteristics associated with masculine stereotypes (e.g., aggressiveness on patrol). They assumed that observed differences resulted from personal or psychological peculiarities of the women rather than from negative experiences once in the department. The evaluations failed to measure the accomplishment of specific police behaviors. They lacked clear standards for weighing frequent policing tasks relative to atypical but critical events and for determining "good" police performance. They overemphasized gender stereotypes. Fewer than half the items in the evaluations related to specific behaviors; many assessed whether officers met such masculine stereotypes as

being forceful and decisive. Common but unpopular tasks were de-emphasized in favor of items involving violence.

4. Others argue that given the history of police racism, for a black person to join the police is a form of "working for the enemy." For the stresses of being "blacks in blue" see Alex (1969) and Leinen (1984).

4
□

Women Officers Encountering
the Gendered Police Organization

Departmental policies and informal practices gender police work in ways that disadvantage women officers. These processes begin with recruitment and selection, are reinforced through training and assignments, and permeate encounters with citizens.

Although departments have opened the doors to the station house, they have resisted changes to ease women's integration. Standards for evaluating performance, behavior, and appearance are designed for men, from displays of physical bravado to the tailoring of uniforms. Women face dilemmas because men do not want women to behave like men and do not accept women who "act mannish" as equals. On the other hand, women who act "feminine" are regarded as inadequate officers. These dilemmas and barriers affect women officers' work lives and identities by shaping occupational opportunities, creating unique stresses, increasing turnover rates, and leading to several adaptive strategies for survival and success in policing.

Gendered Organizational Logic:
Policies and Practices

GENDER AND TRAINING

Police training includes several phases. Recruits receive brief but intensive academy training (about 4 months), followed by several months of on-the-job training patrolling under the supervision of an experienced officer. They remain subject to summary dismissal throughout their probationary year.

The Training Academy

At the training academy, new recruits learn law and legal procedures, first aid, and policing skills, as well as the importance of group solidarity and paramilitary discipline. The training emphasizes a vocabulary of defensiveness (i.e., be alert to possible danger), professionalization (i.e., be responsible and independent), and depersonalization (i.e., view the public in a detached, unemotional way) (Harris, 1973). Like military training, the police academy functions as a rite of passage and is intended to replace civilian patterns of behavior with the perspectives of the new organization.

The academy curriculum, instruction, and experience are gendered in a number of ways, all designed to strengthen "the male macho image" (Pike, 1992, p. 262). The curriculum emphasizes the development of physical and technical skills, in which men are likely to have an initial advantage, over interpersonal skills at which women are more likely to excel.

Dealing with the physical differences between men and women has posed dilemmas for police departments and recruits. Officers must gain control of others, occasionally by use of physical force. Academy training includes self-defense techniques as well as physical training, although the extent to which strength and fitness are necessary is unclear. The largely symbolic nature of the physical training prior to the 1980s is illustrated by the absence of any requirement in many departments that officers maintain even minimal standards of fitness after the rookie year.

Men enter the academy with a physical advantage. They are usually larger and stronger than women and are more likely to have had previous athletic and bodybuilding experiences. Men also are more likely to have played in contact sports that introduced them to important elements in the police culture, including controlled use of violence, teamwork and group loyalty, uniform behavior, tolerance of physical pain, and a willingness to inflict pain on others (Gray, 1975).

Many departments have eliminated preemployment physical testing and have replaced the academy's physical agility tests, with their emphasis on push-ups and pull-ups not directly relevant to the job with health and fitness tests. However, these changes are far from uniform. All-around wellness standards have stimulated officer resistance. As one man administrator observed, "The idea that [a woman] must do the same number of push-ups as me is hocus-pocus, but it's been bred into many officers including the women" (S. Martin, 1990, p. 65).

Instructional methods and content also exemplify the gendered nature of the academy and police organization into which recruits must fit. Classroom characterizations of women highlight their difference from men and their inappropriateness for patrol through humor and stereotyped images (Pike, 1992). Women often appear as sex objects in jokes and training films, heightening gender boundaries. Recruits are told that women victims and suspects pose unique problems for officers related to women's sexiness (Pike, 1992). Women officers are portrayed as having stereotypic interpersonal skills but as disadvantaged by their lack of physical strength and aggressiveness.

"War stories" emphasizing the physical aspects of training and danger on patrol reinforce women's outsider status. Charles (1981) found that men recruits equate personal safety with physical prowess, even though the primary cause of officer deaths is improper police actions. The men rate their women classmates lower not only on physical measures but on many technical and general measures, despite similar actual scores.

Gender differences also are fostered by teasing and flirting. All recruits get teased as a rite of initiation, "to see if they can take it," but teasing of women highlights the fact that they are regarded as sex objects (Pike, 1992). Similarly, flirting reinforces the response to women as sex objects, the occupational working definition of police officers as macho and masculine, and the gendered nature of the organization, by highlighting women's visibility and difference from men.

Academy training also may foster inequality by permitting or encouraging women to seek exemptions, particularly to physical standards. Some women are passed on, permitted to "whine" or claim a medical exemption, by instructors who "let them slide." This treatment identifies those women as different from officers who learn to "suffer in silence," increases men's resentment of the presence of all women, and heightens the concern about women colleagues' ability to carry out patrol duties. It also divides women into those who seek exemptions and those who play by the rules and feel obliged to prove that the exemption seekers are not typical (S. Martin, 1980).

Administrators face a dilemma in deciding whether to foster a "women's caucus" or include training sessions designed to help women deal with heightened visibility on the street and hostility in the station house. Ignoring these issues fails to address concerns of women recruits. But addressing them highlights women's visibility as tokens, engenders men's resentment that women get "special treatment," and upsets women who do not want to be "singled out."

Field Training and Patrol:
Cycles of Success and Failure

Following academy training, rookies usually undergo supervised field training for several months. During this period of on-the-job training, they learn the "tricks of the trade," including the informal rules of the street cop culture. Subsequently, rookies are certified to patrol alone, although supervisors tend to assign them as "floaters" to cover for officers on leave or off duty. As openings occur, they obtain permanent beat or scout-car assignments.

The rookie's field training assignment and initial behavior on patrol are the basis of both self-confidence and a career-long reputation that affects opportunities. All rookies face reality shock when they begin street patrol. Both overprotection or underinstruction retard development of patrol skills. Gender-based differences in interaction compounded by gendered patterns of socialization in the academy and expectations of women's patrol performance influence rookies' responses, creating self-fulfilling prophecies for many women officers (S. Martin, 1980).

These patterns were most evident for the first generation of women, who faced organized efforts to drive them out, including insufficient instruction, coworker hostility, the silent treatment (which, in the words of one officer, "made eight hours seem like eight days"), close and punitive supervision; exposure to danger and lack of backup, and paternalistic overprotection. One woman said, "I was at the precinct 10 days before I knew I had a partner 'cause . . . [the men] called in sick and I was put in the station" (S. Martin, 1994, p. 141). Another stated:

My first day on the north side, the assignment officer looked up and said, "oh shit, another fucking female." . . . My sergeant called me in and said the training officer doesn't want to ride with you but I've given him a direct order to work with you. (p. 390)

Although such overt expressions of hostility are less frequent today, supervisors still tend to keep new women from the busiest beats, and partners tend to protectively seize the initiative. Women that object to such treatment often are labeled "bitches" or un-feminine. This pattern results in the following cycle of protection, incompetence, and demotivation:

[Rookie] officers . . . face unfamiliar and unpredictable situations on the street. In successfully taking action and overcoming their fears, most officers gain confidence as they develop policing skills. The ability to cope with the paperwork, the law, the courts, and most importantly, the citizens they encounter all bolster confidence. . . . The officer who does not have or take the opportunity to develop street patrol skills as a result of

limiting assignments, inadequate instruction, or overprotection is likely to act hesitantly or fail to act in a confrontation.
Because an incompetent officer is regarded by colleagues as a
potential danger to themselves as well as the officer in question,
they are anxious to get such an officer off the street or minimize
his or her street activities, thus perpetuating the cycle of
incompetence on patrol. (Martin, 1980, p. 129)

This paternalistic pattern creates a catch-22 for women. They are
protected and not really expected to behave like the men on patrol,
then blamed for failing to meet performance standards. Occasionally such paternalism is formalized as a policy. For example, the
Chicago Police Department's rule prohibits women from working
on the wagon (that takes arrestees to jail), which results in some
men's criticizing them for shirking their fair share of unpleasant
assignments.

This cycle leads to pressure on women to leave street patrol
"before anyone gets hurt,"[1] thus depriving some individuals of
opportunities to become effective patrol officers. Women as a group
also are hurt by being divided into those who seek paternalistic
protection and those who reject it and criticize the protected women.
It creates problems for women supervisors, who encounter hostility
when they fail to give protected women special treatment. And it
contributes to men's resentment of women, whom they blame for
playing by different rules, rules that, in fact, are created by their
men supervisors and supported by their own behavior. Both the
"pushes" of the cycle of protection and the "pulls" of opportunities
opened by Equal Employment Opportunity (EEO) efforts to assign
women to all units have steadily channeled women out of patrol
and into more "feminine" positions.

GENDERED ASSIGNMENT PATTERNS

Within police precincts, there are quiet and active beats, permanent and rotating patrol assignment, and other assignments (e.g.,
to a vice unit or station-house duties). Most precinct officers are
assigned to a permanent scout-car beat, which they may have for

many years. Statistical data on day-to-day assignments by officer gender are virtually nonexistent, but interview data suggest that women are slower to get permanent scout cars and are assigned to quieter beats and to the station house more often than men with similar seniority (S. Martin, 1980, 1990).

Over the course of a policing career, most officers either have temporary assignments to nonpatrol details or obtain transfers to better assignments. Some are promoted. The most coveted assignments are those that offer higher organizational status, opportunities for additional pay (often through overtime), greater autonomy, and less continuous supervision. These characteristics describe the work of detectives and tactical unit officers, who are freed from responding to calls for service and from wearing a uniform but who have outside crime-fighting assignments associated with masculinity. Support staff assignments to the academy or administrative units also offer better working conditions, including regular daytime hours, but are less valued because of their association with management and feminine labor (Hunt, 1984).

The limited statistical data on nonpatrol assignment patterns suggest wide variation across law enforcement agencies in the extent and nature of the division of labor. Given the differences in desirability and prestige associated with particular specialized duties, based in part on their gender-associated characteristics, it is not surprising that there are gender and race-ethnic variations in their distribution. Sulton and Townsey's (1981) survey indicated that white men were overrepresented in investigative and traffic units; white women and men of color were overrepresented in juvenile and technical units, including dispatcher assignments. These variations reflect patterns that prevailed prior to women's assignment to patrol; they also reflect men's greater seniority (a criterion for distributing desirable assignments) and a gendered organizational logic.

Susan Ehrlich Martin's (1990) survey of municipal departments serving populations over 50,000 found that by 1987, women were slightly underrepresented in detective and vice units and overrepresented in administrative and other units. Case studies conducted in five of those departments identified consistent patterns of gender differences with respect to the number and types of prior assignments and the current assignments of officers. In three of the four departments for which assignment data were available, the number of different assignments an officer had over a career was significantly greater for women than men of similar race-ethnicity, rank, and length of police service. This difference may indicate that women had more opportunities and greater mobility than the men because many were members of the first cohort to benefit from affirmative action policies. Alternatively, it may be that women tended to transfer out of assignments when they met with hostility and harassment. Both factors probably operated simultaneously.

Consistent differences between the assignments of men and women at the time the data were collected also were found. As shown in Table 4.1, when assignments were divided into three groups—patrol, other line units (i.e., traffic, investigation, vice, and other patrol support), and administrative and staff support—women in all four agencies were more likely than men to be in staff support units. In three of the four, they also were less likely to be assigned to patrol; the pattern for investigation and patrol-support assignments was inconsistent. These data suggest that rather than being integrated into police work, women are being re-ghettoized into an enlarged pool of assignments considered appropriate for women. For example, women have become evidence technicians and administrative sergeants, the powerful but "paper-pushing" assistants to shift commanders.

GENDERED ORGANIZATIONAL LOGIC
AND WOMEN'S OCCUPATIONAL MOBILITY

Both formal rules and informal practices affect career opportunities and gender differentiation in police agencies. Organizational factors affecting mobility include the number and types of assignments and promotions available, rules regarding transfers and promotions, the availability and distribution of training opportunities, and EEO policies. The actual distribution of opportunities also is shaped by the informal work culture, sponsorship by influential

TABLE 4.1 Assignments of Sample Officers in Four Municipal Departments by Gender

Percentage assigned to:	Washington, D.C.		Birmingham, Alabama		Detroit		Phoenix	
	W	M	W	M	W	M	W	M
Patrol[a]	70	78	57	53	51	64	66	80
Investigation or field support[b]	11	16	24	40	25	23	18	7
Community relations, technical and administrative units	19	6	19	7	24	12	17	13
	100%	100%	100%	100%	100%	100%	100%	100%
	$\chi^2 = 9.04$		$\chi^2 = 6.58$		$\chi^2 = 5.72$		$\chi^2 = 6.14$	
	$p < .02$		$p < .05$		$p < .06$		$p < .05$	

Source: S. Martin (1990, p. 42), printed by permission of the Police Foundation.
a. In Washington, D.C., within each of the department's 7 districts, officers may be assigned to patrol or to specialized units (e.g., vice, detective, or youth squads). There also are similar citywide specialized units. Data in the table indicate officer's primary assignment (i.e., district or specialized citywide unit); information on assignments within patrol districts was not available.
b. Includes detectives, vice and narcotics units, traffic, special operations, and tactical and tactical support units, except as noted above.

individuals, and apparent "fit" with others in the unit; these factors can make or break careers.

Both formal rules and informal practices hinder women's careers in policing by pressing them into certain assignments and expecting them to perform in ways that conform to popular cultural images of femininity. In addition, women learn that they do not fit in the gendered organization through the division of space (e.g., the absence of a locker room and women's bathroom, particularly in older police stations), images and symbols (e.g., offensive "pinups" adorning the station), rules regarding appearance (e.g., standards for hair length and jewelry), and uniforms (designed for and tailored to men's bodies).

The linkage of formal and informal aspects of the gendered logic of the police organization is made clear by Michael Charles (1981), who observed that women are evaluated by peers "not only on job performance, but their ability to 'fit in' the social setting as well" (p. 222). Because the officer's ability to fit in is at least as important as job performance in the police culture, lack of acceptance into the social culture of the work group "creates almost insurmountable obstacles for the officer," which further hinder performance and substantiate fellow peers' negative perceptions, thus "producing a revolving door dilemma from which it is difficult to escape" (p. 222).

Women officers are overrepresented in staff assignments and underrepresented in patrol support positions for several reasons related to the logic of sexism (Hunt, 1990). First, in elite tactical units, such as gang squads and SWAT teams, the work involves handling heavy equipment (e.g., battering rams), there is fierce competition for assignments, and the few women who attain them often feel isolated and transfer out (S. Martin, 1990; Price et al., 1992). In contrast, prevailing images of women assume that they have office skills and that inside work is feminized and not real policing. Many of the men encourage women officers to reduce the burdens of tokenism encountered on patrol by transferring to assignments viewed as gender-appropriate. In addition to a more comfortable work environment, staff assignments tend to have fixed

performance standards for men. For example, instructions for the Chicago Police Department's rating forms suggest that in assessing the quantity of work, raters consider only arrest activity, traffic enforcement, court attendance (which stems from the prior two), and award history. Public service, crime prevention, and other types of activities receive no notice. Similarly, in rating personal relations, supervisors are instructed to consider the employee's ability to cooperate in team efforts and whether the employee is "someone with whom most other members are able to work comfortably" (S. Martin, 1990, p. 79). Under this system, women are doubly penalized. If men are not comfortable working with a woman or overprotect her, it is she who is negatively evaluated for "inadequate" personal relations. In addition, a woman's crime prevention activities are not rewarded in the same way as arrests in the measure of quantity of work but are recognized only as reflecting a presumably positive attitude toward service to the public.

Examinations of actual performance scores in two other jurisdictions suggest the effects of gender stereotypes and the probable biases of the mostly men raters on evaluations. A study of the 1984 and 1985 rating reports of 26 women and 51 men who joined the Minneapolis Police Department after 1980 found that women's median scores were worse than men's on all but 3 of the 24 measures included in the evaluation form (Byrne & Oakes, 1986, pp. A11-A12). The gender gap was greatest in categories related to aggressiveness. For example, in control of conflict through both physical skill and voice command, 40% of the men, but only 5% of the women, received the top two ratings. Men even got higher ratings on appearance, ostensibly because they look more like police. Women outscored men in only two measures of report writing, and they were rated equal in relationships with the public.

In Martin's 1990 study, a sample of men and women officers in Phoenix matched by race-ethnicity and length of service received identical overall ratings and differed significantly in only 4 of 20 standard categories. Men were significantly more likely to be rated as exceeding expectations with respect to job knowledge, skills, and effectiveness under stress; women were rated higher on the appearance of their workstations. These ratings generally conform to gender stereotypes and illustrate how evaluations are another mechanism for constructing competence and equating it with masculinity.

Instead of viewing women's performance as negative deviations from the norm of street cop culture that emphasizes crime fighting, variations in policing styles might be viewed as potential sources of alternative definitions of social control. The insistence on assessing women's performance by the standard of masculinity obscures the fact that the crime-fighting model embraced by "a predominantly male-oriented police system has failed to prevent, deter, or resolve crimes that have been brought to its attention" (Bell, 1982, pp. 119-120).

UNIFORMS AND APPEARANCE RULES: FORMALIZING GENDERED IMAGES

Police uniforms distinguish officers from other citizens and are symbolically important to both the public and officers. Officers stand for inspection as part of roll call, sometimes are disciplined for shoes that are not polished, and are quick to criticize those who do not convey pride in "wearing the blue."

An officer who is unable to move freely cannot perform the job effectively. The first cohort of women assigned to patrol were outfitted in skirts and carried their guns in pocketbooks. Although uniforms were soon changed, a new and largely symbolic debate arose: Should women's gear be identical to that of men or designed for women? Whatever resolution was adopted by various departments, the decision made clear the gendered nature of how an officer should look (i.e., like a man). Until rules regarding hair length were changed in response to protests from the men in the 1970s, women were required to have hair as short as the men or tuck long hair under their hat. Long hair was considered a potential danger to the officer. Similarly, jewelry and makeup rules have generated debates of a largely symbolic nature over the extent to which women officers may be permitted to appear different (i.e., feminine) and still be accepted as police.

Doing Gender on the Street:
Dilemmas of Police-Citizen Encounters

GENDER AND POLICE WORK

When women workers enter men's turf, they usually are required implicitly to accept men's definitions of that work and the behavioral scripts designed by and for men workers. Thus, even when women do police patrol, job tasks and service styles remain gendered. A central element of policing across situations and tasks is the need to gain control and maintain respect for police authority. Although both men and women officers may perform policing tasks, the meanings of such activities remain associated with manhood and must be addressed as the officers do masculine dominance. For women in policing, this means finding ways to deal with citizens' perceptions, interactions, and challenges to authority.

In police-citizen interactions, the officer seeks to take control but faces uncertainties arising from incomplete information about the citizen and the situation. Citizens often are reluctant to talk to an officer or may behave in inappropriate ways. They may seek to disrupt normal interaction by disavowing the officer's identity as a member of the police and the authority associated with it and relating "person to person," refocusing the interaction on irrelevant statuses, such as gender or race-ethnicity, to gain an advantage (Goffman, 1961).

Citizens generally defer to police officers, who tend to have higher status than most citizens they encounter. At any time, however, reference to an officer's irrelevant lower status characteristic may reverse the flow of deference and threaten the officer's control of the situation. Such interruptions are more prevalent for officers with devalued race-ethnic and/or gender statuses. Thus, how officers and citizens "do gender" in these situations depends on the sex categories of the participants, the specific circumstances, and the meaning of gender in the situational context. A woman cop may be called "officer," but she still is judged in terms of gender stereotypes and pressured to prove that she is "an 'essentially' feminine being, despite appearances to the contrary" (West & Zimmerman, 1987,

p. 140). Her sex category may be used to discredit her engaging in certain patrol activities, whereas her involvement in law enforcement may be used to discredit her performance as a wife and mother.

Because police work has been so closely associated with men and masculinity, the ways that men officers do gender as they do dominance have been treated as natural and thus have been virtually invisible. The close association of authority and control with masculinity, however, makes interactions with citizens more problematic for women cops, who must find ways to limit attention to their sex category or take advantage of it.

Work organizations do gender by constructing and legitimating a gendered image of workers and by calling for enactment of scripted behavior (i.e., stereotypic sequences of actions for familiar or recurring situations); men and women workers do gender by differentially enacting these gendered scripts (Hall, 1993). Just as what constitutes providing good service in restaurants depends on both the restaurant and the server's gender (Hall, 1993), work roles are engendered both by police departments and individual officers, and the concept of "good service" also varies in police work across situations and interactions. In contrast to food service, however, good police work involves taking control of whatever situation arises.

Police-citizen encounters are scripted, and the traditional script calls for masculine behavior (i.e., dominance or control), particularly in dealing with criminal offenders, most of whom are men or boys. However, it also may require providing service or emotional support to victims and their families, which may be viewed as feminine and so devalued (Hunt, 1990). Thus, gendered scripts in policing relate to the definition of the encounter as crime fighting or providing service and of the citizen as a suspect who requires control or a victim who merits support.

The interpersonal resources available to officers and citizens' expectations of culturally dominant images of masculine behavior tend to put women at a disadvantage on street patrol. Women police, in order to gain and maintain credibility as officers, must avoid smiling and appearing friendly (except, of course, as "Officer

Friendly," a title that explicitly reverses the stereotype of police for the sake of community relations), and they must demand deference rather than deferring to others.

Scripts in police work also are based on race and class. Many officers dislike working in upper-class precincts, which have less crime but also are characterized by different patterns of police-citizen interactions. Although there is greater civility, officers' blue-collar social status is lower than that of most citizens they encounter, and the officers resent these citizens' frequent demands for service, as well as reversal of the flow of deference owed to the officer.

DOING GENDER IN PATROL WORK

In police-citizen encounters, four possible combinations of gender and social category may arise: men officers with men or women citizens, and women officers with men or women citizens. Each combination has different expectations and management problems, as police relate to citizens by doing gender while doing dominance or otherwise enacting the police role.

When men officers interact with men citizens, their shared manhood can sometimes be effectively used as an interpersonal resource for doing gender. Generally this is to the citizen's advantage: It says, in effect, "act like a man [read: exercise self-control], and I won't have to exert my authority as an officer to overpower you." It also benefits the officer by minimizing the necessity of using force and enables him to act as a "good guy," giving a little to gain compliance. When suspects or offenders attempt to define the situation in terms of shared manhood, however, officers may view the interaction as a denial of the deference owed to their office. When a man officer relies too heavily on the authority of the badge or rejects a man citizen's effort to be treated as a man, the result is a duel of manhood, with a high probability of verbal or physical confrontation that might have been avoided (Martin, 1980).

As a result of men officers' double-status superiority over women citizens, few problems usually arise in such interactions, except those related to sexuality. Men officers may use the authority of their office to control or gain compliance from women who may have gotten "shrill" by calling on them to "act like a lady" (read: behave in a calm, dignified manner) to gain chivalrous treatment. If invoking the rules of chivalry works, the officer has maintained control while enhancing his sense of manly generosity. If it fails, he still may treat the woman as a wayward "girl" on whom he will not waste his time, or he may use force.

The flirting script or sexual flattery may be used by male officers, particularly with prostitutes. They may be manipulated to become informants in exchange for leniency in enforcing laws related to sexuality that reinforce gender power relations.

Interactions between women officers and men citizens are problematic because police expect to take control of situations and be shown deference by citizens; men may defer to the office but resist being controlled by or deferential to a woman. Thus, expectations regarding how a man relates to a woman and to a police officer generally differ and often conflict. In fact, women officers generally are given deference, either out of gender-blind respect for the uniform or because doing so does not challenge a man citizen's manhood if he chivalrously complies. Conversely, fighting a woman (particularly when men are witnesses) may cause a man citizen to lose status, whether he wins or loses the physical encounter.

The problem for a woman officer, however, is that men may revoke their deference, particularly if she is "unladylike" and acts "like a cop." Because women are often at a physical disadvantage, they may have to rely on the deference of men citizens as a control strategy. Although women officers generally try to minimize rather than activate their gender status, they recognize that men seek to redefine situations so as to affirm men's status superiority.

When women officers encounter sexist or sexual comments that intrude on but do not alter the outcome of an interaction, they generally ignore them, as is expected of officers in the face of a variety of citizen verbal abuse. In dealing with offenders, some women draw on citizens' stereotypes that they are "trigger happy" or are emotional in the face of danger. Some draw on familial roles or social stereotypes such as matriarch or "aggressive bitch" in asserting authority.

Other strategies by which women officers gain situational control involve use of various verbal and nonverbal cues to convey through voice, appearance, facial expression, and body postures that they are to be taken seriously, regardless of their physical stature. Learning to transmit these messages, however, often requires changing such habits as smiling and literally learning how to stand up to people.

In dealing with women citizens, women officers get both greater cooperation and more resistance than do men. For example, a study involving structured observation of new patrol officers found that women were both more positive and more negative to women officers in general, and similarly they had stronger positive and negative reactions to advice and assistance provided by women (Bloch & Anderson, 1974).

The dynamics of police-citizen interactions are affected not only by the gender of the participants (including witnesses) but also by their age, race-ethnicity, class, and sexual orientation. Thus, black officers, who historically were prohibited from arresting white citizens, may draw on racial bonds in dealing with black citizens but may have to overlook racial slurs or condescension in gaining white citizens' compliance.

USING GENDER

Effective police officers of both genders are flexible, able to use both the crime fighter script (associated with masculinity) and the service script (associated with femininity), according to situational demands. They draw on all the interpersonal resources available to them and appeal to gender-appropriate behavior, as well as citizens' respect for police authority, to gain cooperation. They use citizens' expectations and values to their advantage, doing gender in a way that diminishes social distance and maintains control at the same time. They rely on the authority of the badge and tools of policing only when necessary. In interacting with citizens, they may invoke gendered familial authority roles (i.e., mother, big brother).

Ineffective officers may either too rigidly rely on their formal authority, and enact only the crime-fighting aspects of their role, or alternatively emphasize only the community service script and fail to maintain control of interactions when they are challenged. The former shortcoming is more characteristic of men officers, the latter of women officers. Thus, ineffective men tend to provoke fights and generate citizen complaints that might have been avoided by a less bullying attitude; they demand deference, equating doing masculinity with doing police dominance. Ineffective women, in contrast, cannot overcome the handicaps women face in seeking to control men. On patrol, they fail to take control or assert the authority of their office as cops in situations that require such action.

Women's Response: Adaptations, Costs, and Survival Strategies

Women have responded to barriers to their integration into police work in several ways. In response to work-related stresses, some have left policing; others have sought assignments that are more comfortable than patrol. Although all women officers must deal with conflicting expectations as both women and officers, their policing styles and mechanisms of adaptation vary. Most have responded by adopting work-related attitudes similar to those of the men of their race-ethnic group. Identifying with the perspective of dominants is a mechanism subordinates often use to cope with discrimination.

ATTITUDES TOWARD POLICE WORK

Both men hostile to the entry of women and women's advocates have assumed that women officers would behave differently from men on patrol. Men feared women would not respond aggressively; advocates expected that women would have greater commitment to public service, more calming demeanors, and more empathetic and less violent encounters with citizens. These assumptions were based on extrapolations from the work of Gilligan (1982) and cultural feminists on women's differing socialization experiences and perspectives on morality and justice. The limited data comparing job-related attitudes of men and women officers have neither supported the belief that women view their occupational role differently from men nor refuted the possibility of some differences (e.g., Bloch & Anderson, 1974; Worden, 1993).

A recent study comparing the attitudes of men and women in 24 departments, based on data collected in 1977, found few gender differences in officers' perceptions of the public, their occupational roles, colleagues, and departments (Worden, 1993). Women were as ambivalent as men about restrictions on their autonomy on the job. They were mildly but equally positive in their views of the public and, as length of police experience increased, women's views of citizens converged with those of the men. Unexpectedly, white women were as complimentary about their colleagues and as positive about their departments as places to work as were white men. Compared to white officers, black women and men shared less positive views of their colleagues as officers. Worden (1993) interprets the absence of gender differences in perceptions of the workplace as telling less about women's objective experiences in policing than about their experiences with hostile working environments in other occupations.

Despite these attitudinal similarities, women had lower expectations of promotion than men and lacked self-confidence in handling a variety of policing situations. This suggests that the gendered work environment has a negative effect on their identity and self-image as officers.

The general failure of gender to explain much variation on an array of attitudes suggests that women do not have a single, unified, or distinctive perspective on policing. Similarly, despite frequent claims that women and men patrol differently, this difference has not been systematically measured in the past two decades. Differences on patrol may arise, moreover, not as a result of different approaches to policing by men and women but as a consequence of the gendered interactions, both with citizens and fellow officers, that reinforce women officers' identities as they do gender on the job.

POLICE WORK AND STRESS

Occupational stress has been linked to dissatisfaction, absenteeism, burnout, performance problems, and physical illness (Fletcher, 1988; Wright & Saylor, 1991). Several studies of police agencies (Morash & Haarr, 1995; Wexler & Logan, 1983; White & Marino, 1983) have found that both levels of stress and the primary stressors of men and women police are similar. These include relations within the organization (e.g., problems with supervisors), organizational climate (e.g., lack of management support), job circumstances (e.g., too much or too little work), ambiguities built into the occupational role, and career advancement issues. Morash and Haarr (1995) found that the strongest predictors of stress for both men and women were the lack of influence over day-to-day operations, overestimates of physical abilities, inadequate equipment and uniforms, and lack of advancement opportunity.

Women officers also face stressors specifically associated with being a woman, including the lack of acceptance as officers and the denial of information, sponsorship, and protection (Wexler & Logan, 1983). Morash and Haarr (1995) observes that two sources of stress, sexual harassment and language harassment (i.e., deliberate exposure to profanity and sexual jokes), were significantly correlated with workplace problems for women. In contrast, the strongest predictors of men's stress were being "set up" in dangerous situations and being ridiculed by coworkers.

The circumstances related to the men's and women's unique work stresses differ. Nevertheless, each represents a gender-related challenge to the individual's self-definition as masculine or feminine (in terms of hegemonic masculinity and emphasized femininity), respectively.

TURNOVER:
ADAPTING BY LEAVING

A recent study examining a wide spectrum of occupations found that women are entering a variety of male-dominated occupations more easily than might have been expected. However, they also are leaving those jobs quickly. As a result, their employment is less a permanent achievement than a temporary pass through a revolving door (Jacobs, 1989).

Data on gender differences in turnover rates in policing are limited and inconsistent. Women's turnover rate was found to be significantly higher than men's in the California Highway Patrol (1976) and a California sheriff's department (Fry, 1983). In contrast, Sulton and Townsey (1981) found similar turnover rates for men and women in municipal departments.

Susan Ehrlich Martin (1990) found that women had higher turnover rates than men in both municipal and state police departments, but that the gender difference was substantially larger in the latter. For example, in 1986 in municipal departments, 4.6% of the men and 6.3% of the women separated for reasons other than retirement. In state police agencies, only 2.9% of the men but 8.9% of the women left their departments. Thus, women's turnover rate in state police agencies was nearly three times that of men. These data suggest that formal equality of opportunity does not adequately address the problems women face arising from isolation and a hostile organizational environment, but that there is variation among departments and types of agencies.

Although quitting may be appropriate for some officers, and it appears to be the only way to solve problems or eliminate stresses for others, it has two negative effects for women as a group. First, it diminishes efforts to increase women's representation; second, it means that women accumulate seniority more slowly than men. This may reduce competition for women's jobs and enhance individual women's mobility opportunities, but it reduces the likelihood of women increasing their representation in specialized assignments and supervisory positions.

COPING STRATEGIES, ADAPTATIONS, AND WORK STYLES

Faced with openly discriminatory treatment and the burdens of performance pressures, group boundary heightening, and encapsulation in stereotyped roles (Kanter, 1977), women actively develop coping strategies. For example, Martin (1980) identified two opposite ideal types or patterns of behavioral adaptations used by female officers, which she characterizes as POLICEwomen and police-WOMEN. Because most women, in fact, seek to embody characteristics of each pattern and reject either extreme, few can be neatly categorized as fully embracing or typifying either coping strategy. The typology, nonetheless, highlights the nature of the dilemmas women assigned to patrol face in being accepted as both officers and women.

Those whom Martin (1980) characterized as POLICEwomen identify with the police work culture and seek to gain acceptance by being more professional, aggressive, loyal, street-oriented, and macho than the men. In resisting traditional gender-based stereotypes, acting like men, and even outproducing them, however, they face the negative stereotypic labels of dyke or bitch, which imply that they are not real women. They crave acceptance but never can quite become "one of the boys"; those who are sexually active are labeled "easy," which makes clear the persistence of the double standard by which men control women's sexuality.

The deprofessionalized policeWOMEN, conversely, are unable or unwilling to enact fully the street patrol role. They tend to be uncomfortable on patrol, fearful of physical injury, and reluctant to assert authority and take control of situations. Often feeling helpless or uncomfortable with men's crude language, and trying to remain "ladies," they accept the paternalistic bargain. They welcome or tolerate men's protection and often conform to such gender stereotypes as seductress, mother, pet, and helpless maiden in interactions with men officers (Kanter, 1977). Unable to prove themselves exceptions among the women, many policeWOMEN embrace the service aspects of policing, display little crime-fighting initiative, and seek nonpatrol assignments and personal acceptance as feminine women (Martin, 1980).

Most women officers cope with the gendered work organization and its sexism by tending to enact one of these two broad patterns. Nevertheless, many are not consistent and respond with elements of each pattern at various times. In addition, they actively seek to resist traditional gender arrangements and stereotypes. These efforts have contributed to the modification of definitions of femininity and masculinity and to the emergence of new cultural patterns and occupational role identities. Some women have successfully combined valued attributes associated with both masculinity and femininity in their behavioral repertoire and have developed self-definitions perceived to be "feminine, trustworthy, and professionally competent" (Hunt, 1990, p. 26). Young (1991) characterizes these "new policewomen," as

> self-contained, self-consciously feminine women, unwilling to play the traditional role of homemaker, wife, and mother or become the butch 'burglar's dog' taking the part of a surrogate male. Many . . . remain overtly feminine, yet operate in the macho world of policing without inhibition. They are professional, competent, and attractive and in consequence are feared and revered, for they have upturned the prescribed homogeneity of the male ideology which assigns women a clearly defined place on the margins and which they are expected to fill gratefully. (p. 240)

Many women have achieved this new status by striking a balance between traditional feminine stereotypes into which men press them and the "opposite but equally negative gender stereotype" (Jurik, 1988, p. 292). Balancing strategies include projecting a professional image, demonstrating unique skills, emphasizing a team approach, using humor to develop camaraderie and thwart unwelcome advances, and gaining sponsorship to enhance positive visibility (Jurik, 1988).

Women in policing demonstrate professionalism primarily by displaying physical courage, being willing to use physical force in threatening situations, remaining on patrol, and playing by the rules. While adhering to this masculine street-cop model of police behavior, women have expanded the definition of professionalism to include improving their skills (e.g., by learning new languages), treating the public well, emphasizing close links with the community, and working very hard (Heidensohn, 1992, pp. 147-150).

In addition, women have withstood or faced down sexual harassers, often demonstrating a sense of humor in the process. In reacting to the sexualized environment, many women have relied on witty rejoinders rather than feminine responses or complaints when they were the butt of jokes or teasing. Yet in "giving it back," they have had to avoid acting or appearing to act in a sexual or flirtatious way, because "a woman cannot operate by men's rules and get away with it" (Cockburn, 1991, p. 156). Others have laughed at the men's jokes or suffered in silence, trying to fit in, avoid making waves, and "think of the larger picture."

Most have dealt with sexual propositions informally. Solutions have ranged from drawing their gun on a wayward scout-car partner to threatening to call the offender's spouse, relying on support from a trusted friend or partner, silently regarding this treatment as the cost of doing the job, seeking transfers away from tormenters, and resigning. Some have acquiesced, gaining a degree of protection and support. A few have brought formal complaints and lawsuits. Often such complaints set off retaliatory waves that drive out women; a growing number, however, have resulted in large settlements for women (Cooper, 1992, p. 1).[2]

Sponsorship by a supervisor or peer often leads to acceptance for women officers. Sponsorship based on what officers perceive as a sexual bargain, however, can result in ostracism and limit long-term career success.

Women rarely have adopted a unified or organized response. Several factors have prevented formation of strong women's organizations within or across agencies. These include divergent occupational and gender-role perspectives across racial lines, mistrust and racism, and men's success in using a divide-and-conquer strategy to keep women competing with each other and relying on individualistic strategies to gain acceptance.

For both black and white women, acceptance by men of the same race is more important than support of other women, for work-related and social reasons. Men have more policing experience and "muscle," and they are available in greater numbers than women officers. Because women on patrol must depend on them for backup, men's support may be a matter of life and death. In addition, social activities including dating and marriages occur along racial lines. Men of both races control "their" women's on-duty behavior by threatening them with social isolation both on and off the job (Martin, 1994) or categorizing them as lesbians.

MESHING PERSONAL AND OCCUPATIONAL LIVES

As in other occupations, women in policing face strains on family life that employers' policies tend to ignore or exacerbate. In many departments, patrol officers have rotating shifts, uncertain demands for overtime related to arrests, and unexpected call-ups for emergencies. These demands, plus the stressful nature of the work, put strains on family life for all officers. Because women still bear the greater share of responsibility for household maintenance and child care, however, these strains fall more heavily on women officers.

Pregnancy compounds women officers' problems. Because police officers risk physical injury, most departments allow or require pregnant officers to leave patrol assignments once their pregnancy becomes known. At the end of 1986, however, only 25% of municipal agencies had policies related to pregnancy and only 74% of these routinely reassigned pregnant officers to a light-duty position. In 14% of the departments, a woman was forced to go on extended leave when she was unable to continue her normal assignment, and 12% of departments had not had to deal with a pregnant officer (S. Martin, 1990). Smaller departments were more likely not to have a light-duty option than large ones.

Many women forced to leave policing for 6 to 8 months in order to have a child resign from police work. Thus, organizational policies related to parenthood are not gender-neutral; women but not men may have to choose between having a child and a police career.

Summary

Women entering policing encounter a strongly gendered organization. Policies related to training, assignments, and performance evaluations are far from gender neutral. Women also are disadvantaged by overprotection and underinstruction and double standards regarding appearance and performance.

In the informal social world of the police, women remain outsiders, excluded from activities, sponsorship, and information networks important for career advancement. Unable to become one of the boys, they encounter a sexualized workplace in which they are the object of men's sexual initiatives and innuendos.

Patterns of gender differences begin during training, continue in field training, and lead to differences in mobility. Women are more likely than men to leave street patrol, and when they transfer, they tend to go into community service and staff support positions, whereas men tend to transfer into more prestigious line units.

Women officers' work attitudes do not differ substantially from those of men officers, and their job performance is equally competent. Nevertheless, their experiences on the job are different, because as women they must negotiate a way through gendered organizational processes for distributing assignments and power, gendered interactions with colleagues and citizens, and a gendered work culture. They must deal with sexual harassment, uncertain backup, social isolation, and dilemmas regarding language, sexual behavior, appearance, and demeanor. Such behavioral choices reproduce cultural images of a gendered work organization and gender identities of men and women cops.

To deal with work-related stress and dilemmas, two primary coping strategies are available: POLICEwomen act like or outdo the men; policeWOMEN emphasize their femininity but fail to effectively exercise control on the street. A growing number of women have merged elements of these strategies by striking a balance in doing gender and police work, achieving recognition as real policewomen and providing a new model for women.

Notes

1. Ironically, overly aggressive men who provoke fights in which others get hurt often are praised for "maintaining respect."

2. A Long Beach, California, jury awarded a $3.1 million settlement in a sexual harassment case to two female officers who faced death threats, dog bites, pummeling, and denial of backup from men colleagues. The Livermore, California, Police Department, with fewer than 70 sworn personnel, has settled two of the three sexual harassment lawsuits filed against it in 4 years, costing citizens more than $275,000 in awards to the victims and attorney fees (Cooper, 1992, pp. A1, A10).

5

Women Entering the Legal Profession

Change and Resistance

Nature has tempered women as little for the judicial conflicts of the courtroom as for the physical conflicts of the battlefield. . . . Our . . . profession has essentially . . . to do with all that is selfish and extortionate, knavish and criminal, coarse and brutal, repulsive and obscene in human life. It would be revolting to all female sense of innocence and the sanctity of their sex.

Chief Justice C. J. Ryan of the Wisconsin Supreme Court, opposing admitting Lavinia Goodell to the bar, 1875. Cited in Epstein, 1983, p. 269

 Although the practice of criminal law occasionally may be coarse, as Justice Ryan notes, this decision reflects the images and stereotypes that associate the law with masculinity. These images were used to justify the virtual exclusion of women from the prestigious and powerful legal profession in the United States until the 1970s. Despite Justice Ryan's vivid language, the reasons for men's resistance to women lawyers "likely has to do with the law's close relationship to power in our society" (Morello,

1986, p. x). The legal profession structures power relations between groups and classes by shaping the rules and laws that open or limit opportunities without resort to force, making it the quintessential masculine power role (Hagan, Zatz, Arnold, & Kay, 1991).

For many years, the legal community, by controlling its own membership, was able both to limit the number of lawyers admitted to practice and to control the character of those admitted. It did this by exercising both formal control over admissions to law school and bar membership and informal referral and social mechanisms. These processes enforced the understanding that outsiders such as women and racial minorities would be excluded from the legal community or would be kept on its fringes in low visibility, low prestige specialties, serving others like themselves (Epstein, 1983).

Since the 1960s, the legal world has undergone several major changes. The number of lawyers has more than doubled. The nature and organization of legal work also changed. There are fewer lawyers in solo practice and more who work in large law firms and in salaried positions with corporations and government agencies. New areas, such as public interest law, have emerged, and the number of women lawyers has grown significantly. Thus, women's presence in the law occurred as part of the changing legal context; the growing representation of women stimulates further change in the organization and activities of lawyers.

Women now make up nearly a quarter of the legal profession and nearly half all law students, but their numerical gains have not yielded equivalent increases in power or opportunities. As the American Bar Association's Commission on Women in the Profession concluded in 1988: "[The] persistence of both overt and subtle barriers denies women the opportunity to achieve full integration and equal participation in the work, responsibilities, and rewards of the legal profession" (p. 1).

This chapter explores the history of women in the legal profession, the nature and organization of the work done by attorneys, the changes that have occurred across the legal landscape, and the ways that gendered legal culture and its images have severely disadvantaged women lawyers. Chapter 6 looks more closely at the organizational logic that prevails in key legal settings and the strategies adopted by women lawyers to address the barriers that inhibit legal careers. In these chapters, we present a general discussion of women's integration into the legal profession rather than focusing explicitly on criminal law, because no such specialized data are available and because most of the barriers to women are encountered across legal settings.

Historical Overview:
Barriers to Women in Law Before 1970

In 1638, Margaret Brent became executor of the estate of Lord Calvert, governor of the colony of Maryland (Morello, 1986). Although it is known that she was the first woman to practice law in colonial America, little else is known about women practicing law from colonial times until the mid-1800s. Women were barred from both law school and state bar associations. It is possible that a few women appeared in court on their own behalf and that others practiced law in the frontier areas (Bernat, 1992). However, few women pursued legal careers.

In 1869, Iowa became the first state to admit a woman to the bar (Morello, 1986). In other jurisdictions, however, women applicants were denied membership. For example, in 1872, Myra Bradwell, who was denied admittance by the Illinois State Supreme Court, appealed to the U.S. Supreme Court, claiming her rights under the Equal Protection Clause of the Fourteenth Amendment had been violated. The Court, denying her appeal, stated: "A woman has no legal existence separate from her husband [so that] a married woman is incapable, without her husband's consent, of making contracts which shall be binding on her or him", unmarried women are "exceptions to the general rule" of marriage (*Bradwell v. Illinois*, 1872, p. 137).

The Court's decision in *Bradwell v. Illinois* permitted states to exclude women from practicing law. Because admission to a state bar is the prerequisite for practicing law in that state, women had to challenge their exclusion state by state in order to gain the right to practice law. It was not until 1920, 51 years after women first became lawyers in the United States, that women were permitted to practice law before the courts in every state (Feinman, 1986). Women also were excluded from membership in the American Bar Association (ABA) until 1918 (Abel, 1989) and from the prestigious Association of the Bar of the City of New York until 1937 (Epstein, 1983). Consequently, they were kept from the networks through which lawyers gain contacts, referrals, and power.

Between 1870 and 1950, American lawyers as a professional group successfully controlled the market for their services. They developed local, state, and national bar associations; created codes of ethics; and established disciplinary procedures to control the quality of legal services. They also maintained tight entrance requirements into the profession through control over the standards and admission practices of the emerging law schools (Abel, 1986). Thus, the ABA and state bars limited the numbers and controlled the characteristics of new lawyers. As a result, despite the vast economic growth in the United States during the first half of the 20th century, the population-to-lawyer ratio was the same in 1950 as it was in 1900, and the legal profession consisted of white men, most of them in solo practice.

By the end of the 19th century, the professionalization of legal practice had led to an increasing proportion of lawyers with formal legal education. Until 1900, the most common route to the bar was "reading the law" and serving as an apprentice or "clerk" to a working lawyer. As apprenticeship routes disappeared, even these limited opportunities for women to enter law were reduced by women's exclusion from the academic route. Although in 1869, Washington University in St. Louis became the first law school to admit women (Morello, 1986), access to legal education remained very limited. Many law schools, particularly the most elite, denied admittance to women altogether. Columbia University only opened its doors to women in 1928 and Harvard in 1950.

Even when women were admitted, quotas and other restrictive barriers kept their numbers small (Epstein, 1983). With a sufficient supply of qualified men applicants, and in the absence of antidiscrimination laws, the academic gatekeepers excluded or limited the numbers of men and women of color and white women. For many decades, law classes typically had a maximum of three women. Although academics protested that the low numbers were due to women's lack of interest, statistics that appeared in the *Harvard Law Record* in 1965 suggest a pattern of discrimination. Despite increasing numbers of women applicants, women constituted about 3% in each class between 1951 and 1965 (cited in Epstein, 1983). Women remained less than 5% of the enrollment at ABA-approved law schools until the 1970s (Abel, 1989). Both faculty and men students made the educational environment inhospitable to women. Women were called on only on "Ladies' Day," which for many professors and men students was a show put on at the women's expense.[1]

In 1972, passage of Title IX of the Higher Education Act prohibited discrimination based on sex in the enrollment of students and hiring of faculty. Facing denial of federal financial assistance if they continued to discriminate, law schools finally began to admit more women and allow them to compete equally with men. Women's enrollments since that time have grown dramatically; they now constitute more than half the students in some law schools.

The next hurdle for women lawyers was finding a job. Even women with training at elite schools faced employment discrimination that was openly practiced well into the 1970s. For example, a 1963 survey of 430 law firms found that "female status" was the characteristic that got the most negative rating in selecting new recruits (Epstein, 1983). Thus, it is not surprising that in 1965, fewer than 20% of the 104 firms responding to a *Harvard Law Record* questionnaire employed any women lawyers (cited in Epstein, 1983).

Women who obtained legal work often were offered opportunities in low-status specialties deemed appropriate for women, such as domestic relations and probate law. They received lower pay and were denied partnerships and opportunities for leadership in bar associations. For example, when current Supreme Court Justice

Sandra Day O'Connor graduated third in her class at Stanford Law School in 1953, the only job she was offered was as a legal secretary (Epstein, 1983, p. 84).

Women also were rarely found on the bench. The first woman justice of the peace was appointed in 1890, but it was not until 1979 that a woman had served at some level of the judicial system in all 50 states (Slotnick, 1984). Similarly, the first woman on the federal bench, Frances Allen, was appointed by President Roosevelt to the Circuit (Appellate) Court in 1934. The next was appointed to the U.S. District Court in 1949 by President Truman. By 1977, only eight women had ever served in the federal judiciary at the District or Appeals Court level (Martin, 1982).

Women were not the only group excluded from the practice of law. In fact, the club-like homogeneity of law firms that hire only white Anglo-Saxon Protestant men (WASPs) has only gradually, and often grudgingly, moved toward greater representativeness. The first step was made by Jewish and Catholic men during the 1950s and 1960s. White women broke through by the late 1970s. Informal barriers against people of color remain high.[2]

Changing Laws and Job Queues: Opening Legal Practice to Women

In the past three decades, major changes have occurred in the legal profession. These include an increase in the number of law schools and lawyers, a shift in the type and organization of legal employment, and diminution of the legal profession's control over lawyers' behavior. Each of these changes has affected and been affected by the expanded role of women in law.

CHANGING LABOR QUEUES
AND DEMOGRAPHICS IN THE LEGAL PROFESSION

Since 1960, there has been a phenomenal growth in the number of lawyers and in the ratio of lawyers to the general population. In 1960, there was one lawyer for every 627 citizens in the United

States; by 1984, that ratio had become one lawyer per 364 people (Curran, 1986). One consequence of this growth is the legal profession's gradual loss of control over its composition. Restrictions on the training of lawyers prior to 1960 led to a shortage of lawyers, expansion in the number of law schools, and willingness to turn to less expensive women lawyers. Greater demand also led to higher starting salaries, which, in turn, made the law a more attractive career option. The civil rights, women's, consumers', and environmental movements of the 1960s expanded new areas of the law and the demand for lawyers. As racial and sexual barriers to entry into law fell, the number of potential aspiring lawyers more than doubled, and the number of law schools rose by 25%. As a result, the rate at which new lawyers are being trained is three times greater than what it was in the mid-1960s (Abel, 1986, p. 11).

There have been dramatic changes in the demographic composition of the legal profession over the past 30 years. These include a vast increase in the proportion of white women, a small increase in men and women of color, and an increasingly young and diverse profession dominated by elderly white men.

Because men's enrollment in law schools has remained stable while women's has multiplied, most of the growth in the profession represents an increase in the number of women law students and lawyers. In 1960, women made up only 3.5% of the enrollees at ABA-approved U.S. law schools; in 1970, they accounted for 8.5%; in 1980, 33.6%; and in 1986, 40.2% (Abel, 1989, p. 285).

CHANGES IN THE TYPE AND
NATURE OF LEGAL EMPLOYMENT

The organization of legal work also has changed. The solo legal practitioner no longer dominates the profession, and within private practice, large firms have grown in size. They now compete for clients by adding specialties, opening branch offices, and striving to enhance profitability by increasing the ratio of associates to partners. The proportion of all lawyers who were in solo practice declined from 61% in 1948 to 33% in 1980. At the same time, the number of firms with 100 or more lawyers grew (Abel, 1989).

Another trend is the increase in the proportion of lawyers who are salaried workers. More lawyers work for government and private industry, and a higher percentage of the lawyers working in large firms are salaried associates. Thus, a profession that was 85% self-employed in 1948 and about 60% self-employed in 1980, will be less than half self-employed by the turn of the century (Abel, 1986, p. 14).

These changes in the size, composition, structure, and function of the legal profession have affected its self-governance by breaking down the control formerly exercised by the ABA and state bar associations and subjecting lawyers to more external regulation. The changes also have increased stratification of the legal profession according to practitioner background, clientele, function, and re-ward. At the bottom of the status ladder, the solo practitioner faces an increasingly hostile economic environment, declining prestige, and dwindling numbers. At the top, large firms have grown in size and prominence but are increasingly bureaucratic. Sociologist Richard Abel (1986) has suggested that by increasing heterogeneity within the profession, "stratification may come to be associated with racial and gender differences" (p. 16). As in other occupations undergoing rapid integration, changing job queues and expanded demand for women have enabled them to enter the field, but women have come into law as it becomes more stratified, bureaucratized, and specialized, and as it suffers declining prestige.

THE CHANGING LEGAL ENVIRONMENT

Civil rights laws have contributed to change in the legal profession by opening the doors to law schools and legal work for women and people of color. Title VII of the Civil Rights Act of 1964, the 1972 Amendments to Title VII, and the 1972 Educational Amendments Act were of particular importance to aspiring women lawyers.

The 1972 Amendments to Title VII extended antidiscrimination provisions to all employers with 15 or more workers, including small law firms, as well as to state and local government agencies and educational institutions. It also allowed the U.S. Department of Justice to bring "pattern or practice" lawsuits. This provision was applied to include the placement offices of law schools, which served as employment agencies; as they became targets for lawsuits, they radically altered their gatekeeping functions.

The 1972 Educational Amendments Act prohibited sex discrimination in all public institutions of higher learning receiving federal monies, including major university law schools. This not only opened enrollment to women students but affected the distribution of scholarships and the hiring and promotion of women faculty members. It also made it illegal for law firms to openly refuse to interview or hire women.

WOMEN LAWYERS USING THE NEW LAWS

Opening employment opportunities in law to women required legal action against the legal establishment. This action has only gradually brought about changes in the legal profession's treatment of women in practice, teaching, and the job market. At first, women students at New York University and Columbia law schools, with the participation of Columbia Law School's Employment Rights Project (ERP), set out to end exclusionary practices in elite Wall Street firms. Pooling information about job interview experiences, they concluded that these firms were not taking women's applications seriously. They complained to their school's placement office and, with help from the ERP (and funding from the Equal Employment Opportunity Commission), several women filed complaints with the New York City Human Rights Commission against 10 firms on behalf of all women law students in New York. In 1976, 7 years after initiation of their suit, all the firms agreed to settlements similar to those reached following findings of employment discrimination in two test cases.

In the first case decided, *Kohn v. Royall, Koegel, and Wells* (1973), the court determined that the firm had systematically discriminated against women in hiring. The firm agreed to a complex formula, including a guarantee that it would offer at least 25% of its positions each year to women. In the other case, the court found that Diane

Blank's interviewer from the firm of Sullivan and Cromwell had admitted that the firm was biased, discouraged her interest in the firm, failed to examine her resumé, and asked about her lawyer-husband's career. Sullivan and Cromwell also agreed to a settlement, including a provision that in addition to hiring women, it would not hold social events in clubs that excluded women. The other eight firms cited in the initial complaint adopted similar guidelines (Epstein, 1983, pp. 184-189).

Despite antidiscrimination laws, women law students and faculty had to keep up pressure on law school placement offices through the 1970s to force law firms to recruit women seriously or face sanctions. In some instances, women students sued placement offices (e.g., University of Chicago Law School). By the end of the decade, law firm recruiting had changed; although old prejudices remain, most firms have eliminated blatant discrimination.

The next legal barrier was posed by the partnership decision. In *Hishon v. King & Spalding* (1984), the U.S. Supreme Court legally recognized that promotion to partnership is an area covered under Title VII. Earlier, the courts had treated partnerships as voluntary associations that must be congenial for all concerned, because partners are liable for the negligent acts of any co-partner. In *Hishon*, the Court rejected the argument that the choice of partners was protected under the First Amendment right to freedom of association. It ruled that Title VII does not force partnerships to accept less qualified individuals. Nevertheless, consideration for partnership is a "term, condition, or privilege" of the original employment contract covered under Title VII, and, as such, a partnership decision must be made on a fair and equal basis without regard to the applicant's sex (Madek & O'Brien, 1990). The next hurdle for women, addressing discrimination in the actual decision-making process, still is not fully resolved. Because the decision to admit an individual to a partnership usually involves both objective and subjective factors and a collaborative decision, identifying the real cause of such decisions often is impossible. In a 1989 decision, *Price Waterhouse v. Hopkins*, a fragmented Supreme Court failed to establish either clear grounds for determining when discrimination has occurred or the rules of the fight.

The facts of the case are clear. Ann Hopkins, a senior manager at the Price Waterhouse accounting firm, was denied a partnership in a "mixed motive" case (i.e., one in which there were multiple reasons for denying partnership, only some of which were related to her gender). Hopkins had generated more new business for the firm than any of the 85 men who applied for partnership at the same time; she was also known to be a demanding and difficult supervisor. In the usual manner, Price Waterhouse solicited comments from partners about candidates who had applied for partnership. Among the 32 comments regarding Hopkins were 13 supporting admittance and 8 for rejection. The decision was put on hold, and when two of Hopkins's supporters withdrew their support, partnership was denied.

The lower courts ruled that once a plaintiff has established that an illegal motive played a significant part in the decision to deny partnership, the burden of proof shifts to the defendant to show that no discrimination actually occurred. In the Price Waterhouse case, the lower court suggested that Hopkins's management style was a legitimate reason for putting her partnership application on hold. Nevertheless, the firm still was liable because the partnership process gave unacceptably great weight to negative comments that reflected unconscious sexual stereotypes by men evaluators. Among the suspect comments were statements that Hopkins needed a "course at charm school" and, from her primary supporter, that she would improve her chances of becoming a partner if she would "wear makeup, have her hair styled, and wear jewelry" (at 1116-1117).

The U.S. Supreme Court overruled the lower courts and raised the threshold for showing discriminatory intent. The Court was split, with Justice O'Connor in the middle as the swing vote on two issues: the amount of evidence needed to show a discriminatory motive that triggers a shift in the burden of proof from plaintiff to the defendant and the degree to which discriminatory intent is the cause of the decision. Such a split decision suggests that further litigation or legislation related to partnerships will be necessary to resolve these issues (Madek & O'Brien, 1990).

CHALLENGING DISCRIMINATORY PRACTICES:
GENDER-BIAS TASK FORCES

Women lawyers soon encountered discriminatory practices and gendered interactions in the courthouse that threatened their livelihoods. Because these practices often were perpetrated or tolerated by judges, women lawyers could not safely challenge them individually. Instead, attorneys from the National Organization for Women's Legal Defense and Education Fund, in cooperation with the National Association of Women Judges, designed a program to call attention to gender bias in the law, decision making, and courtroom interaction in state judicial systems. To make this change strategy palatable to judges and other gatekeepers in the legal system, the program was focused on collecting state-specific information about gender bias. Such bias was defined as existing when

> people are denied rights or burdened with responsibilities solely on the basis of gender; . . . people are subjected to stereotypes about the proper behavior of men and women which ignore their situations; people are treated differently on the basis of gender in situations where gender should make no difference; [and] men or women as a group can be subjected to a legal rule, policy, or practice which produces worse results for them than for the other group. (Maryland Special Joint Committee, 1989, p. iii)

Thus, gender bias includes both overt discrimination and more subtle practices.

The program was designed as part of the judiciary's continuing judicial education efforts and employed a new approach, the creation of gender-bias task forces, to document such bias in the courts (Schafran, 1987a). The first such body, the New Jersey Supreme Court's Task Force on Women in the Courts, was established in November 1982 by that state's chief justice to investigate three issues: Whether gender stereotypes affect the substantive law or have an impact on judicial decision making; whether a person's gender affects his or her treatment in the legal and judicial environment; and, if so, how to ensure equal treatment for women and men in court.

Its *First-Year Report,* published in June, 1984, found substantial gender bias (detailed in Chapter 6, this volume) and led to creation of similar task forces and the introduction of judicial education about gender bias in many states. As of October 1989, 30 state task forces on gender bias in the courts were in various stages of formation, data collection, report writing, and implementation of recommendations published. In 1987, the American Bar Association initiated a similar Commission on Women in the Profession, chaired by Hillary Rodham Clinton. Its 1988 report to the ABA House of Delegates called on that body to recognize the persistence of discrimination against women in the legal profession and to affirm its commitment to ending barriers that prevent "full integration and equal participation of women in all aspects of the legal profession" (ABA Commission, 1988, p. 1). Thus, the legal establishment finally went on record as opposing discrimination more than 20 years after the first surge of women into the profession.

Lawyers' Jobs, Specialties, and the Division of Legal Labor

Although women made up 24% of the legal profession by 1990 (ABA Commission, 1993), their numerical gains have not yielded equivalent increases in power, status, and income. Table 5.1 shows that men and women lawyers clearly have different employment patterns. In brief, women are proportionally underrepresented in private practice and overrepresented in government and corporate work; within each of these organizational hierarchies, they are concentrated on the bottom rungs of prestige and income. This section looks at the organization and work of lawyers as well as their distribution across specialties and workplaces to set the stage for examination of the factors responsible for and the impact of these employment patterns.

TABLE 5.1 The Employment Distribution of Men and Women
Lawyers in 1980

	Percentage of Total		Women as Percentage
	Women (N = 44,185)	Men (N = 498,020)	of Lawyers in Job Type
Private practice	56.0	69.0	6.6
Federal judiciary	.8	.5	13.3
Federal government	7.0	3.4	15.5
State/local judiciary	3.0	3.1	7.9
State/local government	10.2	5.2	14.9
Private industry	9.2	10.1	7.5
Private association	1.9	.7	19.5
Legal aid/public defender	4.8	1.2	26.0
Education	2.0	1.1	13.5
Retired/inactive	5.1	5.7	8.2
Total	100%	100%	

Source: Data from Curran (1986, p. 41, Figure 5), used here by permission of the
Law & Society Association.

THE ORGANIZATION
AND WORK OF LAWYERS

In complex societies, the critical rules of social life are codified in
law and their meanings interpreted and enforced by a group of
experts on their proper application and use. These specialists in
legal rules are lawyers, whose occupational specialty often is traced
back to ancient Rome.

The work of lawyers is advocacy or action directly or indirectly in
defense of a client's interests in the courts and other legal organizations and social institutions (Krause, 1971). In theory, the lawyer
functions to gain for the client those redresses or privileges that are
defined within the broader context of legal norms and statutes. This
occurs through the court system, where the rules of the legal system
are applied. Legal work revolves around the court setting, where the
rules of the legal system interact with specific interests of clients or
relationships between clients and the state.

The public image of lawyers' activities focuses on the drama of the adversarial process in highly publicized criminal trials, pitting the prosecution against the defense with the judge serving as a referee. However, not all proceedings in court are adversarial. Most laws are civil; they are related to facilitating, regulating, or channeling activities (e.g., transmission of property, marriage) in a given society.

In court, the lawyer's role is to adjust the needs, requests, and rights of the client in response to another party's assertion of rights, the rights of the state, or requests of the state for certain behavior (e.g., the payment of taxes). The judge's role is to exercise the authority of the legal system to constrain the activities of lawyers in their role as advocates.

In the United States, the division of legal work may be examined along two major dimensions: the specific kind of legal work done and the particular setting of the practice. In each, there is stratification based in the nature of the client served. Criminal law generally deals with the poor, whereas much of civil law has to do with business matters. More prestige and rewards accrue to lawyers who work for the elite; lawyers become identified with the kind of clientele with whom they associate. Similarly, types of work settings also involve stratification. Usually solo lawyers work with poor or middle-class individuals; Wall Street and other lawyers in large and established law firms have powerful corporate clients. In between are smaller group practices, governmental legal activities, and house-counsel work. Lawyers also are stratified by specialty. Most lawyers enter civil work, and the elite among these go into business-related legal specialties. The work of Wall Street lawyers often involves helping to manage the private sector of the world economy. However, most lawyers work in small firms on cases involving middle-class individuals and families, such as wills, torts (i.e., personal injuries), and divorces. In addition to becoming practicing attorneys, a number of people with law degrees pursue careers in business, politics, or government.

As a profession, a key characteristic of the practice of law is autonomy or authority to assert control over work (Freidson, 1970).

This affects the work and work culture in several ways because it rests on an institutional foundation, organizational constraints, and professional tasks. Although it is assumed that there are boundaries between a lawyer's work and private life, these are fluid because they are subject to open-ended demands from clients and from processes such as networking. At the task level, lawyers are expected to be endlessly available to pursue their careers in a single-minded manner. At the organizational level, they are assumed to be willing to work overtime without direct compensation as a sign of "commitment" (Sirianni & Welsh, 1991, p. 424). At an institutional level, professional autonomy rests on a system of private social support that is required to ensure release time from private (e.g., home and family) obligations. In addition to long work hours, professional success also requires some time when lawyers are inaccessible to clients but free to pursue leisure activities or professional networking to make contacts and garner new clients (Seron & Ferris, 1995).

With respect to both work time and leisure time, professional men have an advantage over women because they can expand hours spontaneously, flexibly, and informally and thus can more easily meet the organizational policy that they put work first. The professional model thus rests on men's experience of release from domestic burdens; it gives men an implicit advantage that becomes visible by focusing on the ability to control professional time. This, in turn, rests on a "negotiated release from private time to have access to professional time" (Seron & Ferris, 1995, p. 27).

PRIVATE LAW PRACTICE

About two out of three lawyers are in private practice, as shown in Table 5.1. Nevertheless, the kinds of practice, their positions within firms, and the types of legal work they do vary considerably, and women are much less likely to enter private practice than are men.

Within the world of private practice, women are more likely than men to be in solo practice (56% vs. 48%) (Abel, 1989, p. 97). However, among lawyers in firms, women are more likely to enter large firms that offer higher starting salaries, greater prestige, and more advancement potential than small or medium-size firms. Nevertheless, this apparent advantage is offset by the fact that although the absolute number of partners has grown, increased firm size and changes in employment patterns have reduced the percentage of lawyers who are partners. This has had a more pronounced effect on women's chances for partnerships than on men's, and its greatest impact has occurred in the proportionate reduction of women partners in small firms (Hagan et al., 1991).

IN-HOUSE COUNSEL AND CORPORATE LAW

By 1986, about 13% of lawyers worked in corporations, making such businesses the largest employer of lawyers after law firms (Fisher, 1984). Women constituted 13% of this group (Curran, Rosich, Carson, & Puccetti, 1986), but they are not distributed evenly across in-house counsel departments of different sizes or types of business firms. Sociologist Sharyn Roach (1990) observed clear gender differences in the routes by which men and women found such jobs and in their current positions, salaries, and promotion opportunities, despite similarities in their educational credentials.

Men employed as in-house counsel disproportionately work for corporations in the manufacturing sector and in large departments that offer substantial salaries and opportunities for advancement. In contrast, women in-house counsel are concentrated in the financial services sector and in medium-size legal departments offering lower pay and fewer mobility opportunities.

WOMEN AND MEN IN GOVERNMENT WORK

A disproportionately large number of women attorneys are employed in government work, particularly at the state and local levels. In 1960, according to U.S. Census figures, 28% of the women but only 14% of the men lawyers in the labor force worked for government (Epstein, 1983, p. 97). In 1980, those figures were 17% and 9% respectively, as shown in Table 5.1. An additional 4.8% of women and 1.2% of men work in legal aid or public defender offices (Curran, 1986).

Several factors have contributed to the concentration of women in government legal work. First, it offers more regular and flexible hours; second, it involves little client contact or "rainmaking" activity (i.e., bringing in clients); third, the greater presence of other women and lower rates of sexual harassment make the environment less hostile (Rosenberg, Perlstadt, & Phillips, 1993). Despite these advantages, women working in government rated their work environments lower, in terms of opportunities for salary increases, professional development, and achieving career goals, than did women working in private legal settings.

Prosecutors and public defenders constitute the small fraction of government lawyers involved directly in the criminal justice system. National data on the number and positions of women in these offices are not available. Nevertheless, several individual women have achieved high visibility as chiefs of important prosecutor's offices. Currently, Janet Reno, the former elected district attorney in Miami, is U.S. Attorney General, the highest legal official in the country, and Mary Jo White is U.S. Attorney for the Southern District of New York (including Manhattan, the Bronx, and six counties north of New York City).

THE JUDICIARY

Only about 4% of lawyers were members of the federal, state, and local judiciary in 1980 (Curran, 1986). Because judges have great power and prestige and because appointment to the bench usually occurs as a "reward" for a successful legal career, it is not surprising that women make up a smaller proportion of the judiciary than of the legal profession. Very few women were judges before 1970; since then, the number of women judges at both the state and federal level has grown, but women still are underrepresented on the bench.

In the past two decades, the number and proportion of women state court judges have grown substantially. In 1970, there were fewer than 200 women, making up less than 1% of the state court judiciary (Feinman, 1986, p. 118). By 1984, their numbers had more than doubled, and women constituted 6% of state appellate judges and 4% of state trial judges. By 1991, their representation had grown to 10% of both state trial court and appellate judges (ABA Commission, 1988). This pattern of growth is similar for the federal judiciary. Change came during President Carter's term (1976-1980), when 40 new women, including seven blacks and one Hispanic, were appointed to the bench.[3] Although President Reagan appointed the first woman, Sandra Day O'Connor, to the U.S. Supreme Court in 1981, he appointed few other women judges during his 8 years in office. By 1992, 14% of Circuit and 13% of District Court judges at the federal level were women (ABA Commission, 1993). President Clinton appointed Ruth Bader Ginsberg as the second woman on the Supreme Court in 1993.

LAW SCHOOL TEACHING

Less than 2% of lawyers go into full-time law school teaching, as shown in Table 5.1, yet they have a disproportionate effect on the law as role models, gatekeepers, and shapers of the next generation of practitioners. In addition, their legal writing affects lawyers' arguments and judicial decisions.

Initially the barriers to women achieving faculty positions in law schools were even higher than those facing legal practitioners. In 1950, there were only five women law faculty members; they accounted for less than 0.5% of tenure track faculty in law schools (Fossum, 1980). By 1977, the number of women had grown to 391 professors, who made up 8.6% of the tenure-track faculty. Nevertheless, most of these women were hired by a few law schools, particularly new schools such as Northeastern and Rutgers (Epstein, 1983).

During the 1980s, the number of women on law school faculties continued to grow. A survey of law school faculty composition during the 1986-1987 academic year indicated that women made up 20% of full-time faculty, including 45% of the teachers of professional skills—legal writing and clinical law (teachers of these subjects are not considered regular faculty) (Chused, 1988). In 1992, the ABA reported that 27% of full-time law faculty (23% white and 4% black) and 7% of law school deans were women.

Despite these numerical increases, women professors are clustered in low-paying, non-tenure track jobs and have gained tenure primarily at low-prestige law schools. Moreover, these gender gaps are growing rather than closing (Angel, 1988; Chused, 1988).

Evidence that women are being denied tenure at high-prestige law schools at disproportionate rates comes from two studies. An ABA-supported study of law schools (Chused, 1988) found the tenuring rate was about half for both men and women law faculty candidates. However, schools with a low proportion of women faculty, including the disproportionate share of prestigious schools, granted tenure to women at lower rates (41%) than men (51%). Conversely, low prestige schools with higher proportions of tenured women faculty granted tenure to women at higher rates (64% versus 50% for men).

Similarly, at five Eastern law schools that range across the prestige spectrum (University of Pennsylvania, Temple, Hofstra, Rutgers-Camden, and Columbia), women made up only 11% of the tenured faculty and were being tenured at a substantially lower rate than men (Angel, 1988). From 1970 to 1987, 31% of the female candidates but 60.5% of the male candidates eligible for tenure actually were granted tenure. This tenure gap occurred at both elite Ivy League and other schools. For example, at Columbia University, 33% of the eligible women but 57% of the eligible men were given tenure; at Temple the proportions were 35% and 75%, respectively.

Data on the representation of men and women of color on law school faculties suggest continuing racial tokenism (Chused, 1988, p. 539). The proportion of full-time black law school faculty increased from 2.8% in 1980-1981 (123 out of 4,444 full-time faculty) to 3.7% in 1986-1987 (181 out of 5,064 full-time professors). Hispanic representation was even lower. In 1980-1981, there were 24 Hispanic law school faculty members nationwide. They constituted 0.5% of all teachers; their number had increased to a total of 33, constituting 0.7% of law faculty by 1986-1987 (Chused, 1988).

A total of 54 women of color were on law faculties (including those in traditionally minority-operated institutions), accounting for 8.8% of the women faculty and 1.2% of all faculty in 1980-1981. By the 1986-1987 academic year, their number had nearly doubled to 101, but they still constituted only 9.8% of women and 2% of all faculty (Chused, 1988).

Gendered Legal Occupational Culture and Barriers to Women

In many ways the legal culture is a quintessentially man's world from which women have been excluded. Professional opportunities are defined by informal social networks, private (formerly all-men's) clubs, and bar associations that order status and power. Each serves as a barrier that reinforces the other. Thus, in circular fashion, the images of the law as masculine strengthen men's resistance to including women in informal socializing and bar association activities; their absence from informal networks and professional activities, in turn, supports the view that women do not fit in the profession.

Participation in the informal social world of lawyers, after long hours of legal work, means that a legal career is defined as total commitment to a workaholic schedule. Such work-related expectations were created when the prototypic lawyer had a wife taking care of the home and family. Most men regard this aspect of the legal culture as simply one of the inevitable and necessary norms of the profession. For women, such work-related expectations generate difficult choices on a daily basis.

Because the prototype of the lawyer is a man, a woman applicant for a legal position does not seem to fit. Once hired, the characteristics generally associated with masculine dominance are used to explain men's successes; their failures are explained as "bad luck." Thus, men's success is regarded as a function of innate analytic and rhetorical abilities that presumably make them more suitable for practicing law. But women's success is attributed to luck, chance, or inappropriate use of their sexuality; their failures are explained as inability to "think like a lawyer" (Rhode, 1988). Gender-based schema affect promotion and salary decisions as well.

Scripts prescribe norms of professional interaction, such as who can do what, with whom, and under what circumstances. They also reflect broader cultural beliefs about gender dominance and deference. Men's positions of power and authority give them the right to control the structure and content of professional conversation. By controlling the professional context, men behave in ways that show that other men are taken seriously and accorded respect. Conversely, the way men talk about women and their appearance treats them as invisible, devalues them, and affects their ability to perform effectively.

For example, when a judge allows the opposing attorney to label a woman attorney's appearance a distraction, it signals others that it is acceptable to use a woman's looks as the basis for objecting against other women attorneys. Similarly, a judge may defer to a man attorney who monopolizes argument time or displays an aggressive style, but penalize a woman who displays the same behavior as "shrill" or too aggressive. Yet, if a woman adopts a less combative, more soft-spoken lawyering style, it is assumed she does so because she is a woman, and she is treated as less effective. When a man displays a similarly noncombative style, it is viewed as simply a different style and may be regarded as negotiating skill.

By not fitting the professional image, women lawyers are highly visible and face constant dilemmas. Either they must model their professional behavior after a masculine image and suppress their femininity, or they must "act like women" and thus exhibit characteristics incongruent with the professional prototype, which leads to being discounted by men colleagues. Women lawyers who act like men are resented for being inflexible or too tough; those who act like women are, by definition, not acting in a professional (i.e., masculine) manner. Thus, women lawyers have to seek ways to be "demure but tough" (Rhode, 1988, p. 1189).

Many men do not want to be women's mentors because they are uncomfortable interacting with women as peers and are concerned about accusations of sexual intimacy. With few women mentors or role models available, women have had difficulty learning the norms of informal behavior in the male-dominated community, "fitting in," and forming client and collegial relationships. The situation of Elizabeth Hishon, cited in her denial of partnership suit, illustrates these problems. One reason cited by her detractors was that she did not socialize much; she was quiet and "just didn't fit in." Yet while her suit was pending, the partners staged a bathing suit competition among law student associates. Similarly, feminist legal scholars have been charged with producing propaganda rather than scholarship; yet their critics assume that traditional legal canons are value-free, rather than representing a masculine perspective and interests.

Lawyers meet, socialize, secure clients and business contacts, plan policy, provide leadership opportunities, and set the rules of their profession through informal gatherings and formal meetings of the ABA and in the 1,700 state and local bar associations in the United States. Through the 1970s, women lawyers were denied memberships in many private clubs and positions of influence on prestigious committees by local, state, and national bar associations. These exclusionary practices greatly hampered their legal careers.

The effects of gender contributed to women's limited role in bar organizations in several ways. Their areas of specialization in law lacked prestige. Many women had less time to spend on after-hours bar association work due to family obligations. Women who sought bar involvement often were unknown to the men in power. They were "invisible" both because they rarely encountered these men through their work activities (e.g., research and writing rather than trial work) and because of their absence from men's social networks. The latter source of invisibility, in turn, arose from discriminatory exclusion from the private clubs where social and business contacts were made.

Today, women are no longer denied membership in bar associations, but the continued importance of informal networks and mechanisms for securing clients and making informal social contacts with powerful bar members puts them at a disadvantage.

Outside of the courtroom or law office, women lawyers encounter an occupational culture hostile to their presence. Because lawyers require clients, getting referrals and rainmaking are important criteria for success. Men lawyers obtain powerful clients and career-enhancing legal contacts through participation in informal networks developed in private clubs and bar association activities. Women have been excluded or kept in marginal positions in these organizations until recently. Clubs now are formally open and bar associations increasingly include women in important activities. Nevertheless, their structures, decision-making logic, and controlling images continue to pose problems for women lawyers.

Even informal interactions such as making small talk with colleagues pose dilemmas (Epstein, 1983). A woman lawyer who is friendly is suspected of "coming on"; one who is too serious is rejected as unfriendly. Ignoring sexist jokes and comments signals tacit approval; failure to laugh leads to being labeled "humorless." Women get touched and interrupted more but cannot make "a thing" about this without being labeled thin-skinned. They cannot simply behave like lawyers; they must *negotiate* their interpersonal power and find an acceptable style. Thus gender serves as a "screen" for professional interactions so that a woman lawyer is evaluated, above all else, as a woman.

Women perceive that they are "at a disadvantage because they are operating in an alien culture" (ABA Commission, 1988, p. 13), but they have difficulty in conveying their perceptions convincingly to men. Their disadvantage becomes cumulative through the organizational logic and opportunity structure in the profession, which calls for total career commitment, raising tensions between family and workplace issues. These and women's coping mechanisms are the focus of Chapter 6.

Summary

Before the 1970s, the number of women in law and their career opportunities were very limited. They were excluded from many law schools and denied job opportunities and bar association leadership roles. In the past two decades, large numbers of women have entered law. At the same time, the legal profession has undergone several major changes. These include rapid expansion of the number of lawyers, changes in the nature of practice (i.e., a decline in solo practice and growth in large firms and in salaried work in public sector and corporate organizations), development of new areas of law (e.g., public interest law), and the opening of the profession to white women and to men and women of color. Nevertheless, the law remains stratified by specialty and type of practice and, increasingly, by gender and race-ethnicity.

Despite similar academic records, men and women follow different legal careers. Women are overrepresented in government employment and public interest work and underrepresented in private practice. Women in private practice are concentrated in less prestigious and remunerative specialties, earn less, and take longer and are less likely to make partner during their career than their men counterparts.

The legal culture poses formidable informal barriers to women. The prototype of the lawyer is a man; scripts and behavioral images of the successful recruit or partner are gendered. Referrals of clients and opportunities for leadership rest on participation in social networks and bar association activities. These, in turn, rest on visibility in the "right" specialties and firms, which select those that fit in. Women are perceived as too emotional and insufficiently analytical to succeed in law. Less frequently given the opportunity to move onto the occupational fast track, women face subtle but often self-perpetuating cycles that limit their career choices.

Notes

1. To help end "Ladies' Day" at Harvard, women of the class of 1968 on the designated day dressed in black, wore glasses, and carried black briefcases. When the professor asked the question whose punch line was "underwear" and which was supposed to

6

The Organizational Logic of the Gendered Legal World and Women Lawyers' Responses

A fair trial in a truly adversarial setting may be impossible when one of the attorneys is reduced to a laughingstock by a judge. In this way justice is defeated. Clients, confronted with such bias, are given a none-too-subtle message: get yourself a male lawyer or lose the case.

Florida Supreme Court
Gender-Bias Study Commission, 1990, p. 920

Women pursuing legal careers encounter gendered images and sexist treatment in the courtroom and other work-related settings. This undermines women's credibility in the eyes of others and their self-image as lawyers. In addition, gendered organizational logics operating through formal policies and informal practices reinforce each other, creating rules of the game that are stacked against women. Together these create dilemmas that require women lawyers to maneuver through diverse, stressful, double-bind situations in the workplace and to make life choices not required of most of their male counterparts.

Women still encounter patterns of discrimination in law school classrooms, job recruitment, financial rewards, and promotion and partnership decisions. They also face more subtle but insidious barriers, including selective recruitment into lower opportunity specialties and a lack of mentors. Consequently, they are not assigned to the "big" cases, introduced to the "right" clients, or sponsored for prestigious bar association committees. The long-term impact limits women's opportunities for partnerships, judgeships, and other career options. Women lawyers also experience sexual harassment and masculine images of lawyers that hinder their ability to practice law.

This differential treatment, now under scrutiny by the legal community itself, has been termed *gender bias* and pervades the organizational logic, legal culture, work-related interactions, and professional identities of lawyers (Gellis, 1991). When such treatment occurs in the courtroom, it undercuts women lawyers' credibility and professionalism, creates double standards of performance, and affects the justice afforded litigants.

Organizational and occupational barriers confronting women in law vary across worksites and specialties. Nevertheless, across the legal landscape, the division of legal labor is gendered, as are the symbols and images of the profession (e.g., the language, dress, and ideology of law) and the interaction processes through which dominance and submission are displayed before other lawyers and clients. These reinforce gender differences and result in gendered identities, which, in turn, sustain the organizational logic that supports and magnifies the growing difference in wealth and power among lawyers.

This chapter examines the organizational logics or mechanisms operating over a legal career and within various specialties that limit the career options of women; their consequences in terms of income differentials, career patterns, and occupational identities; and the manner in which women in law have sought to address and alter these limits on their careers.

Gender Bias in Law School, Recruitment, and Hiring

Gender bias for women seeking legal careers begins in the law school environment, which emphasizes a middle-class masculinity. Several studies have found that, although women perform adequately in law school and make up nearly half of all students, they are more dissatisfied with and alienated from what they regard as an inhospitable educational system than are men. Weiss and Melling (1988) identified four aspects of women's alienation from law school: alienation from themselves, from the law school community, from the classroom, and from the content of legal education. Alienation from the law school community, for example, includes discomfort with the competitive environment, sexist attitudes of men, and a masculine atmosphere that is part of the gendered legal culture.

Further exploring women law students' alienation, Homer and Schwartz (1990) surveyed all students at Boalt Law School in 1988. In accord with several previous studies, they found that women are much less likely than men to participate in class in any other way than being physically present. The majority of white women, as well as men and women of color, stated that they never asked questions or volunteered answers in class; nearly two thirds of white men stated they had done both with some frequency. Homer and Schwartz (1990) suggest that this reluctance to participate, which may have begun in the instinct for self-preservation, now reflects "a countercode of classroom ethics" (p. 37) and an active decision not to compromise the integrity of their beliefs by submitting them to the narrow legal analysis of the classroom.

Homer and Schwartz (1990) also found that women students were significantly less likely than men students to feel as competent as their classmates, as intelligent and articulate as they had felt before law school, and as confident that their talents are respected. Self-doubts were even greater among women of color than among white women. For example, 43% of women of color, 36% of white women,

30% of men of color, but only 19% of white men indicated that they had lost confidence during law school (Homer & Schwartz, 1990, p. 33). For many white women and people of color, law school leads to a feeling of schizophrenia, as they learn to cultivate the legal logic that tends to isolate them from their communities and each other and to undermine their values and sense of self. As Angel (1988, pp. 810-811) observed, "we were treated to three years of 'the reasonable man's' perspective on the world" and a curriculum that often is remote from women's concerns. Thus, the core of legal pedagogy and reasoning epitomizes the link between law and masculinity.

Mary Jo Frug (1992) identified several ways in which apparently gender-neutral law courses and casebooks on contract law are gendered. First, the parties in cases are predominantly men, and they represent many different occupations and roles; the few women in illustrative cases are found in stereotypical women's occupations and domestic roles. Language in both text and cases sometimes uses "he" to refer to people of both genders. In addition, cases used to illustrate principles such as mutuality of assent are drawn from commercial settings in which men predominate, even though issues of concern to women, such as reproductive technology and cohabitation, also might illustrate contractual principles. Frug (1992) adds:

> By confining issues that particularly concern women to domestic relations or sex discrimination courses, casebooks combine with standard law school curriculums to perpetuate the idea that women's interests are personal, concerning only themselves or their families. Men, in contrast, are concerned with the rest of life. (p. 71)

As new lawyers, women encounter barriers in recruitment, job interviews, and selection. Although questions about their marital status, plans for pregnancy, and husband's occupation are prohibited, several gender-bias task forces have documented numerous instances of women still being asked just such questions (ABA Commission, 1988; Gellis, 1991). Nevertheless, one recent study of women lawyers found that among those reporting differential treatment in recruiting and hiring (i.e., about half of the sample of 200 women), more reported gaining personal benefits from such treatment than reported discrimination (Rosenberg et al., 1993). It is unclear whether those women actually benefited from employers' efforts at affirmative action or simply attribute their selection to gender preference rather than their own qualifications.

Gender Bias in the Firm, Office, and Agency

On the job, women lawyers' activities and rewards differ from those of men. By the mid-1980s, women should have had enough time in the profession to have attained their share of partnerships, yet they did not. At least four recent studies have shown that in large and medium-size firms, women have worse prospects for moving into partnerships than men; in small firms, women's prospects are even poorer. Abel (1989, p. 98) found that in the cohort of lawyers who entered private practice after 1970, 71% of women but only 48% of men remained at the associate level (i.e., were not partners) by 1984. A study of the Harvard Law School class of 1974 found that by 1985, only 23% of the women had made partner, compared with 51% of their men classmates (Abrahamson & Franklin, 1986). After 9 years of experience, 95% of men but only 76% of women had made partner in New Hampshire law firms (New Hampshire Bar Association, 1988). Hagan et al.'s (1991) study of lawyers in the United States and Canada found that a woman's probability of making partner was 39% less than a comparable man's, and that women who became partners did so about 26% more slowly than men.

Women's career progress is hindered by several factors; these are more difficult to identify in law than in policing or corrections because law firms vary widely, rarely have written policies to examine, and are secretive about practices that rarely have been studied. Nevertheless, across widely varied firms and specialties certain patterns prevail and cumulatively result in gender-differentiated career trajectories.

First, new employees of a firm are assigned to cases and specialties by senior partners. Women still are guided toward specialties, such as trusts and estates or domestic relations, that have lower status, visibility, and opportunity for interaction with clients. Women also continue to report being assigned different types of cases than men colleagues. Senior partners or supervisors continue to steer women away from "major litigation, commercial matters, heavy client contact, extensive travel, or late night responsibilities," and relegate them to support roles such as preparing documents, even when they have a leading role in preparing a case (ABA Commission, 1988, p. 11).

This pattern often appears to result from the lack of a mentor to serve as role model and sponsor, guide a young associate through firm or agency politics, and distribute business referrals to him or her. It also arises because employers assume women have feminine personality traits that land them in dead-end specialties. Assumptions that women are less motivated or not tough enough to handle business law and courtroom stresses, for example, lead to tracking into "less challenging" work such as domestic relations cases. This puts women in a no-win situation. "Tough" women face disapproval from both men and women colleagues for adopting a masculine model of behavior; women who conform to culturally emphasized feminine behavior are viewed as behaving in unlawyerly ways.

Women lawyers in various legal workplaces in one midwestern capital reported discrimination in both assigned activities and rewards (Rosenberg et al., 1993). Substantial proportions of women working in private law firms (45%) and courts (46%) claimed they received less interesting and challenging assignments. Moreover, discrimination in work assignments was the factor that most negatively affected women's view of the work environment and undermined their expectations of opportunities for professional growth, promotion, and commitment to law (Rosenberg et al., 1993).

There are also consistent differences in the income of men and women lawyers, differences that can only partially be accounted for by factors other than discrimination. Differences in the type and size of the firm in which they work, legal specialty, and partnership status contribute to these income differences. For example, a study conducted by the bar association of New Hampshire found that the average salaries of full-time attorneys in private firms in that state in the mid-1980s were $50,373 for men and $30,892 for women. After controlling for firm size and length of legal experience, the income gap was still $10,404. In full-time non-solo private practice, men nonpartners had a salary advantage over women nonpartners of $1,054 per year. The income advantage to male partners over women partners was $9,114, and it was greater in firms with more than 10 lawyers than in smaller firms (New Hampshire Bar Association, 1988). Similar income differentials were found in Florida and Indiana (Gellis, 1991).[1]

A survey conducted by the Florida state bar in 1986 found that men outearned women at every stage of their legal careers in every specialty area. Florida's Gender-Bias Study Commission also reported that among assistant state attorneys, men averaged about $3,600 more than women annually, and among assistant public defenders, men earned about $3,000 more annually than women (Florida Supreme Court, 1990).

Sociologist John Hagan's (1990) study of factors contributing to the large differences between the incomes of men and women lawyers in Toronto, Canada, distinguished between the effects of discrimination and nondiscriminatory "composition" factors. The latter include differences attributable to specialty, experience, and practicing in a growing sector of the law. Among lawyers in private practice, men not only earn more than women after controlling for experience and specialty but also get a much larger financial return than women both from going to an elite school and from years of experience. Thus, for each year of experience the gender income gap grows larger.

Men also gain more in income than women from moving up career ladders in large law firms. For example, men who are managing partners in medium-to-large firms average nearly $84,000 more per year than men who are partners in small firms. In contrast, women managing partners in medium-to-large firms earn only $24,000 more than women partners in small ones (Hagan, 1990).

After separating out all the income differences due to nondiscriminatory composition effects identified above, Hagan (1990) found that 29% of the difference in income between men and women lawyers was due to discrimination. Women pay a penalty simply for being women, a penalty amounting to more than $12,000 annually.

These findings led Hagan to conclude that changes in growth patterns in particular sectors of law have benefited men more than women. Men have gained more in income than women from moving up career ladders in large law firms, from translating higher-status specializations into higher income, from elite education, and from length of experience. They also have gained more in leaving large firms and going into business, a pattern that women have not been able to achieve.

The Impact of Gender Bias
on Women Attorneys in Court and Beyond

To be credible or believable is crucial for an attorney, particularly in the courtroom. Yet in this setting, women attorneys often are subjected to treatment that undermines their ability to act as effective advocates for clients and, therefore, biases the rendering of justice.

The nature, extent, and impact of gender bias in the courtroom and other legal environments has been amply documented in the past few years (Bernat, 1992; Epstein, 1983; Feinman, 1986; Florida Supreme Court Gender-Bias Study Commission, 1990; Gellis, 1991; MacCorquodale & Jensen, 1993; Maryland Special Joint Committee, 1989; Rosenberg et al., 1993; Schafran, 1987a, 1987b). The legal world clearly is filled with sexist jokes, disparaging or patronizing treatment, inappropriate terms of address, remarks that call attention to a woman's gender, and other displays of disrespect. In addition, women lawyers encounter inappropriate touching and quid pro quo sexual harassment. The extent of the bias and how it hampers women's work performance and undermines their self-image will be elaborated in this section.

TABLE 6.1 Percentage of Women Lawyers Reporting
Inappropriate Behaviors in State Gender Bias Reports

	Inappropriate Names		*Comments on Appearance*	
State	*Attorneys*	*Judges*	*Attorneys*	*Judges*
Indiana	64	—	59	—
Maryland	73	45	76	54
Minnesota	59	35	59	42
New Hampshire	67[a]	18	56[a]	11
New Jersey	85	61	68	54
Rhode Island	80	—	53	—
North Carolina	57	32	35	18

Sources: Gellis, 1991, 1972, in the *Indiana Law Journal*, by the Trustees of
Indiana University and Fred B. Rothman & Co. Reprinted by permission.
Vasu & Vasu, 1991.
a. Outside courtroom; comparable figures for the same behavior in chambers or
court are 40% and 23%.

SEXUAL HARASSMENT

Sexual harassment is a widespread problem for women in law. As
shown in Table 6.1, several gender-bias task force reports documented the frequent occurrence of two forms of harassment that
make the work environment a hostile one—inappropriate terms of
address and comments on appearance. In addition, they found that
women lawyers often encounter disparaging remarks, sexist jokes,
and quid pro quo harassment. For example, the Indiana gender-bias
report found that 11% of the women lawyers in that state had
experienced physical sexual harassment and 40% reported verbal
harassment related to their work (Gellis, 1991). In Maryland, 47%
of the women the task force surveyed said women attorneys were
subjected to verbal or physical sexual advances by other counsel
(Maryland Special Joint Committee, 1989). A quarter of the women
lawyers in a midwestern capital reported unwanted sexual advances
in a professional situation, and 85% of them said such incidents had
occurred more than once in the prior year (Rosenberg et al., 1993).

The effects of being a token include both greater visibility on the
job and social invisibility due to boundary heightening (Kanter,

1977). For women in law, what is noticed is their physical appearance (see Table 6.1); what is ignored is their legal skill or reputation.
A survey of lawyers in Pima County, Arizona, that tested the effects
of tokenism found that women reported frequent compliments on
their appearance but infrequent praise for handling a case or for
their legal reputation; men reported compliments on their legal
activities but not on their appearance. Moreover, 38% of the women
but only 6% of the men believe men counsel get more attention and
credibility from judges than women; no respondents believed
women get more. This gives women a message that they are valued
only for appearance (MacCorquodale & Jensen, 1993).

Sexist jokes abound in and around the courthouse. In the Rhode
Island gender-bias study, 53% of the women reported hearing sexist
jokes; in the Minnesota study, 63% of the women respondents had
heard such jokes or demeaning remarks (Gellis, 1991); in Maryland,
78% of the women had heard such remarks or jokes made by men
attorneys, and 55% heard them from a judge. In the Pima County
study, more than 80% of the women heard judges and attorneys
make sexist jokes and remarks at least occasionally, more often at
social events than at meetings, and rarely in court (MacCorquodale
& Jensen, 1993).

The frequency and type of sexual harassment varies across types
of legal worksites. Comparing three types of private sector work
settings (solo practice, law firm, and in-house counsel) and three
categories of public sector settings (government agencies, courts,
and other settings) in one city, Rosenberg et al. (1993) found that
harassment was widespread, but it was more common in private
than public sector work. As shown in Table 6.2, nearly a quarter of
the women overall and nearly half of those employed in law firms
experienced sexual advances.

Several illustrations suggest the nature and impact of such incidents. The Indiana Commission on Women in the Profession
reported that one county bar association invited its members to
attend a dinner in which a featured event was "to get drunk and
come on to babes." In response to a letter of complaint from a
woman bar member, the association printed her letter on the

TABLE 6.2 Percentage of Women Lawyers Reporting Disparagement and Harassment by Workplace

Treatment	N^a 100 (161)	Private Sector			Public Sector		
		Solo 11.8 (19)	Firm 26.1 (42)	In-House 9.9 (16)	Government 37.3 (60)	Court 7.5 (12)	Other 7.5 (12)
Disparagement							
Act as secretary	17.5	22.2	17.5	25.0	16.3	—	25.0
Inappropriately addressed	66.0	75.0	73.7	68.8	66.6	61.5	30.8
Gender emphasis remarks	64.5	78.9	78.6	68.8	65.0	33.3	33.3[b]
Addressed by first name	32.0	29.4	28.9	33.3	39.2	25.0	16.7
Harassment							
Unwanted advances	24.0	26.3	43.6	25.0	18.4	—	15.4[b]

Source: Rosenberg et al., 1993, p. 424; reprinted by permission of *Gender & Society*.
a. The number of responses to these items varies slightly.
b. Kendall's tau *B*: *p* = .01.

placemats used at the dinner (Gellis, 1991). Similarly, an attorney testified at hearings in Florida that her sexual harassment complaint to a judicial ethics commission was made public and, as a result, she was ostracized by the legal community.[2]

Sexist jokes and remarks heighten group boundaries by reinforcing tokens' feelings of isolation, polarizing gender divisions, and testing women's loyalty (Epstein, 1992; Kanter, 1977). When a sexist joke is told, others wait to see if the woman will react "like a woman," with offense and anger, or will respond like "one of the boys" by laughing, even if it is at the expense of women. Such jokes also reflect the status hierarchy, because they are told about outgroups rather than those in the power structure. A woman telling a joke about men's sexuality would be regarded as displaying bad taste.

UNDERMINING WOMEN LAWYERS'
CREDIBILITY IN THE COURTROOM

Women lawyers often face condescension and displays of disrespect in the courtroom from judges and other attorneys. Such behavior may undermine a client's confidence in his or her attorney's ability to handle a case and may diminish credibility in the eyes of jurors and other court personnel. When it occurs in open court, a lawyer faces a bind: confront the issue and threaten the interest of the client or remain silent and accept a tarnished professional image. For a lawyer whose livelihood depends on attracting clients, often by having a track record of winning cases, the effects of such disrespectful behavior may be devastating. Thus, doing femininity and successful trial work often are in conflict.

Women attorneys overwhelmingly report disparaging and condescending treatment by both attorneys and judges. About 85% of the women responding to the Wisconsin gender-bias study reported that judges behaved in a condescending manner toward women and minorities; 91% of the women reported similar conduct by men litigators.

Other forms of disparagement that reinforce gendered cultural images are the allusion to a woman's gender characteristics or sexuality and restatement of their arguments. Women are addressed through infantilizing terms (e.g., honey, doll) (shown in Table 6.1), by their first name, or by another term that emphasizes social status (woman attorney), whereas men are addressed as "Mister" or by a term emphasizing professional status (counselor). Men also are condescending when they repeat and restate arguments made by women but not by men attorneys.

Women lawyers are frustrated by the lack of respect shown them by both judges and attorneys. For example, 57% of the women attorneys responding to the Maryland Special Joint Committee (1989) agreed that judges appear to give less weight to women attorneys' arguments than to those of men attorneys. They also believe they are repeatedly forced to prove themselves capable, whereas men's competence is taken for granted (Gellis, 1991).

The perception that women are less competent lawyers than men was demonstrated by an experimental study using college students as jurors (Hodgson & Pryor, 1984). To explore the relationship between an attorney's gender and perceived credibility in a criminal court simulation, students read a summary of a mock breaking-and-entering case, then listened to the audiotaped closing remarks of a man or woman defense attorney. The women students' ratings of the woman attorney were significantly lower than those of the men students on 6 of 12 credibility scales; men students gave similar credibility ratings to the male and female attorneys. Although there was no statistically significant difference in the proportion of the clients of the men and women lawyers who were given guilty verdicts, the respondents were significantly more likely to say they would retain the man than the woman as their lawyer (65% and 39.7% respectively; $\chi^2 = 7.29$; $p < .01$).

MEN'S PERCEPTIONS OF GENDER BIAS

Men often claim to be unaware of the diverse forms of gender-biased behavior. Thus, whereas more than two thirds of the women in nearly every gender-bias survey indicated they had experienced various forms of discriminatory treatment, less than a third of the men reported observing such behavior. For example, in Indiana,

69% of the women but only 17% of the men lawyers observed the incidence of sexist jokes and other displays of disrespect for women colleagues (Gellis, 1991).

Not only do most men not perceive gender bias, but their responses suggest that many regard complaints of discrimination as imaginary or as an overly sensitive reaction to their well-intentioned acts. These views persist despite the consistency of survey data and a study based on systematic observation of court proceedings in Rhode Island that found an average of 1.64 incidents of gender bias every hour in the court (Gellis, 1991).

Organizational Logic and Limiting Opportunity Structures

In law, as in many occupations, there is an "opportunity structure" or set of positions that usually lead to obtaining the credentials and visibility needed to achieve a highly coveted position such as judge, law school dean, or police chief (Cook, 1984; Kanter, 1977). Women face a "glass ceiling" or limit on opportunities to climb beyond certain lower steps on the career ladder so they are not ready or positioned to reach the top.

The processes through which differences in types of work settings, areas of specialization, income, and other employment outcomes arise for men and women in law rest, in part, on gendered organizational logic. Across the spectrum of legal practice, the rules and informal practices on which advancement decisions are based continue to rest on the masculine professional model. In it, work comes first, work-related social and professional organizational activities play a key part in cultivating contacts that contribute to the career, and domestic and family responsibilities are limited. Because the time demands on which this model rests are open-ended and unpaid, professions require a system of "social capital" or private social support that allows the professional to give work tasks priority and ensure release time from private (e.g., family) obligations (Seron & Ferris, 1995).

Women who do not play by these professional rules (e.g., those who wear skirts that are too short, eat lunch at their desk, take advantage of flexible working hours or maternity leave, or do not attend bar association meetings) may be disadvantaged in promotion decisions or relegated to the "mommy track." How such gendered organizational logics operate at various career stages and sites are illustrated at three points in a legal career: the selective job recruitment mechanisms, the selection of judges, and the tenuring of law professors.

ORGANIZATIONAL LOGIC AND GENDERED JOB RECRUITMENT

Sharyn Roach Anleu (1992) examined the processes by which women and men with similar educational credentials get routed into different legal career trajectories. She found that large corporations and law firms seek to hire the "best lawyers" available in the segment of the labor pool from which they seek recruits, but they draw from different pools. From law school, graduates may go to large or smaller law firms or corporations with legal departments. Manufacturing companies offer salaries that are competitive with the most prestigious law firms; men apply to both and see what happens. These companies are more likely to hire men because they are overrepresented in the top schools. Manufacturing companies also tend to recruit seasoned associates from outside law firms, particularly those they have worked with previously (i.e., people with corporate law experience). Men are overrepresented in this labor pool as well.

In contrast, women graduating from law school tend to be attracted to in-house legal departments, which provide work settings in which there is greater security, less competition, and a more hospitable environment than law firms provide. Women are disproportionately hired to work in financial services companies, where salaries are lower, law departments are smaller, jobs less competitive, and promotion opportunities fewer than manufacturing companies. If experienced lawyers are sought, financial services companies recruit people with skills in banking, insurance, and finance law, which are considered to be among the "feminine" areas of legal practice. Because women are more likely to have acquired these skills, the available supply of lawyers for positions with these companies outstrips demand and depresses salary levels. However, women do not reach top positions in these companies, because such positions are filled with lawyers from outside the firm. Women also are encouraged to move into management to move up, and this reduces competition for top-level legal positions. Thus, career opportunities are controlled by management and disadvantage women.

GENDER BARRIERS TO A JUDGESHIP

A judgeship may be the final step and highest achievement in a long legal career. Not surprisingly, women are underrepresented on the bench because they have few of the experiences considered prerequisites for a judgeship. The fast track to a judgeship traditionally has involved graduation with honors from an elite university and law school, a prestigious clerkship, partisan political experience, experience in the U.S. Department of Justice, and partnership in an elite law firm. Women are disadvantaged with respect to each of these career elements.

Women's continued underrepresentation in elite law schools contributes to the fact that they have not gotten a proportionate share of clerkships with judges, but that is only part of the picture. Between 1971 and 1983, for example, the proportion of women selected for U.S. Supreme Court clerkships was always below their representation, even in the elite schools (e.g., 3 of the 32 Supreme Court clerks in 1980 were women) (Cook, 1984, p. 320).

Women also are disadvantaged along each route to the bench. In private practice they are slower and less likely to make partner than their men counterparts. They also are greatly underrepresented on elite law school faculties. The third route to prestigious judgeships, through service on local or municipal courts, often is blocked by political power brokers, many of whom regard a candidate's manhood as an unwritten qualification for a judgeship.

The selection processes for professional experiences that serve as stepping stones to judgeships are controlled by senior gatekeepers who are men. These gatekeepers tend to prefer working with people like themselves, because similarity is a basis for trust and easy social interaction (Epstein, 1983; Kanter, 1977). In addition, the judicial selection process itself rests in the hands of nominating bodies appointed by bar associations that apply different standards to men and women applicants. In Florida, for example, the Judicial Nominating Commission gives greater weight to certain areas of law perceived as traditionally masculine (e.g., commercial law) while disparaging areas of specialization (e.g., family law) perceived to be more feminine. The commission is biased in favor of lawyers in private practice; women are disproportionately in public sector work. Furthermore, women's managerial experience in the home is ignored, but discussion of plans to bear children often creeps into the judgeship interview (Florida Supreme Court Gender-Bias Study Commission, 1990). A comparison of the men and women appointed to the bench by President Jimmy Carter (1976-1980) illustrates how women's limited experience and lack of political power, judicial selection criteria and mechanisms that fit the careers of men, and the influence of state bars and the American Bar Association (ABA) combine to limit women's opportunities for selection. To increase the number of white women and people of color on the federal bench, President Carter altered the traditional selection criteria and process. First, he modified appointment procedures to expand the number and types of people participating in the judicial selection process by establishing circuit (appellate) court nominating panels and encouraging use of merit selection panels to nominate judges to the district (lower) courts. In addition, Carter expanded the eligible pool of potential women judges by seeking women with different career characteristics than the men in the eligible pool.

As a result of the change, Carter's women judges were younger (most were under 50; most of the men were over 50) and less likely to be partners in traditional law firms. They were also more likely to have worked in a prosecutor's office than the men he appointed

(24% versus 48%, respectively) and were more likely than the men to have had judicial experience (58% vs. 55%, respectively) or to come from a law school faculty (13% vs. 6%). The women judges also were more likely than the men to have attended an elite college and law school and to have graduated from law school with honors, but less likely to have been politically active (Slotnick, 1984). Men of color appointed by Carter also were drawn from the lower judiciary and were more likely than white men to have represented criminal defendants (53% vs. 23%, respectively) prior to coming to the bench.

Thus, Carter's white men candidates tended to follow the well-worn path to a federal judgeship: after long legal experience, largely in successful private practices and participation in partisan politics, their "merit" was rewarded by appointment to the bench. Because white women and men and women of color followed different legal career paths, Carter used alternative procedures and selection criteria in order to appoint them to the federal bench. President Reagan went back to older procedures, adding an ideological test, and, not surprisingly, only 11% of judicial appointments in his first term were women. This illustrates the importance of organizational logic in shaping opportunities to favor white men.

BARRIERS TO LAW SCHOOL TENURE

Gendered organizational logic also contributes to the difficulties women have in getting tenure at prestigious law schools (see Chapter 5). Tenure decisions formally rest on such criteria as good teaching, research, and service. But what good teaching means is not clear.[3] Both senior faculty members and students expect a teacher to adopt an adversarial, Socratic stance; they mistrust a teacher who is willing to explore different approaches and values. The research and writing of women faculty may be judged negatively because it often concerns "insubstantial" subjects such as family law and women's issues. Women's extensive service contributions often are denigrated. For example, little weight is given to advising women law students or serving on the university committees on the status of women, both of which take considerable time (Angel, 1988).

In addition, the informal decision criteria often rest on collegiality, which generally means how well the individual fits with the rest of the faculty and how well he or she is liked. As Angel (1988) notes, when "the rest of the faculty" are men judging women, the latter often don't seem to fit.

Women's Responses to Gender Bias: Adaptation and Innovation

Women lawyers have adopted a variety of coping strategies for dealing with gender bias. Like women in policing and corrections, they attempt to strike a balance between identities that will be regarded as too tough or too feminine, to seek sponsors or mentors, and to avoid sexual harassers or deal with harassment informally. Other adaptive strategies include reducing stress by choosing work settings and legal specialties deemed more appropriate for women and avoiding those where they are less welcome, by delaying or avoiding marriage and children, by changing jobs or seeking part-time work when they have a family, or by leaving the legal profession.

At the same time, women lawyers' strategies differ somewhat from those of women in policing and corrections, due to the structure of the legal world and the nature of the work. First, they have organized more effectively than women in other criminal justice system (CJS) occupations. They have formed local women's bar associations and have stimulated gender-bias task forces in many states. Second, they have used their training to develop feminist jurisprudence, which challenges the premises of legal reasoning, and they have applied it in lawsuits challenging discriminatory practices of their own employers—law schools and law firms, as previously illustrated.

WOMEN'S BAR ASSOCIATIONS
AND GENDER-BIAS TASK FORCES

To foster their careers, women have established separate women's bar associations. The Women Lawyers Club (which became the National Association of Women Lawyers) was formed in 1899; by 1951, its more than 1,000 members represented about 20% of women lawyers. Although the number of members grew to 1,600 by 1980, they made up only 2% of women lawyers in that year (Epstein, 1983, p. 259).

Women's bar associations have helped women participate in professional life by serving as friendship groups and centers for mutual support, giving leadership opportunities, and providing visibility. However, they also have been criticized for diverting women from full integration into the profession (Epstein, 1983, p. 258). As leadership opportunities in state bars and the ABA opened to women, many have resisted joining a separate organization.

The rationale and findings of gender-bias task forces make clear the nature and extent of discrimination in the law and have forced the legal profession to confront its own injustices. Nevertheless, their recommendations remain advisory, and actual outcomes have not been systematically evaluated.

FEMINIST JURISPRUDENCE AND LEGAL ACTION

By doing their jobs as lawyers, women have written and presented arguments affecting employment opportunities for women in many occupations, including the legal profession. The efforts of feminist lawyers not only have reshaped the law regarding employment discrimination, but also increasingly have challenged the gender bias of legal reasoning and the ways it affects such diverse areas of law as contracts, family relations (including treatment of domestic violence and child support law), and criminal sentences. Thus, they have questioned the law's entire perspective on and treatment of women.

Initially, feminist legal scholars challenged rules or laws that treated men and women differently, focusing on so-called women's issues such as rape and pregnancy. They also demanded to be admitted to law schools and allowed to practice on equal terms with men. But they discovered formal equality could be a double-edged sword and began exploring a variety of biases in the legal system. For example, they noted that ostensibly objective legal rules rest on the perspectives of "the reasonable man." Feminist jurisprudence is branching out to explore what law and legal process would be like if it embodied a worldview that is more inclusive, less abstract, and more caring, and if it took the reality of women's lives into account. Initially regarded as radical, the feminist jurisprudential examination of the assumptions of the justice system has penetrated the mainstream of legal thinking. For example, in 1994 the ABA Commission on Women in the Profession sponsored a symposium titled "Is the Law Male?: Bringing Feminist Legal Theory into the Practice of Law."

The issue now identified as sexual harassment clearly illustrates the perspective of feminist jurisprudence, its close links to feminist theory in other disciplines, and its impact on the law. Until 1978, what is now call sexual harassment was simply an unnamed condition that women had long endured. Feminist theorist Catharine MacKinnon labeled certain types of behavior sexual harassment and provided a legal theory that enabled women to identify certain behaviors as a form of actionable employment discrimination covered by Title VII (MacKinnon, 1978). As noted in Chapter 1, courts have gradually accepted MacKinnon's reasoning.

THE TIME CRUNCH:
MESHING WORK AND FAMILY LIFE

Because the legal profession demands an open-ended commitment of practitioners' time and energy, women lawyers face a particularly acute time crunch. Moreover, the work pressures and conflicts faced by lawyers have increased over the past two decades due to increases in the number of lawyers, their salaries, and firm size. The average number of hours billed annually by lawyers working in firms (which does not fully reflect the time devoted to their profession) has risen from about 1,700 in the 1960s to between

2,300 and 2,500 today. This translates into 12 hours a day, 6 days a week for people who expect to make partner. A study of graduates of the University of Michigan Law School with full-time jobs 5 years after graduation found that childless women and men worked an average of 52 hours per week, while women with children averaged "only" 49 hours a week (Chambers, 1989).

Meshing work and family is the last and greatest hurdle for women in law. Women carry most of the family responsibilities, particularly those related to child care, and balance the perceived demands of home and work differently than their men colleagues (Chambers, 1989; Epstein, 1983; E. Martin, 1990). These "choices," in turn, have affected women's career opportunities.

Joan Williams (1990, p. 351) observed that women lawyers internalize both an ideology of work success and a belief that successful motherhood is essential to adult life. Meeting expectations of the ideal worker, however, prevent women in law from meeting their children's daily needs for care and affection. This leaves three options: avoid having children, spend very little time with them, or join the mommy track, reducing career activities and opportunities for advancement.

Each option reflects a system of gender privilege rather than a free choice, demonstrating that, in fact, men and women are not similarly situated with respect to legal work. Men but not women generally have access to the domestic labor of their spouses. The work schedule of elite American lawyers both reflects and reinforces this system of gender privilege. It ensures that a disproportionate number of women will be effectively barred from elite jobs by choosing to marry and have a family, because they, but not their husbands, work a second shift that begins when they return home (Hochschild, 1989).

MARRIAGE AND CHILDREN

To reduce career-limiting domestic demands, women may remain single or hire a housekeeper. In the past, women attorneys were forced to choose between career and marriage. Men attorneys were not only expected to marry; their wives sometimes were interviewed informally to assure that they understood the firm's demands on their husband's time and that they "fit" into the social life of the firm. According to U.S. Census data on the marital status of lawyers and judges by sex, in 1960, 32% of the women but only 8% of the men were single; 46% of the women and 87% of the men were married; and 22% of the women and only 5% of the men were separated, divorced, or widowed (cited in Epstein, 1983, p. 330). More recent figures indicate that higher proportions of women lawyers are marrying, but they are still more likely to be single or divorced than men lawyers (Florida Law Record, 1990; Gellis, 1991; New Hampshire Bar Association, 1988).

The parental role is even more demanding and likely to conflict with professional life, particularly for women who have primary responsibility for child care. Consequently, many women lawyers have opted to remain childless. Among lawyers who have children, a higher proportion of women than men report delaying having children because of their careers, taking parental leave when they have children, and remaining on leave longer than their men counterparts (New Hampshire Bar Association, 1988).

The availability and length of maternity leave, as well as its impact on women's careers, vary among employers. A survey of large law firms, government, and corporate employers of lawyers found that the vast majority had maternity leave policies and paid leave of between 6 and 12 weeks. However, policies regarding total length of maternity leave, including unpaid leave, and paternity leave varied widely (Stanford Project, 1982).

Child care responsibilities, even more than maternity and child-birth, create demands for more flexible hours and part-time work. Many studies have found that child care demands have affected women lawyers' choice of job, legal specialty, and the hours they work, and choosing to take maternity leave or work part-time is likely to hurt their careers. One third of the firms in the Stanford Project (1982) survey reported that part-time work or extended leave would negatively affect partnership opportunities and decisions.

The absence of part-time opportunities and inflexibility of law firms regarding accommodations for pregnancies and families exacerbates the frustration of women in law. It also highlights the gendered nature of legal organizations. Family responsibilities are not viewed as an acceptable reason to ask for professional scheduling adjustments; lawyers who ask for extended leave are said to display "reduced professional commitment" or demand "special treatment." In contrast, when a man who is a member of a law firm decides to run for the presidency of the state bar, his activities on behalf of the firm also are limited for a defined period of time, yet his commitment to the firm or the law is not questioned (Florida Supreme Court Gender-Bias Commission, 1990).

Even accommodations, such as provision of an on-site child care facility, have proven to be a double-edged sword. Such actions have enabled firms to increase expectations of young lawyers, pressuring them to work later and come in on weekends, bringing the children if necessary.

RESHAPING THE PROFESSION: WORK-FAMILY BALANCE AND QUALITY OF LIFE

The increasing number of women in law has led some scholars to speculate on women's impact on the law and legal practice and its effect on them. Studies find that women lawyers generally are satisfied with their careers (Chambers, 1989; Gellis, 1991; Rosenberg et al., 1993). For example, Chambers (1989) found that 5 years after graduation from the University of Michigan Law School, women members of the classes of 1976-1979 were as satisfied with their careers as men. Nevertheless, there also was widespread dissatisfaction with specific aspects of work and life situations. In Indiana, women were more likely than men to be dissatisfied with their financial rewards, opportunities to advance on the job, role in management decisions, and respect shown them by coworkers (Gellis, 1991). In the Midwest study, 50% reported seriously considering a change in job or career during the past year, including 14% who considered leaving law altogether (Rosenberg et al., 1993).

Lawyers' marital and family status are related to work satisfaction. Single persons of both sexes are less satisfied than those with spouses or partners, and among women lawyers, those with children are significantly more satisfied than those who are childless. For women but not for men, having children is significantly related to career satisfaction (Chambers, 1989).

Both parenthood and the legal work environment affected lawyers' satisfaction with the balance they have achieved between professional and family life. Only 40% of the Michigan Law School graduates in private practice but 55% of lawyers working outside private practice were "quite satisfied" with the balance between family and work. Women were more content than men with that balance, and women with children were more likely to be quite satisfied (56%) than other women (41%) (Chambers, 1989).

There are several possible reasons why women lawyers with children are significantly more satisfied with their legal careers and with the balance of work and family lives than are men and childless women. First, women generally report higher job satisfaction than do men in the same occupation. Second, they may have achieved a healthier balance between career and the rest of life by accepting and resolving the work-family tension and adjusting personal standards accordingly. Third, this group comes closer than others to "having it all."

The ABA Commission on the Status of Women in the Profession (1988) noted that the pressures on lawyers to produce more billable hours has resulted in "dehumanized" lawyers unable to relate to others with compassion or "render legal advice with a built-in sense of reality" (pp. 16-17). The commission also observed that women have taken the lead in challenging the pressure to become "24 hour-a-day workaholics" and forcing the legal profession to examine the direction it is moving. Similarly, Schafran (1989, p. 1112) notes that the critical mass of women lawyers is forcing more and more employers to make changes. These include providing leave for mothers and fathers, opening day-care centers, and allowing part-time lawyers to continue on the partnership track; indeed, it has "opened a dialogue about the profession as a whole" (Schafran, 1989, p. 1112), although the outcome is still evolving.

Women's challenges to the profession, however, often accentuate the ways in which women are outsiders and the tendency to treat their criticisms of the profession as a lack of career commitment. Many recommended alternative work schedules and part-time options (e.g., Marks, 1990; Nielsen, 1990) that accept and accentuate women's differences but keep the existing rules of the game for workforce participation by creating an alternative mommy track.

Joan Williams (1990) proposed a more radical vision that identifies three possible structural changes to resolve the work-family dilemma. In the first option, both parents would rein in their professional ambitions when their children are young; this would lead to two classes of both men and women lawyers. The second option, to have government or employers provide adequate child care, fails to increase men's responsibility for children's needs. Instead, it would alter norms of "ideal parenting" to resemble more closely traditional fatherhood. The third alternative, which Williams prefers, is to "restructure the entire society's work around the time commitments of responsible parenting" (p. 357), by allowing people to slow down during parenting years. This solution, however, would require a whole cultural shift regarding work-family relations, so that employers who demand 12-hour days and parents who work them would be regarded as irresponsible.

Summary

This chapter has examined gender bias in diverse legal settings. For many women, legal education is an alienating experience. Across diverse legal worksites, women are paid less and advance more slowly than men with similar education and experience, and the differences are magnified over time. Also, women are more likely than men to be denied partnerships in firms and tenure at elite law schools. Some of these differences are due to composition factors, such as women's specialties. However, even after controlling for confounding factors, women lawyers still pay a price simply for being women.

In various work settings, women encounter deprecating and harassing behaviors. Sexist jokes and demeaning comments are common and affect women's morale, satisfaction, commitment, and professional advancement opportunities. They also undermine women's credibility as lawyers and their ability to effectively represent clients.

Organizational logics limit women's opportunities for advancement. The path to partnership, the bench, or tenure on a law faculty favors those who fit in, and such people are men. This is the result of several factors. Fewer women than men are able or willing to pursue the workaholic life of lawyers, particularly those on the fast track. To achieve a judgeship, for example, usually requires a prestigious clerkship and partnership in a commercial law practice. In addition, women encounter gatekeepers with gendered images of judges and law professors.

Although some attribute gender differences in career patterns to the fact that women bear children and continue to shoulder responsibility for their rearing, both women who choose to forgo families and those who work part-time or take a leave of absence face "a system of complex and interrelated barriers . . . which pushes [them] to make fundamentally different 'choices' than men, both in terms of the directions of their careers and in terms of their personal lives" (Gellis, 1991, p. 942). Many women opt for work in less high-pressure environments than law firms or in specialties that are less prestigious and financially rewarding than commercial law. Those who are wives and mothers also must find a balance between extraordinary work demands and family responsibilities without institutionalized assistance. Whether the women who are challenging the pattern of success based on continuous and total commitment will succeed in altering the profession rather than reshaping themselves to fit the mold remains to be determined.

Notes

1. This income difference may help explain why 24% of women responding to the Indiana Commission's survey, compared with

14% of men, said they were dissatisfied or very dissatisfied with their financial rewards (Gellis, 1991).

2. Nearly 40% of respondents to the survey of the Florida Supreme Court Gender-Bias Study Commission reported that they wanted to file a complaint but did not do so because of the fear of ostracism, other reprisals, and the failure of the commission to take action (Florida Supreme Court Gender-Bias Study Commission, 1990).

3. Angel (1988) describes the bind women face regarding student evaluations:

> If the student evaluations and "they" (the tenured faculty) like the faculty member being evaluated, the student evaluations are valid. If the student evaluations are good and "they" don't like the faculty member, the evaluations show that students are being spoon-fed and are not being intellectually stimulated. If the student evaluations are bad and "they" like the faculty member, the evaluations reflect that the teacher is being "tough on the little bastards." . . . If the student evaluations are bad and "they" don't like the faculty member, the evaluations just prove how awful the faculty member is. (p. 830)

7

Women in Corrections

Advancement and Resistance

For more than a century, women working in corrections in the United States were volunteers or specialists, assigned to supervise women inmates and juvenile offenders. Since the late 1970s, the number and types of jobs for women in corrections have expanded significantly, like those in policing and law. Nevertheless, the number of women working in correctional jobs traditionally held by men is still small relative to women's percentage of the total workforce. Moreover, as old forms of gender subordination have eroded, new and sometimes invidious forms have emerged. These constitute formidable barriers, but many women have developed innovative strategies to challenge them.

This chapter examines the history of women's work in corrections, especially their entry into the men-dominated occupation of correctional security officers (COs) in men's prisons. Despite women's advancements over the past two decades, the close association of corrections work with culturally dominant notions of working-class masculinity continues to sanction work cultures that oppose women.

157

History of Women in Corrections:
1860s to 1960s

In 1793, Mary Weed became the first known woman correctional administrator. As the principal keeper of the Walnut Street Jail in Philadelphia, she was known for her humane administration over men and women inmates (Morton, 1992). Before 1861, women correctional workers were extremely rare.

Between 1860 and 1900, small groups of U.S. women took up women prisoners as their special cause. They followed Elizabeth Fry in England, where they organized volunteer programs to visit and aid women inmates (Rafter, 1990). At the time, women were housed in the same facilities as men but were usually segregated into crowded, isolated areas. Reformers guided by religious beliefs visited prisons and questioned prevailing images of women inmates as depraved (Freedman, 1981; Rafter, 1990).

Gradually, women prisoner aid societies joined with prison boards and other social welfare groups to advocate changes in the treatment of women inmates. Reformers were predominantly elite and middle-class women with the desire and free time for social activism. Prison reform was one of several movements aimed at underprivileged and disenfranchised groups. Women reformers had been active in other causes such as the abolition of slavery, temperance, and aid to the needy (Rafter, 1990). They tried to transform societal images of women inmates by portraying them as victims of economic disadvantage and sexual exploitation by men. Women reformers argued that women were different from and morally superior to men (Freedman, 1981), and that all women, rich and poor, shared a common bond of innate, womanly spirit. Their vision of appropriate womanly behavior was a middle-class construction of femininity that disapproved of the ordinary behavior of lower-class women and girls.

At a prison conference in 1870, women and other reformers demanded separate prisons for women. They envisioned women's institutions as homelike atmospheres of rehabilitation that would be controlled and run by women. Women reformers also worked to establish the modern juvenile justice system to serve as a "protective parent" for wayward youth, especially lower- and working-class girls. Their design of the juvenile system actually inspired some of the reforms recommended for women's institutions (Rafter, 1990).

Women gained authority over public institutions that housed women, and, by the end of the century, were employed in the growing fields of charities and corrections. They became administrators and jail matrons in women's prisons and juvenile detention centers (Freedman, 1981). Women were able to enter correction work in the late 19th and early 20th centuries by emphasizing womanly qualities (Heidensohn, 1992; Rafter, 1990).

Middle-class women held the professional jobs of reforming women and girls of the lower, more "dangerous" classes (Rafter, 1990). They claimed that their inherently emotional and sympathetic natures prepared them for work as professional role models for "fallen women" (Freedman, 1981; Rafter, 1990). Their activism made professional work both an acceptable component of middle-class femininity and an avenue for imposing middle-class constructions of femininity on women and girls in the lower classes (Odem & Schlossman, 1991).

By 1900, separate women's prisons were a reality in many states, but their success was partially due to their increasing resemblance to men's prisons and their reliance on programs that conformed to middle-class gender stereotypes. Women's prisons took on more of the institutional and warehouse-like character of men's prisons, and increasingly were headed by men.

From 1900 to 1920, progressive women reformers tried unsuccessfully to drop sexual distinctions and to diversify training. Although reformers did carve out new categories of work for women in corrections, their specialist strategies reinforced culturally emphasized images of femininity and ultimately limited women's work opportunities (Freedman, 1981).

From the 1930s to the 1970s, women worked as administrators, security officers, and counselors in juvenile and women's detention facilities and as probation and parole officers for women and juvenile offenders. Women also worked as volunteers and as administrative and clerical staff, but they were rarely allowed to supervise men inmates (Feinman, 1986). Women inmates and prison matrons became second-class citizens in a correctional system planned around the demands of men's prisons (Rafter, 1990).

During this period, correctional work, especially in women's and juvenile facilities, was characterized by long hours and low pay. The director of the New Jersey Reformatory for Women reported in 1940, "Our cottage staff work practically 24 hours a day and receive $50 to $70 a month, plus maintenance. Men guards in reformatories for men work 8 hours and receive a minimum of $150 per month" (Hawkes, 1991, quoted in Morton, 1992, p. 84).

Despite these barriers, a few women were recognized as outstanding in the field. In 1863, Edna Mahan, superintendent of the New Jersey State Reformatory for Women, was the first woman to receive the American Correctional Association's achievement award; she revived the Women's Correctional Association. Grace Oliver Peck chaired Oregon's Institutions Committee and worked to modernize its entire correctional system (Morton, 1992).

The gender ratios of men and women correctional workers remained steady throughout the 1950s. In the 1960s and 1970s, the civil rights and women's movements began to sow the seeds of change for women correctional workers.

Social Change and Changing
Queues for Women COs: 1960s to the Present

Only in the last two decades have women begun to participate fully in all areas of corrections. The occupational area that has been the most resistant to the inclusion of women has been security work in men's prisons.

Because most prisons are for men and most resources are devoted to men's programs, women have a large stake in obtaining employment in men's facilities. Women began working as COs in men's prisons in the late 1970s. This expansion of women's roles was prompted by a confluence of factors both external and internal to correctional organizations.

SOCIOLEGAL CHANGES AND WOMEN COs

Civil rights and women's movements of the 1960s and 1970s launched ideological and political attacks on the principle of "separate but equal" in all realms of social life. With regard to women prisoners, critics exposed the inequality of their vocational training and longer indeterminate sentences. Radical feminists even advocated closing women's prisons (Feinman, 1986).

Liberal feminists focused on opening up all correctional jobs to women (Feinman, 1986). Legal pressure is frequently cited as the major impetus for expanding women's roles in corrections (Feinman, 1986; Zimmer, 1986). The equal employment opportunity legislation and regulations discussed in Chapter 1 were crucial to their expansion.

Some courts continued to deny employment opportunity to women in men's prisons. In 1977, the U.S. Supreme Court allowed Alabama to exclude women from CO positions in men's facilities because they represented a threat to security (*Dothard v. Rawlinson*, 1977). The suit was filed by Diane Rawlinson, who was denied a job as a CO because her weight was below minimum requirements. As noted in Chapter 1, her class action suit challenged these requirements, as well as a regulation that prevented women COs from "continual close proximity" to inmates in maximum security prisons for men—the "no-contact rule."

The Supreme Court held that height and weight requirements were not legitimate BFOQs because they disproportionately disqualified women. However, the Court also affirmed the no-contact rule, citing the danger of attack on women by "predatory sex offenders" and arguing that their vulnerability would weaken security and endanger others. There was little evidence for either assertion, but the majority opinion was strongly influenced by the extremely dangerous (and unconstitutional) conditions that characterized Alabama prisons (Hawkins & Alpert, 1989; Jacobs, 1983; Zimmer, 1986).

The general instability within prisons during the 1960s and 1970s, including riots and increasing court intervention, prompted numerous changes in these institutions. Federal and state courts mandated due process requirements for inmate discipline, required releases for inmates in overcrowded facilities, named receivers to manage several state prisons, and demanded the introduction of job skill and "resocialization" programs (Irwin, 1980; Jacobs, 1983, pp. 33-60). Prisons were increasingly centralized and bureaucratized in the hope that they would become more rational organizations (Jacobs, 1983). Reformers wanted to replace traditional, informal, and arbitrary prison management with formal and universal rules and regulations (Marquart & Crouch, 1985). These changes indirectly supported the hiring of women in nontraditional correctional jobs.

CHANGING LABOR AND
JOB QUEUES FOR WOMEN COs

With the intention of ensuring that line COs exercised their responsibilities in a manner consistent with these reforms, new administrators concentrated on upgrading job qualifications (Task Force on Corrections, 1973). Policymakers and administrators believed that the professionalization of prison custodial staff would produce more humane, treatment-oriented practices (see Johnson, 1987; Owen, 1988).

Prior to the 1970s, white men predominated as COs in men's prisons. Embarrassing publicity, which revealed that all of the COs at Attica Prison during the 1971 riot were white, and federal mandates for equal employment opportunity pressured prisons to hire more "minority" COs (Hawkins & Alpert, 1989). COs of color were expected to be more sympathetic to the needs of inmates of color. Correctional agencies began recruiting blacks and other people of color in the early 1970s. For example, in Illinois, "recruitment trailers and sound trucks were sent to the inner city to interview and hire guards from African American communities" (Jacobs, 1977, p. 126).

Changes in penal philosophy, which favored rehabilitative and service functions and emphasized equal employment practices, encouraged the assignment of women to security jobs in men's prisons. Policymakers believed that the addition of women to prison staff would promote more humane treatment of inmates. Women COs were expected to bring to the prison culturally emphasized feminine qualities, including a greater sensitivity to inmates, communication skills, and conflict diffusion abilities (Kissel & Katsampes, 1980; Owen, 1988).

Shortages of men workers also stimulated the growth of women's employment in corrections. Prisons, especially in isolated rural areas, were unable to find enough men for CO positions. For example, when Louisiana's Angola prison could not find enough local men to service its inmate population, administrators took men off the guard towers and replaced them with women (Crouch, 1980, p. 36).

Years of economic recession, growing numbers of households headed by single mothers, and increasing social acceptance of women working in nontraditional jobs increased the numbers of women seeking jobs in corrections. The harsh unemployment picture for other jobs in the 1970s, the relatively low entrance requirements, and improvements in the pay level and professionalization combined with affirmative action policies to attract women to CO ranks (Belknap, 1991; Zimmer, 1986).

Women's Movement Into CO Jobs in Men's Prisons

A 1988 survey of federal and state prisons reveals that women make up about 43% of the total correctional workforce (Morton, 1991b). By 1988, women had closed the gap between their representation in the general workforce (43% of workers were women) and their composition in corrections. Nevertheless, women make up 65% of the CO force in women's prisons, but only 13% of the CO force in men's prisons. However, the 13% figure represents a doubling of 1978 estimates (Morton, 1991b).

States vary widely in the percentage of women COs assigned to men's prisons. Mississippi reported that 36.1% of COs in men's facilities were women; North Carolina reported a low of 3.1%, as shown in Table 7.1. The Federal Bureau of Prisons reports that approximately 7% of its COs are women.

Researchers have anticipated that the greatest resistance to women COs would occur in maximum security prisons. Indeed, women constitute a smaller proportion of COs in maximum- than in medium- and minimum-security facilities, but differences are slight and have diminished over the past decade. Women make up 12.7% of COs in men's maximum-, 13.4% in men's medium-, and 15% in men's minimum-security prisons (Morton, 1991b).

In local jails, 21.5% of the total CO force in 107 of the largest U.S. facilities are women. In some counties (e.g., Fulton County, Georgia, which includes parts of Atlanta), women constitute more than 40% of the jail guard force, but these figures are misleading because jails are mixed-sex institutions, and women employees may supervise women inmates (Zupan, 1990).

Despite these advances, women continue to account for a small minority of administrators in corrections. Women constitute less than 10% of the wardens and supervisors in adult correctional institutions, including women's prisons (Hunter, 1992). In juvenile correctional facilities, they make up 39.5% of the staff but only 23% of the wardens and supervisors (Young, 1990).

The same conditions that produced changes in women's roles in prisons generated opportunities for women in community corrections. In probation and parole, women initially were restricted to supervision of women clients, but a 1974 survey revealed that cross-gender supervision had become common practice in all state probation and parole agencies (Schoonmaker & Brooks, 1975). Recent data indicate that 49.1% of probation employees and 50.6% of the workforce in parole agencies are women (Goldhart & Macedonia, 1992; Hunter, 1992).

Other than supervising inmates in prisons for women and juveniles, women in corrections most frequently have worked in administrative or clerical support positions. In these jobs, women have performed daily, taken-for-granted, operating tasks and often contributed extra hours and talent to expanded roles without the accompanying pay and title (Morton, 1992, p. 77).

Characteristics of Women COs in Men's Prisons

Although there are no comprehensive national studies of women and men COs, several case studies provide information on the demographics of women COs. Nancy Jurik and Gregory Halemba (1984) found that women COs in a state prison were more highly educated, more likely to come from professional urban families, and less likely to be married than men COs. In her New York and Rhode Island samples, Lynn Zimmer (1986) found that women and men COs had similar education levels. Before assuming their CO positions, the women either were unemployed or had worked in low-paying, jobs traditionally held by women. Both studies revealed that men had more law enforcement and related work experience than did women.

A large proportion of women COs are women of color. The limited data on gender-by-race composition suggest that men and women COs of color make up anywhere from 20% to 80% of the CO force in prisons across the country (Maghan & McLeish-Blackwell, 1991; Owen, 1988; VanVoorhis, Cullen, Link, & Wolfe, 1991). Jess Maghan and Leasa McLeish-Blackwell (1991) reported that 24.7% of New York City Department of Corrections COs were women. Of these, 84% were black, 10% were Chicana, .2% were Asian American, and 6% were white. Joanne Belknap (1991) reports that 43% of the women COs in her jail sample from a midwestern city were black; 57% were white.

Women may enter correctional occupations for different reasons than men. In some samples, women were more likely to report

TABLE 7.1 Comparison of Employment of Women COs in Men's Facilities: 1978-1988

1988 Rank	State	Total Number of COs	Number of Men COs	Number of Women COs	Percentage of Women COs (1988)	1978 Rank	Percentage of Women COs (1978)
1	Mississippi	1,022	653	369	36.1	a	a
2	South Carolina	2,671	2,006	665	24.9	5	13.9
3	North Dakota	100	78	22	22.0	15	8.1
4	Indiana	1,912	1,557	355	18.6	12	8.5
5	Alaska	583	480	103	17.7	b	b
6	Texas	8,301	6,877	1,424	17.2	b	b
7	Washington	1,594	1,328	266	16.7	22	5.4
8	Tennessee	2,147	1,805	342	15.9	26	4.7
9	Louisiana	2,732	2,302	430	15.7	1	18.2
10	Michigan	7,802	6,588	1,214	15.6	8	12.5
11	California	9,057	7,653	1,404	15.5	10	9.8
12	Colorado	875	745	130	14.9	27	4.6
13	Virginia	3,567	3,038	529	14.8	9	10.7
14	Kansas	1,115	950	165	14.8	6	12.6
15	Kentucky	1,080	925	155	14.4	3	15.9
16	Minnesota	856	738	118	13.8	17	7.2
17	Ohio	3,301	2,846	455	13.8	28	4.6
18	Oregon	385	332	53	13.8	23	5.4
19	Nebraska	371	322	49	13.2	30	4.2
20	Vermont	215	187	28	13.0	18	6.7
21	Oklahoma	1,102	964	138	12.5	4	13.9
22	Massachusetts	1,584	1,393	191	12.1	35	3.0
23	Georgia	3,595	3,189	406	11.3	24	4.8
24	New York	14,283	12,683	1,600	11.2	34	3.2
25	Missouri	2,132	1,899	233	10.9	13	8.4
26	New Hampshire	211	188	23	10.9	31	4.2
27	Hawaii	596	533	63	10.6	a	a
28	Delaware	604	541	63	10.4	14	8.2
29	Wisconsin	1,375	1,233	142	10.3	25	4.7
30	Nevada	438	394	44	10.1	7	12.6
31	Utah	287	259	28	9.8	b	b
32	Idaho	195	176	19	9.7	21	5.6
33	Illinois	5,369	4,855	514	9.6	11	9.3
34	Arkansas	760	690	70	9.2	29	4.5
35	West Virginia	349	317	32	9.2	37	2.9

TABLE 7.1 *Continued*

1988 Rank	State	Total Number of COs	Number of Men COs	Number of Women COs	Percentage of Women COs (1988)	1978 Rank	Percentage of Women COs (1978)
36	Alabama	1,697	1,544	153	9.0	20	6.2
37	Iowa	743	688	55	7.4	16	7.3
38	Maine	217	202	15	6.9	44	0.0
39	FBP, D.C.	4,611	4,299	312	6.8	n/a	n/a
40	Connecticut	1,500	1,423	77	5.1	39	1.7
41	Rhode Island	521	498	23	4.4	43	0.0
42	Pennsylvania	2,892	2,798	94	3.3	b	b
43	North Carolina	3,931	3,811	120	3.1	33	4.0
44	Arizona	a	a	a	a	41	1.4
45	Florida	a	a	a	a	38	2.8
46	Montana	a	a	a	a	42	0.6
	TOTAL	98,678	85,987	12,691	12.9		6.6

Source: From the American Correctional Association (ACA) publication, "Women correctional officers: A ten-year update," by Joann B. Morton (1991a), in J. B. Morton (Ed.), *Change, challenge, and choices: Women's role in modern corrections* (pp. 22-23). Laurel, MD: ACA. Reprinted with permission of the American Correctional Association.
a. No response or data not usable.
b. Responded that in 1978 they did not hire women as COs in male facilities.

intrinsic reasons, such as an interest in human service work or in inmate rehabilitation, as primary reasons for taking the job. Men more often ranked salary, job security, and having no other job as primary reasons for becoming COs (Jurik & Halemba, 1984). Zimmer's (1986) women respondents ranked salary and a lack of alternative employment options as most important. Belknap (1991) found that women COs working in a county jail chose the job for the salary, benefits, and experience, but they hoped to eventually get jobs as police officers. The black women in her study were more interested in a career in corrections and less interested in moving into police work than were their white counterparts.

Relative to white women COs, women COs of color are more likely to be single heads of households. Maghan and McLeish-Blackwell (1991) found that 46% of black women COs in their survey were single. They were attracted to corrections by salary, benefits, and potential job security.

Researchers have also examined women COs' attitudes on gender issues. The women in Zimmer's (1986, pp. 43-44) sample appeared to be conservative. Only 17% were for the Equal Rights Amendment; 56% disapproved of a woman working during her children's formative years. In Belknap's (1991) sample, the women COs held more liberal attitudes on gender issues, focusing on parity between men and women in the workplace.

CO Jobs as a
Resource for Doing Gender

Despite improved opportunities, women have encountered difficulties surviving and advancing in corrections (Jurik, 1985, 1988; Morton, 1992; Owen, 1988; Zimmer, 1986). Women entered CO positions approximately 5 years after most men's prisons began hiring men of color. Like men of color, women of all race-ethnicities confronted overt and covert hostilities and exclusion from coworkers and supervisors. In her study of San Quentin prison, Barbara Owen (1988) reported that men of color and women COs were harassed on the job and by phone in their homes. Their hiring or promotion elicited cries of reverse discrimination from white men staff (Owen, 1988).

Despite problems shared with men of color, women COs face unique problems, including paternalistic protectionism, sexual harassment, and the refusal of their right to work in men's prisons. By the early 1970s, racial discrimination, which was legally rejected, was relegated to the informal culture of corrections, but the denial of work opportunities to women in men's prisons remained part of official policy in many departments (Johnson, 1991). Overtly sexist language and conduct were still openly tolerated (Owen, 1988). Women of color face both racial and gender prejudice and discriminatory treatment.

EMBEDDED RESISTANCE

Many analyses of resistance to women have focused on individual attitudes—especially pre-employment gender role socialization—as the cause of resistance to women or of women's performance failure. Although opposition to women COs in men's prisons has come from inmates, courts, coworkers, and supervisors, this resistance is best understood by locating individual attitudes within their larger organizational context (Anleu, 1992). Sociological research has stressed the preeminence of organizational characteristics (e.g., power, opportunity, relative numbers) over individual traits in explaining on-the-job behavior (Feldberg & Glenn, 1979; Kanter, 1977).

Correctional literature emphasizes the culture of the prison, not personality variables, as primary in shaping COs' responses to the job (Irwin, 1980; Sykes, 1958). Craig Haney, Curtis Banks, and Phillip Zimbardo (1973) conducted an experiment to test for evidence of the "guard mentality," a syndrome of traits that guards allegedly bring to the job. These traits reflected popular stereotypes of prison guards. They randomly assigned men volunteers to guard and prisoner groups. Prior to assignment, the researchers ran personality tests on each group to ensure that they had not disproportionately assigned individuals with authoritarian personalities to either group.

The experimental prison environment turned normal college students into a group of prison guards who derived pleasure from threatening and dehumanizing their peers (Haney et al., 1973, p. 84). A normative culture among guards emerged that defined strength and weakness according to power. As Haney et al. noted,

Not to be tough and arrogant was seen as a sign of weakness . . . , even good guards who did not get drawn into the power syndrome . . . respected the implicit norm of never . . . interfering with the actions of a more hostile guard on their shift. (p. 90)

THE NATURE OF WORK IN CORRECTIONS

The structure and organization of penal institutions varies, but the CO job involves a variety of ambiguous and conflicting tasks centered around controlling unwilling inmates (Sykes, 1958). Although prisons assume some responsibility for rehabilitating, educating, and training inmates, "custody and control are the nucleus" of the entire job (President's Commission, 1967, pp. 45-46). COs' primary duties are the supervision of residents and the maintenance of security, order, and discipline. Control is fostered by physical barriers, regimented schedules, and the regulation of all inmate movements. Several times a day, prisoners must return to their cells or dormitories for the count. If an inmate is missing, all other activity stops until the counting error is corrected, the missing inmate found, or an escape detected.

Outsiders are closely monitored to prevent the introduction of contraband, especially weapons and drugs. COs also are responsible for monitoring physical objects such as the packages, prison equipment, or supplies that might be used as weapons.

Beyond the preventive control functions, COs are responsible for policing inmate violations of rules, ranging from illegal acts, such as assault, to infractions peculiar to prison, such as violations of grooming standards. COs constantly face danger. Even more than police, they work with a clientele who resent the restrictions imposed by their imprisonment. COs can "act tough" and punish troublemakers or relinquish some of their authority to reduce the danger of being taken hostage, assaulted, or killed.

To enforce the myriad of rules, COs must rely on inmate cooperation. Such cooperation arises through tacit agreements between officials and inmates regarding which rules will be strictly enforced. Because COs are outnumbered by inmates, they learn to enlist cooperative inmates and give them special privileges for keeping other inmates "in line" (Hawkins & Alpert, 1989, p. 344). Either this corruption of authority or excessive toughness has negative consequences and may lead to physical harm (Sykes, 1958; Zimmer, 1986, p. 22).

Despite the potential for danger, much CO work is repetitive and uneventful. Correctional institutions, like police departments, are hierarchical paramilitary organizations, but COs have less discretion than police. Prisons also are bureaucratic organizations, and consequently, COs spend considerable time writing reports and managing activity records. Salary and prestige are low, turnover is high, and work hours include nights, weekends, and holidays (Hawkins & Alpert, 1989).

Changes in corrections in the 1970s and 1980s have made the work of COs more tedious and dangerous. Rising incarceration rates have produced serious overcrowding in prisons (Hawkins & Alpert, 1989). Organized and increasingly powerful inmate gangs have made the prison more volatile (Irwin, 1980). U.S. Supreme Court decisions have afforded new rights to prisoners, and resulting procedures sometimes require increased documentation and justification for formerly routine decisions (Jacobs, 1977). Reforms emphasizing inmate services and programs introduce new job tasks for which many COs are ill-prepared (Jurik, Halemba, Musheno, & Boyle, 1987).

CORRECTIONAL OFFICER
WORK CULTURES AND MASCULINITY

COs' work and prison organizations give rise to distinctive work cultures. Many COs feel underappreciated because their occupation is not highly regarded by the public. Danger makes COs dependent on one another for backup, and the unusual hours and isolated locations of prisons encourage them to socialize after work. As in police departments, correctional administrators have developed rules that COs cannot follow "to the letter" and perform their jobs. Nevertheless, rule violation leaves COs constantly vulnerable to arbitrary punishment. These conditions increase the informal sanctions against COs who "snitch" on other COs for rule violations.

Occupational cultures are not gender-neutral. The social control and danger dimensions of the work, as well as past identification of the job as a working-class occupation, encourage an association of

CO competence with dominant notions of working-class masculinity. Because overt displays of fear can undermine authority, CO occupational cultures have stressed physical and verbal aggressiveness as essential qualities for controlling inmates (Zimmer, 1986). Women COs threaten the association between the CO job and working-class masculinity.

Several factors also foster conflict among COs. Limited promotion opportunities generate considerable competition (Hawkins & Alpert, 1989, pp. 338-339). Some COs resent advances in inmates' rights and attempt to sabotage related regulations. Other COs are generally supportive of inmates' rights and associated policy changes (Jurik & Musheno, 1986).

Despite their differing views, most COs believe that they are treated unfairly and denied many due process rights granted to inmates (Hawkins & Alpert, 1989, pp. 352-353). Many COs are alienated and isolated (Poole & Regoli, 1981). They often feel caught in the middle, having to enforce rules developed by courts or prison administrators, rules in which they have little input (Jurik & Musheno, 1986). Yet, if problems arise from enforcing the rules, COs are accountable for the consequences. In response to these problems, some COs have tried to organize in unions. However, unionization efforts have divided COs when unions have worked against affirmative action programs (Jacobs, 1977). Some COs have sought other avenues of prison reform, including support for inmates' rights movements (Johnson, 1987; Jurik & Musheno, 1986; Toch, 1980).

Despite the unified image presented in prison literature (Haney et al., 1973), COs are not a monolithic group (Gilbert, 1990). Racial and gender integration and the reform-professionalization ethic have undermined solidarity based on social similarity and fragmented the "old guard subculture" (Jacobs, 1977; Marquart & Crouch, 1985).

Even before the entry of women and COs of color, researchers identified diverse CO work styles. For example, Lucien Lombardo (1981) distinguishes COs according to whether they regard their authority as emanating from their own personal legitimacy or from their formal position. Michael Gilbert (1990) identifies four CO occupational styles: the professional, who seeks compliance through communication; the reciprocator, who just tries to get along; the enforcer, who rigidly enforces the rules; and the avoider, who minimizes contact with inmates.

Other researchers have argued that it is doubtful if a single guard subculture ever existed (Klofas & Toch, 1982; Lombardo, 1981; Poole & Regoli, 1981, p. 268). In any case, corrections work today involves multiple occupational cultures, each with its own images and work styles (Johnson, 1987; Jurik & Musheno, 1986). Work styles and strategies vary across and within race and gender groups (Owen, 1988; Zimmer, 1986). Prison reforms, affirmative action recruitment, and the upgrading of CO educational credentials have fostered some work cultures supportive of prison reform, bureaucratic rationality, and professionalism; others continue to oppose these changes. Despite their growing diversity, work cultures continue to be influential in shaping CO behavior (Crouch, 1980; Owen, 1988). These diverse cultures provoke struggles in daily interactions over the job and definitions of CO competence.

Sites of Struggle:
Gendered Interactions, Gendered Identities

The nature of CO work and gendered occupational cultures shape the routine social interactions of women COs with men inmates, coworkers, supervisors, and those outside the work environment. Cultural images of correctional work converge with popular images of femininity and masculinity to make daily work in the prison a resource for doing gender.

Drawing attention to feminine characteristics of women COs becomes a mechanism for highlighting the masculinity of men COs. Doing masculinity is identified with demonstrating competence. Opposing images of feminine incompetence portray women as "little sisters" who accept men's protection or as "seductresses" who accept men's sexual advances (Jurik, 1988; Kanter, 1977). Accordingly, for many men COs and inmates, projecting a masculine identity means demonstrating superiority to that which is feminine. Some inmates, men coworkers, and supervisors support women COs who challenge these images of feminine incompetence and construct opposing images of feminine competence in corrections. However, typically, women who refuse men's protection and sexual advances and seek to demonstrate competence risk being labeled as too mannish, or as "man-haters," "bitches," or lesbians. Thus, images of competence as masculine affect all social interactions in the prison.

The many changes in the correctional system have heightened the struggles between competing notions of worker competence and concurrent constructions of femininity/masculinity. The old guard work culture associates competence with notions of masculinity as a manifestation of physical strength and emotional toughness. Such notions of masculinity are integrally associated with poor, white, working-class, or even rural cultures (Messerschmidt, 1993). In contrast, reform-oriented visions of corrections tend to view such versions of competence as authoritarian and as cultivating a sadistic, violent culture among guards. Reform visions call for more educated (read: middle-class) COs, who are rational and rule oriented. They must oversee inmates using conflict management and communication techniques. If they conform to this vision of bureaucratic professionalism, educated white women and men and women of color can be competent COs. This version of professionalism appears to be gender-neutral and more supportive of women.

MEN INMATES AND WOMEN COs

Men inmates haze new COs, but the hazing is gendered. Inmates may whistle, flirt, openly stare, or otherwise declare their own masculinity and the femininity of women COs. However, those constructions of masculinity are neither uniform over time, nor universal to all inmates. Women COs report that hazing usually subsides once they have demonstrated competence or "established their authority." Women COs have to "prove themselves to be fair and emotionally strong with inmates" (Jurik, 1988, p. 293; also Jurik, 1985; Zimmer, 1986). Some inmates may then assist women COs by providing important information necessary to perform the job, especially if men COs have refused to supply such information (Owen, 1988; Zimmer, 1986).

The relationships between women COs and inmates are organized along race as well as gender lines. Men and women COs of color feel some tension about their authority over inmates of their own race, perhaps from their own neighborhood, who like themselves have been victims of racial discrimination and economic disadvantages. One writer has argued that people of color should not seek employment in the "racist CJS [criminal justice system]" (Jones, 1978). Black inmates may exhibit special resentment toward black women COs, because they regard them as violating racial unity and participating in the white culture's emasculation of black men. Maghan and McLeish-Blackwell (1991) argue that black women COs with incarcerated family or friends experience the "concomitant stress and emotional pain . . . [of] this situation in their lives on and off the job" (p. 93). Alternatively, women COs and men inmates may display highly supportive behavior in interacting with others of their race-ethnicity.

Despite potential problems, surveys suggest that most inmates are positive about the presence of women COs. However, pat searches and situations in which women COs see inmates nude may challenge masculinity and increase tension and resentment among the prisoners (Zimmer, 1986). Inmates have legally challenged women CO's presence in men's prisons, alleging that the women's presence violates men inmates' right to privacy. These lawsuits are discussed in Chapter 8.

MEN COWORKER, SUPERVISOR, AND SUBORDINATE RESISTANCE

Women threaten the close association between the CO job and the production of masculinity. If women can do the job as well as men, the job is no longer a viable resource for constructing masculinity. Although some men are supportive, women COs identify men supervisors and coworkers as their major opposition in men's prisons (Jurik, 1985; Zimmer, 1986; Zupan, 1986).

Some men supervisors and coworkers contrast what they see as masculine and feminine behavior, arguing that women are too weak, physically and emotionally, to work CO jobs in men's prisons. They argue that due to their natural physical weaknesses, women cannot perform adequately in violent encounters and will be injured. Emotional weakness means that women will be too fearful or depressed to do the job, or will be "taken in" by inmates. Men COs may "step in to protect women" in conflict situations with inmates, but then claim that they may be injured while protecting women, or when women fail to "back them up" (Jurik, 1985, p. 379).

Many men supervisors and coworkers are fearful that women COs will become too "friendly" with inmates. They scrutinize and sexualize women's interactions with men inmates, watching for situations in which women get "too close." Women COs complain that men COs' intentions with inmates are rarely monitored. Such concerns disadvantage women because interaction with inmates is a necessary part of the job. This disadvantage is magnified for women COs of color who know inmates as neighbors or relatives. In such cases, the women COs have been transferred to other institutions (Maghan & McLeish-Blackwell, 1991).

Women who advance in rank encounter resistance from men subordinates. The few women in supervisory positions report that men subordinates use both subtle and blatant forms of resistance. Nonverbal gestures (e.g., rolling eyes, inattentiveness, inability to "hear" orders) enable subordinates to challenge the competence of women superiors (Jurik, 1985, 1988; Stambaugh, 1995). If a woman supervisor complains, she appears to be paranoid and a poor manager. Subordinates can undermine authority by going over the head of the woman supervisor and complaining to her superior. If her superior is insensitive to the plight of women in management, the woman loses the respect of both subordinates and superiors.

SEXUAL HARASSMENT

Sexual harassment is another mechanism for constructing masculine dominance over women. Women COs are victims of rumors and allegations of sexual misconduct spread by men and women colleagues (Jurik, 1988). Harassment ranges from outright statements of opposition and propositions by men COs and supervisors to more subtle forms such as joking, teasing, and name calling (Zimmer, 1986, pp. 90-100). One women CO reported that men colleagues' wives had phoned the local child protective services to report her for child neglect because she worked long hours at the prison (Sweet, 1995). Women COs who refuse men's protection or attention are ridiculed as lesbians. Women's perceived or real deviation from heterosexual norms is identified as a serious challenge to old-guard work culture notions of masculinity (Zimmer, 1986).

About 31% of the women COs in Belknap's (1991) jail survey said that sexual harassment had been a problem. Zimmer's (1986) intensive interviews revealed that all of the women respondents reported at least one incident of sexual harassment. Belknap's respondents distinguished between "nonsexual put-downs" and offensive sexual comments or behaviors. The first type of harassment claims that women are less capable or intelligent than men. Overtly sexual behavior includes whistling, pressuring women for sex, or comments on their bodies (Belknap, 1991, pp. 103-104). A pattern of either type of harassment may correspond to the legal concept of hostile-environment sexual harassment.

Perception and reporting of harassment vary among women along age and racial lines. Younger women are more likely than older women to report sexual harassment. White women are more likely than black women to report sexual harassment (45% and 13%, respectively), and white women also are more likely to report that men as a group "put women down" (Belknap, 1991).

Racial variations in perceptions of sexual harassment may be due to the blurring of gender and racial harassment for women of color (Stambaugh, 1995). Some women may define harassment as racial; some may perceive it as sexual. In reality, the two types of discrimination are not as easily separable as sexual harassment laws imply (Crenshaw, 1990). Comments about a black women's sexuality may be linked to racist images of black women as sexually promiscuous (P. Collins, 1991). Owen (1988) reports that white women COs who were married to or dating men COs of color experienced harassment from white men coworkers.

If they are harassed by men COs of their own race, women of color face additional dilemmas. Although women COs of color generally describe men COs of their race as very supportive (see Zimmer, 1986), when these men harass them, women of color feel betrayed by the very group that should understand discrimination. Such harassment reinforces the outsider status of these women. They may avoid reporting it because they fear that such reports will further emasculate men of their own race. They may also believe that their claims of harassment will be taken less seriously than those of white women COs (Maghan & McLeish-Blackwell, 1991).

Evidence demonstrates that supervisor and coworker harassment is a source of mistrust, resentment, and job-related stress for women COs (Cullen, Link, Wolfe, & Frank, 1985; Jurik, 1988; Zimmer, 1986). Harassment reinforces the definition of women as outsiders and subordinates in the organization and punishes them for entering men-only domains.

RESISTANCE FROM WOMEN
COWORKERS, FAMILY, AND FRIENDS

No matter how frequent or severe, work-related stress can be reduced by social supports at home and in the workplace (Cullen et al., 1985). For women COs, stress that accrues from the resistance of inmates and staff can be mediated by the support of women colleagues in the same predicament or from family and friends outside of work. Unfortunately, these spheres are not always supportive of women COs.

Women COs are not a homogeneous group; some women colleagues are hostile and oppose other women (Jurik, 1985, 1988; Zimmer, 1986). Some women COs resent being supervised by other women (Belknap, 1991; Jurik, 1988). Women who have different styles of doing their job sometimes oppose one another (Jurik, 1988; Zimmer, 1986). Women COs of color may encounter racial prejudice from white women coworkers (Owen, 1988; Zimmer, 1986). Although women COs have tried to establish networks for coping with the barriers to women, men supervisors who fear such alliances try to block them (Jurik, 1985, 1988).

Family and friends can also provide support and respite from workday pressures. However, even this dimension of the woman CO's life is not always trouble free. Some women COs encounter resentment of their nontraditional jobs from husbands, dates, friends, or family members.

Some husbands define their wives' careers as challenges to their masculinity. They are insecure if their wives have higher job status and resent wives' long hours and rotating shifts. Zimmer (1986) found that COs' husbands were more supportive if their wives accepted the protection of men colleagues at work. Black and white women COs identify problems with marginally employed or unemployed mates (Maghan & McLeish-Blackwell, 1991). Other COs report that their mates see their job as unfeminine. Some black women COs say that their spouses have a difficult time "seeing me in uniform" (Maghan & McLeish-Blackwell, 1991, p. 93).

Children and parents may fear for women CO's safety. The women COs may respond by hiding fears and refusing to discuss work-related problems with fearful or hostile family members. This containment of emotions can heighten work-related stress. Although women colleagues and outside friends and family often offer support to women COs, this pattern is inconsistent. For women COs, social supports are often hard to find.

PROPONENTS OF WOMEN COs: ALTERNATIVE GENDERED IDENTITIES

Despite the diversity that now characterizes prison work culture, gender remains one of its fundamental organizing features. The exclusionary and hostile interactions surrounding women COs, as well as the negative images of women that justify such exclusion, are part of larger occupational, cultural, and societal dynamics that devalue women (Acker, 1992).

Robert Johnson (1987) has emphasized the emergence of new human service-oriented COs who support correctional reform, professionalization, and women COs (see Jurik, 1985). These supporters include some white men COs and supervisors, as well as white women and men and women of color at all ranks. These work cultures advance a different vision of CO competence from that of the old guard culture. They emphasize the custodial and service/counseling aspects of the job and models of gender-neutral, professional competence.

Some supporters of women, including COs, supervisors, women's rights advocates, and prison reformers, have constructed alternative images of competence that emphasize women's unique capacities and their positive contribution to work in men's prisons. Like 19th-century women reformers and modern cultural feminists, they view women COs as different from men COs in ways that can improve CO-inmate relations and the prison environment. This image of women COs contrasts with that of opponents, who argue that women's differences are harmful to prison order and discipline. Proponents suggest that different gender-role socialization patterns give women better communication skills, which enable them to diffuse conflict more effectively than men can (Zimmer, 1986). Prison literature refers to this phenomenon as the "calming effect" of women COs on men inmates. Men inmates have reported that women COs help normalize the prison environment (Kissel & Katsampes, 1980).

Although other men and some women coworkers and supervisors continue to oppose affirmative action and rationalization principles, pro-reform, professional cultures have presented formidable challenges to anti-reform old guard cultures that devalue women. To the old guard culture, bureaucratic paperwork, limitations on CO discretion, and emphasis on dispute management and communication skills represent attempts to feminize the job (Jurik, 1985; see also Hunt, 1990).

The construction of women as different has several hidden dangers. Readily accepting the existence of preemployment feminine differences from men can reinforce the existence of other more negative and limiting images of feminine capacities. As prison overcrowding has undermined reform agendas, old guard definitions of masculine competence may undermine the importance of feminine virtues.

Difference arguments also overemphasize the power of individuals or small groups to exert change in large organizations (Anleu, 1992). If women do not exhibit the predicted differences in job performance, some may question the necessity of hiring and promoting women. Even if an absence of predicted feminine effects does not reinforce resistance to women, their job performance continues to be judged by comparing it to men's. Finally, these unified images of femininity ignore the diversity of behavior among women COs.

Summary

Women have played prominent roles in corrections since the late 1800s, but it was not until the 1970s that women supervised men inmates. Changes in women's corrections work were precipitated by a variety of societal and organizational-level changes: social activism, economic recession, equal employment opportunity laws, and prison reform efforts.

Despite these opportunities, women have faced many barriers in nontraditional corrections jobs. Their presence limits the CO job as a resource for constructing masculinity. Men opponents construct images of feminine physical and emotional weakness. Racism and diverse occupational styles may divide women COs into hostile camps. At home, being a good wife or mother often means that a woman must downplay or sacrifice her correctional career. The roots of imagery about women's inappropriateness in men's corrections are best understood within the context of the job and its surrounding work cultures. Some work cultures, built on a shared sense of masculinity and dominated by white, rural, working-class definitions of masculinity, have been shaken by the entrance of new types of workers, including white women and men and women of color, as well as college-educated, urban, reform- and bureaucratically oriented administrators and staff.

Drawing on the discourses of reform and affirmative action, prison experts and supportive staff have constructed opposing images of competence arguing that feminine talents are an asset in modern prisons. Women may exert a calming effect through superior communication and conflict diffusion skills. However, these images, as well as those of opponents, continue to assess women's capabilities in corrections by comparing them to men's.

These gendered interactions, identities, and work cultures are located within larger organizational contexts. Chapter 8 focuses on the gendered organizational logic of modern correctional agencies and its impact on the career progression of women COs. It discusses women COs' individual and collective responses to barriers and the significance of their actions for the social control world of corrections.

8

Gendered Organizational Logic and Women CO Response

The gendered cultural imagery and interactions of correctional officers (COs) draw upon, reproduce, and sometimes challenge conditions both internal and external to correctional organizations. Societal divisions of labor, power, and culture shape social institutions such as the state, family, labor market, and prisons. In institutions such as prisons, everyday routines, including interactions, identities, and work cultures, also shape and are shaped by the basic rules and regulations of the prison—its organizational logic.

Chapter 7 addressed the forces outside of corrections agencies that encouraged reform, professionalization, and bureaucratization processes. These conditions fostered the hiring of women COs to work in men's prisons. The discourse of reform and professionalization promoted work culture images and interactions more supportive of women COs. However, recent developments have challenged the reform-professionalization ethic of corrections and exacerbated ongoing tensions in the fundamental logic of corrections organizations. These conditions have fueled resistance to women COs in men's prisons.

This chapter considers how dynamics external to corrections and the internal prison organizational logic contribute to the struggles, adaptations, and innovations of women COs in men's prisons.

Social Context and Organizational Logic of Corrections: 1980s-1990s

Social, economic, political, and legal changes in the 1960s and 1970s altered the labor and job queues for corrections and facilitated women's entry into men's occupations. Concomitant changes in correctional philosophy reasserted the importance of program and service functions for prison inmates and emphasized equal employment opportunity (EEO) hiring and promotional practices. Some argued that women would bring feminine qualities to the prison, including better communication and conflict diffusion skills (Owen, 1988; Zupan, 1992). This ethic challenged the old guard CO culture, which associated competence with notions of masculinity as tantamount to physical strength and emotional toughness. Reform/professional orientations de-emphasized this version of masculine competence and viewed it as part of a culture of violence among guards.

Social developments in the mid-1980s and 1990s heightened organizational tensions between security and rehabilitation, caused greater prison crowding, and weakened the implementation of prison reform and affirmative action programs. These trends have bolstered the resistance to women COs.

REHABILITATION AND SECURITY AS CONFLICTING ORGANIZATIONAL GOALS

The conflict between security and rehabilitative functions is a classic correctional dilemma (Sykes, 1958). The goals of detention and rehabilitation continue to collide in prisons. The rehabilitative ideal officially dominated correctional policy and criminological theory throughout much of the 20th century. In the 1970s, widespread criticism of the rehabilitative ideal resulted in its abandonment by most states and the federal government; it was replaced by a focus on retribution, incapacitation, and deterrence. Although the rehabilitative era has officially passed, corrections continues to be responsible for vocational and inmate educational programs (Hepburn & Knepper, 1993).

After prison riots in the 1970s and 1980s, some reformers advocated a human service orientation for corrections (Hepburn & Knepper, 1993, pp. 315-316; Johnson, 1987). This service philosophy was not supposed to compromise the security function; rather, reformers and administrators hoped that the two goals would be complementary (i.e., active, satisfied inmates would be less violent). In practice, these models are in conflict. Rational management of security matters requires that COs treat all inmates alike and consistently enforce rules, but programs require that COs tailor inmate schedules to individual needs. For example, participation in educational programs requires inmate movement within and outside the prison; this poses security problems in understaffed and overcrowded prisons. If conflicts arise, security concerns win (Jurik & Musheno, 1986).

Reforms that require COs to discipline inmates in a rational and nonviolent manner upset arbitrary systems of social control predominating in some prisons. The resulting milieu, which is dangerous for inmates and staff (Marquart & Crouch, 1985), bolsters fears about women COs in men's prisons (Jurik, 1985).

ECONOMIC RECESSION AND DETERMINATE SENTENCING LAWS

Economic recession in the 1980s, federal cutbacks in aid to state governments, and increasing local demands for public services constrained revenues available to state, county, and municipal governments. Recessionary pressures have restricted the hiring and promotions of correctional staff. Temporary hiring and wage freezes have been implemented in many states, and the staff assigned to inmate programs has been reduced (Hawkins & Alpert, 1989; Jurik & Musheno, 1986).

In the 1980s, federal and state determinate sentencing laws and other efforts to "crack down" on crime increased dramatically. Despite new construction, state and federal prisons and local jails are now seriously overcrowded (Hawkins & Alpert, 1989). Additional funding is spent on adding bed space and security at the expense of inmate programs and services.

Inadequate Implementation
of Reform Agenda

Prison crowding, recessionary pressures, and administrative ambivalence hindered the implementation of corrections reform and affirmative action programs. Agencies failed to adequately plan or devote sufficient resources for the diffusion of these innovations. In fact, corrections agencies have seldom devoted adequate resources to monitor the implementation of new organizational practices (Jurik & Musheno, 1986).

Administrators supported these reforms halfheartedly, and demonstrated little commitment to follow-through during implementation stages (Jurik, 1985). Evaluation procedures were seldom reviewed to guarantee that the job strengths particular to women as a group would be rewarded (Zimmer, 1987).

Even when administrators supported reform and EEO programs, the hierarchical, paramilitary structure of corrections agencies did not foster the training of veteran staff or encourage their understanding of, input into, and support for new policies (Marquart & Crouch, 1985). Many opponents resented the interference in hiring, evaluation, and promotional decisions: "Nobody asked us how we felt. . . . We don't even know why things are changed. . . . Sometimes we know a policy won't work. Those making the policy may never have even worked with inmates" (man CO supervisor, quoted in Jurik, 1985, p. 382). The neglect of implementation processes, and in some cases, the near abandonment of reform and affirmative action agendas, greatly empowered correctional work cultures opposed to women COs.

Debates surrounding men inmates' privacy, sexual harassment, and maternity leave are three examples of implementation problems that perpetuate opposition to women COs. They are discussed in the following subsections.

APPEAL TO THE LEGAL REALM: INMATE SUITS

Institutional and legal struggles over inmate privacy and women's rights to employment opportunities have occurred in men's prisons. By mandating reforms, federal courts indirectly fostered the extension of correctional employment opportunities to white women and men and women of color. However, court intervention also spawned inmate activism that challenged women working in men's prisons.

Early decisions prohibited women's presence in some areas of men's prisons. In *Reynolds v. Wise* (1974), a Texas district court ruled that excluding women from working in men's prison dorms reasonably accommodated inmate privacy interests and did not unduly discriminate against women (W. Collins, 1991).

Most cases during the 1970s and 1980s preserved employment opportunities for women by demanding that prisons accommodate women's employment *and* inmate privacy. In *Hardin v. Stynchcomb* (1982), the court ordered officials to erect privacy screens and juggle work schedules to increase the number of positions available to women in men's prisons.

In the late 1980s, courts became less sympathetic to inmates' rights. They often held that the limited observation of men in the nude by women COs does not violate inmate rights, nor does it require officials to modify the institution or to juggle work schedules (W. Collins, 1991; *Grummett v. Rushen*, 1985).

Consistent with an anti-inmate climate, recent cases have favored security concerns and women's employment rights over inmate rights. However, administrators still use past rulings to restrict women's work assignments (Jurik, 1988).

SEXUAL HARASSMENT POLICIES

Corrections officials are more attuned to legal issues relating to inmate treatment than to legal issues relating to the employee work environment. Many women correctional staff work in a hostile environment as a result of both overt and unconscious sexual harassment. Most sexual harassment complaints involve harassment by men coworkers or supervisors (Morton, 1991a). The sexual harassment policy gap fuels hostilities toward women COs.

One hope has been that with time, the sexual harassment of women COs in men's prisons would decrease. So far, this has not happened (Belknap, 1991; Zimmer, 1986). Although many businesses have used educational and role-playing techniques to prepare workers for sexual integration, prisons have done little in this area (Zimmer, 1986, 1989).

Corrections agencies have been sorely lacking in harassment prevention. Women COs are poorly informed about procedures for lodging a sexual harassment complaint, and many feel that administrators do not support the process (Jurik 1985, 1988; Zimmer, 1986). Women fear that complaints may lead to negative evaluation or job loss at some later date. Women in management find that hostility from subordinates is inadequately covered by sexual harassment law (Sweet, 1995).

Most departments handle sexual harassment complaints internally; this permits information leaks and corruption of the investigation by informal friendships (Sweet, 1995). Unions typically defend officers who are the subjects of such an administrative disciplinary process (Zimmer, 1986).

Sexual harassment policies rarely are sensitive to the work experiences of women COs of color. Their harassment is generally linked to their race as well as their gender, and they may fear making formal complaints even more than do white women (Maghan & McLeish-Blackwell, 1991).

Like other work organizations, corrections agencies have developed, disseminated, and enforced sexual harassment policies. However, in order to promote an environment that welcomes rather than devalues women's contribution, existing practices need improvement. Without strong administrative support, informal hostilities will persist (Zimmer, 1989).

CONFLICTS BETWEEN WORK AND FAMILY: PREGNANCY LEAVE

Despite widespread publicity surrounding the "growing gender equality" in the 1970s and 1980s, women have continued to provide a primary and disproportionate share of home, child, and extended family care (Hochschild, 1989). Balancing these responsibilities with paid work is a dilemma. Predominant models of paid work (e.g., rigid work schedules, absence of paid family leave) presume that employees lack responsibilities for the day-to-day care of children and other family members. Corrections is no exception. The CO's job is inflexible: Absence or tardiness may jeopardize an entire unit; there is a constant demand for shift coverage. Continuing societal patterns whereby women bear the primary responsibility for household and family matters produce conflicts between work and home obligations for women COs, especially working mothers.

The lack of pregnancy leave policies in corrections agencies accentuates the tension between women COs' work and family responsibilities. Maternity leave is generally defined as prenatal and postnatal leave for new mothers. Initially, some corrections agencies forced pregnant women to take leaves of absences or quit. Forced leaves can cause financial hardship and disadvantage women for future promotions (Morton, 1991a). The absence of voluntary pregnancy leave is equally problematic.

An American Correctional Association (ACA) survey reveals that over three fourths of responding state corrections agencies have instituted pregnancy and maternity leave policies (Morton, 1991a). However, 22% of the agencies still have no written policy. Paternity leave was allowed by 39% of the departments surveyed. The conditions of the policies varied greatly across states. Only 14 states provide for the reinstatement of employees on sick leave to their former or equal status jobs. Adherence to these maternity policies is also problematic. Additional study is needed to determine whether corrections agencies follow their policies.

The inadequate implementation of policies and procedures, or an absence of them altogether, forces women to choose between jobs and families. Some women COs find themselves deferring advancement and selecting "mommy tracks" in order to have a family and continue working (Cole, 1992).

Even an effective pregnancy leave policy will not ease all of the family-work conflicts faced by women staff. New federal unpaid family leave policies may help women and men in corrections to accommodate these dual demands. However, the lack of *paid* family leave and other methods of support for child and other relative care will continue to work hardships on women and their families.

Gendered Organizational Logic and Women's Careers

The gendered corrections organization affects the careers of women COs at several crucial points—training, work assignments, and performance evaluations. The societal conditions and organizational tensions described above limit the availability and coherence of training programs; COs must rely on coworkers and inmates. Gendered dynamics also reinforce the importance of supervisor discretion in allocating assignments and conducting performance evaluations (Lombardo, 1981; Zimmer, 1986). At each stage, women bear the consequences for their differentness (Jurik, 1988; Morton, 1991a).

PRE-EMPLOYMENT EXPERIENCE AND TRAINING

Women tend to enter correctional employment with less law enforcement or related experience than do men (Jurik, 1985; Zimmer, 1986). On-the-job training should provide recruits with the requisite skills for their work, especially those with no correctional experience. However, staff shortages and prison overcrowding restrict training. Jurik and Musheno (1986) report that 33% of COs surveyed were offered no entry-level training before their first day of work. Zimmer (1986) found that, in the absence of adequate formal training, and in the face of hostile men coworkers, inmates trained women COs. Owen (1988) and Maghan and McLeish-Blackwell (1991) report that many black women COs received training from black men inmates.

Training should disseminate information about routine procedures, self-defense, and service policies supportive of women COs. Training programs should include information about communication skills and nonviolent techniques for resolving disputes, but conflicts between security and rehabilitative functions produce inconsistent programs. COs in one department reported conflicts in the philosophy of different training classes within the same prison (Jurik, 1985). Training that is provided outside prison work units often seems irrelevant to the day-to-day work of COs.

Without training in communication and crisis intervention skills, COs are inept at alternatives to intimidation tactics of inmate control. The old guard discourse of masculinity—stressing physical strength and mental aggressiveness—endures, and women COs are devalued (Britton, 1995; Jurik, 1985).

WORK ASSIGNMENTS

COs' assignments affect their integration and career advancement. Although most COs hold the same rank, their activities vary greatly. Assignments affect COs' attitudes toward their work, departments, chances for advancement, and themselves. Legal conflicts pitting inmates' rights to privacy against women COs in men's prisons have promoted ambiguity and inconsistency among administrators regarding women's work assignments (Morton, 1991b, p. 37; Zimmer, 1989). Administrators' failure to monitor gender allocation patterns leads to inconsistencies within the same institutions. Assignments reflect supervisor discretion and views of women COs' "proper place" in the prison (Jurik, 1985; Zimmer, 1989).

Based on her national survey of corrections departments, Joann Morton (1991b, pp. 33-36) reported that the number of agencies restricting women COs' work assignments significantly decreased between 1978 and 1988; there was a balanced use of women COs across security levels of men's prisons. Still, 34 agencies, including the Federal Bureau of Prisons, reported limitations on women CO assignments in men's prisons. Only 11 agencies reported no restrictions (see Table 8.1). There were considerable inconsistencies across agencies. Limitations varied from Delaware, where women COs were prohibited from housing areas, to more common restrictions on strip searching and collecting urine samples. All of the limitations dealt with some aspect of inmate privacy, and none dealt with security or women COs' ability. Although most agencies had increased the work assignments available to women COs, a few agencies had lost ground (Morton, 1991b).

The restrictions in women COs' work assignments may not be consistent with court rulings in inmate privacy cases. These inconsistencies stem from administrator ambivalence about women's roles in men's prisons and the practice of leaving work assignments to the discretion of individual supervisors (Johnson, 1991).

One department's policy was to assign women to all areas of men's prisons unless it violated inmates' rights to privacy—strip searches and viewing inmates nude. In reality, the interpretation of their policy varied from prison to prison, among supervisors, and across time. Some supervisors restricted women COs to clerical duties (Jurik, 1988; Morton, 1991b, p. 37). Others prohibited them from working in yards and housing, even when it did not entail seeing nude inmates or conducting strip searches. Consequently, women COs were typically assigned to control rooms that monitor doors and communications, visitation, kitchen areas, and clerical duties (Jurik, 1985).

Without experience in assignments involving inmate contact, women COs' promotion opportunities are limited (Morton, 1991b, pp. 36-37). This situation often leads to the informal identification of "women's slots." Women's COs must then compete for a few valued assignments (Jurik, 1985, p. 385). Ironically, restricted work assignments fuel the resentment of men coworkers over reverse discrimination or the special treatment given to women (Jurik, 1985, 1988; Owen, 1988; Zimmer, 1986). When women are not given the opportunity to demonstrate competence in all aspects of the job, images of feminine incompetence are reaffirmed.

PERFORMANCE EVALUATIONS

Performance evaluations become part of the CO's permanent work record and are scrutinized when COs apply for promotions. Correctional reforms have emphasized "universalistic" and objective criteria based on formal organizational rules, instead of "particularistic" and subjective judgments based on friendship or partisanship. Despite these bureaucratic reforms, subjectivity and discretion surround the evaluation process.

Even if implemented, universalistic and seemingly gender-neutral criteria can disadvantage women for promotion. Zimmer (1987) found that women COs who use unique work strategies may receive less favorable evaluations because their performance differs from men's. Jurik's (1985) content analysis of CO performance evaluation forms in one agency revealed that security was emphasized and service responsibilities were ignored: "Of the 18 categories, . . . only one dealt with any service function . . . administering first aid. . . . Communication skills, conflict diffusion or other service functions were not addressed" (p. 386). Communication and conflict diffusion are skills in which women may excel (Zimmer, 1987). The continued emphasis on paramilitary custodial and security functions supports status quo images of CO work, which equate masculinity with competence.

The evaluation process also formalizes the informal suspicions of women COs in employment records. Supervisors scrutinize and record women COs' interactions with men inmates more carefully than encounters between men COs and men inmates (Belknap, 1991; Jurik, 1985; Zimmer, 1986).

The discretion and ambiguity surrounding the evaluation process increase women COs' vulnerability to sexual harassment. Women COs fear retaliation from supervisors if they resist or complain about sexual harassment (Jurik, 1985; Zimmer, 1986). Ironically, when women receive favorable evaluations, the ambiguities in the

(text continued on p. 197)

TABLE 8.1 1988 Percentage of Women COs by Men's Facility Security Level

State	Maximum			Medium			Minimum		
	Total COs	Number of Women COs	Percentage of Women COs	Total COs	Number of Women COs	Percentage of Women COs	Total COs	Number of Women COs	Percentage of Women COs
Alabama	670	13	1.9	845	121	14.3	67	0	0.0
Alaska	177	23	12.0	406	80	19.7	—	—	—
Arizona	—	—	—	—	—	—	—	—	—
Arkansas	116	0	0.0	505	45	8.9	75 14	18.6	—
California	3,337	506	15.0	4,550	745	16.3	1,170	153	13.0
Colorado	185	24	12.9	571	90	15.7	119	16	13.4
Connecticut	370	15	4.0	996	56	5.6	134	6	4.4
Delaware	568*	63*	11.0*	—	—	—	36	0	0.0
Florida	—	—	—	—	—	—	—	—	—
Georgia	547	97	17.7	155	20	12.9	—	—	—
Hawaii	117	7	5.9	479	56	11.6	—	—	—
Idaho	—	—	—	153	11	7.1	36	6	16.6
Illinois	2,127	191	8.9	2,300	227	9.8	872	74	8.4
Indiana	688	41	5.9	1,126	290	25.5	—	—	—
Iowa	303	17	5.6	383	31	8.0	57	7	12.2
Kansas	812	112	13.7	154	25	16.2	149	28	18.7
Kentucky	242	28	11.5	680	117	17.2	158	10	6.3

Louisiana	1,140	169	14.8	456	241	52.8	—	—	—
Maine	156	9	5.7	25	0	0.0	26	4	15.3
Massachusetts	198	14	7.0	1,338	173	12.9	48	4	8.3
Michigan	1,638	228	13.9	5,682	928	16.3	482	58	12.0
Minnesota	643	74	11.5	70	10	14.2	143	34	23.7
Mississippi	—	—	—	185	29	15.6	837	340	40.6
Missouri	583	79	13.5	1,290	112	8.6	202	29	14.3
Montana	—	—	—	—	—	—	—	—	—
Nebraska	177	23	12.9	141	16	11.3	53	10	18.8
Nevada	37	8	21.6	336	30	8.9	55	3	5.4
New Hampshire	30	5	16.6	156	16	10.2	19	1	5.2
New York	6,875	706	10.2	6,475	791	12.2	564	61	10.8
North Carolina	1,463	76	5.1	1,405	21	1.4	1,063	23	2.1
North Dakota	85*	19*	22.3*	—	—	—	15	3	20.0
Ohio	1,313	109	8.3	1,777	311	17.5	162	27	16.6
Oklahoma	237	36	15.1	593	77	12.9	205	15	7.3
Oregon	251	33	13.1	120	17	14.1	14	3	21.4
Pennsylvania	993	39	3.9	1,899	55	2.8	—	—	—
Rhode Island	328	17	5.1	104	4	3.8	56	1	1.7
South Carolina	1,972*	497*	25.2*	—	—	—	638	153	23.9
Tennessee	705	96	13.6	1,210	200	16.5	116	23	19.8
Texas	8,301	1,424	17.1	—	—	—	—	—	—
Utah	—	—	—	—	—	—	—	—	—

TABLE 8.1 Continued

State	Maximum			Medium			Minimum		
	Total COs	Number of Women COs	Percentage of Women COs	Total COs	Number of Women COs	Percentage of Women COs	Total COs	Number of Women COs	Percentage of Women COs
Vermont	—	—	—	—	—	—	—	—	—
Virginia	2,838	464	16.3	719	64	8.9	—	—	—
Washington	1,031	141	13.6	447	100	22.3	81	15	18.5
West Virginia	208	19	9.1	112	6	5.3	20	5	25.0
Wisconsin	771	78	10.1	358	36	10.0	108	23	21.0
TOTAL	42,232	5,500	12.8	38,201	5,151	13.4	7,780	1,149	14.7
Federal Bureau of Prisons	883	0	0.0	2,772	215	7.7	956	97	10.1

SOURCE: From the American Correctional Association (ACA) publication, "Women correctional officers: A ten-year update," by Joann B. Morton (1991b), in J. B. Morton (Ed.), *Change, challenge, and choices: Women's role in modern corrections (pp. 26-28).* Laurel, MD: ACA. Reprinted with permission of the American Correctional Association.

Note: Data from Arizona, Florida, Montana, Utah, and Vermont are not available.

*Maximum and medium correctional facilities combined.

process prompt men's claims of reverse discrimination or insinuations of promotion due to sexual favors (Jurik, 1985, 1988; Owen, 1988). Without clear and equality-promoting standards for evaluations, women COs must rely on the goodwill of individual supervisors, most often white men.

Women's Response:
Performance, Adaptation, and Innovation

Performance studies agree that women can do the CO job as well as men and without constant victimization by men inmates (Holeman & Krepps-Hess, 1982; Kissel & Katsampes, 1980; Shawver & Dickover, 1986, pp. 32-33). However, women experience higher levels of work-related stress than do men COs (Zupan, 1986). In the absence of consistent organizational support, women COs have to adapt to the masculine organizational culture. According to a woman CO: "It's a macho environment, and I have to act aggressively to succeed. I work here all day, talk loud, act tough. I go home at night and find myself talking in a deep, loud voice to my kids" (woman CO quoted in Jurik, 1988, p. 303).

Given such pressures, it is not surprising that women COs hold views about inmates and behave in many ways consistent with men COs (Jurik, 1985). However, women COs do not simply accommodate to the aggressive milieu: They are innovators. Just as there are cross-gender differences in CO work behavior, work styles also differ significantly among women COs.

WORK-RELATED ATTITUDES

Most research has focused on attitudinal comparisons of women with men COs on a variety of work issues. A gender-role approach predicts that different socialization means that women COs' work attitudes will differ dramatically from those of men COs. Although studies report some variations along gender lines, the similarities between women and men COs' views are striking.

Survey research indicates that men and women COs perceive many work-related conditions similarly, including opportunities for advancement, learning, variety, influence in policy making, and job satisfaction. Notable exceptions are the differential assessments made by men and women about the level of discretion on the job: Men COs want more discretion; women COs prefer more structure (Jurik & Halemba, 1984).

Women COs more often express negative attitudes toward co-workers. Both men and women COs rated administrators and supervisors as the group that causes them the most problems. However, women COs rated coworkers as the next major source of problems in their jobs. Men COs were more likely to list inmates second and coworkers last (Jurik, 1988; Jurik & Halemba, 1984).

Women COs were expected to hold less punitive attitudes toward men inmates. A longitudinal study of men and women COs in the training academy and 6 months later found that women hold less punitive and aggressive attitudes about inmates (Crouch & Alpert, 1982). However, the COs in that study supervised only inmates of their own sex. Other survey research comparing the attitudes of women and men COs who supervise men inmates refutes the hypothesis that women are less punitive and more treatment oriented (Jurik & Halemba, 1984; Zupan, 1986). Zupan (1986) concludes that both men and women COs perceive the needs of inmates similarly but do so inaccurately.

JOB PERFORMANCE

The few systematic evaluations of the job performance of women and men COs reveal more cross-gender similarities than differences. Comparisons of 168 matched pairs of women and men COs found no significant difference between gender groups in performance appraisal ratings, number of commendations or reprimands, or use of sick leave (Holeman & Krepps-Hess, 1982).

There were significant differences across and within gender groups when COs evaluated themselves and coworkers. Women who were asked to compare their performance with that of men coworkers tended to rate themselves more positively (Kissel & Katsampes,

1980). Women who accepted men's protection on the job tended to rate men higher than women (Zimmer, 1986). Men COs tended to evaluate women COs' performance more negatively than did either women COs or inmates (Kinsell & Sheldon, 1981).

Concern for women's safety often leads men COs to be more protective of women than of men coworkers (Kinsell & Sheldon, 1981). Women COs often resent such behavior as unwarranted. The limited available evidence suggests that women COs suffer significantly fewer assaults than men COs; when women COs are assaulted, they are no more likely to be injured than are men (Shawver & Dickover, 1986). Increases in the number of women COs in a prison does not increase the number of assaults against men COs (Shawver & Dickover, 1986).

Inmate surveys (Kissel & Katsampes, 1980) and qualitative research (Zimmer, 1986, 1987) indicate that women COs exert a more calming effect on men inmates than do men COs. Research suggests that women help to "normalize" men's prison environments (Holeman & Krepps-Hess, 1982), but men COs dispute the reality of this "calming effect" (Kinsell & Sheldon, 1981).

WORK STYLES AND INNOVATIONS

The similarities between men and women COs support generalizations about the power of the prison organization to mold all of its workers (Haney et al., 1973; Kanter, 1977). Nevertheless, despite the similarities in men and women COs' attitudes, qualitative performance evaluations and inmate surveys suggest significant gender differences in CO work styles (Belknap, 1991; Britton, 1995; Jurik, 1988; Zimmer, 1986, 1987). Both types of studies report that women COs exert a calming effect on men inmates (Zimmer, 1986). Such findings suggest that women COs do challenge old guard cultural images and bring innovative strategies to their job. Zimmer (1987) argues that

most . . . women who work as guards in men's prisons have neither the desire nor the capacity to perform the job as it has been traditionally performed by men. . . . [They] are . . . more likely to have a social worker's orientation toward the job and to spend . . . time listening to inmate problems. . . . Women rely on . . . skills of communication and persuasion. (pp. 422-423)

In addition to these apparent gender differences in CO work styles, there are significant differences within gender groups (Gilbert, 1990; Johnson, 1987; Jurik, 1988; Zimmer, 1986). These illustrate the various methods of doing gender on the job.

Zimmer (1986) found that women COs adopt one of three roles. In the *institutional role*, women adhere closely to prison rules and try to maintain a professional stance. Although the women try to enforce all rules fairly and consistently, inmates and other staff view them as rigid and inflexible. Corrections researchers claim that it is impossible to enforce all rules and still maintain order in institutions (Sykes, 1958). The *modified role* is a compromise for women who do not think that they can perform the job as well as men. They rely on men COs to protect them from men inmates. Finally, women in *innovative roles* rely on inmate guidance to do their jobs.

Arguing for a more dynamic conception of job performance, Jurik (1988) suggests that women COs use a variety of strategies, not set role types, to challenge organizational policies and informal staff resistance. Women COs use these strategies to "strike a balance," doing gender in ways that avoid negative gender images and combining notions of femininity and competence (Jurik, 1988, pp. 291-292; also Kanter, 1977).

First, women COs adopt a professional demeanor, which they perceive to be a gender-neutral performance strategy. This strategy requires adherence to institutional rules. But in contrast to Zimmer's institutional role, it does not require the enforcement of all rules at all times. The professional demeanor emphasizes consistency and fairness but also flexibility in dealing with inmates and staff. Conflict management techniques replace old guard approaches to inmate confrontations. Sexuality is explicitly excluded from the professional demeanor; sexual comments and overtures are considered unprofessional in workplace interactions.

Emphasizing unique skills allows women COs to identify the contributions that they make to the men's prison. Some define these contributions in terms of their feminine nature or socialization, such as women's "superior" feminine abilities to communicate with and calm inmates. By using this strategy, women COs increase the value of so-called feminine talents and devalue talents that are viewed as the domain of men (e.g., physical aggressiveness or macho demeanor). At other times, women may simply identify talents that are unique to themselves as individuals. By distinguishing unique individual skills (e.g., writing, counseling, public speaking), women COs may reduce their competition with other COs and minimize performance pressures that stereotype them either as failures or as overachievers. Regardless of their alleged source, it is important that the organization value these unique talents in promotion and retention decisions. Moreover, there is always a danger that emphasizing any difference may reinforce gender stereotypes that cause a woman's work to be devalued relative to men's.

Highlighting organizational policy requiring teamwork is another strategy used by women COs. This policy requires that in a potential confrontation situation, COs must call for backup. Enforcement of such rules helps counter criticisms based on women's alleged inherent physical inferiority to men.

Women COs use humor to distance men COs who harass them, while simultaneously avoiding the negative images that plague women who formally report harassment. However, the humor strategy can backfire if a woman eventually reports harassment; supervisors may claim there is no record that she found the harassment offensive. Also, if the humor strategy involves the use of offensive language, women COs can be sanctioned for violating rules that prohibit such conduct.

Finally, sponsorship is a method that women COs use to advance in prison organizations. Supportive sponsors give women COs visibility and information essential to promotion in an organization with a strong informal opportunity structure. Men COs also seek sponsors. However, because powerful sponsors are typically men, women COs face potential rumors about sexual liaisons with their sponsor.

When I . . . got promoted, they said I was sexually involved with the captain. . . . I tried to maintain a good relationship with him, but also . . . to use the attention I was getting to demonstrate my abilities, to show that I was an independent thinker. It was a good thing because, he got . . . transferred and demoted. (woman CO, quoted in Jurik, 1988, p. 302)

The use and effectiveness of these strategies vary over time, across situations, and from one women CO to the next (Jurik, 1988). The strategies used vary for women of different ages, marital statuses, and levels of seniority, and across racial-ethnic groups (Belknap, 1991; Owen, 1988; Zimmer, 1986). These differences may lead to resentment and conflict, not only between men and women, but among women. These conflicts between individuals distract from a collective awareness of organizational problems.

Literature on grassroots corrections demonstrates the mistake of dichotomizing the behavior of men and women COs (Johnson, 1991). In some prisons, progressive, human-service-oriented COs have adopted innovative work strategies, including conflict mediation and other techniques for avoiding oppressive, physically aggressive displays of masculinity with inmates (Gilbert, 1990; Johnson, 1991; Zupan, 1992). Research suggests that changes in prison facilities and policies made to accommodate women COs (e.g., partitions for increased inmate privacy in showers, use of smaller weapons with less recoil) have actually improved the benevolence and efficiency of the organization. To the extent that the contributions and innovations of women COs are recognized and valued in the organization, the place of women will become more secure. Additional systematic and direct observations are needed to assess differences in work strategies both across and within gender groups.

THE COSTS: STRESS AND TURNOVER

Even for women COs who strike a balance and avoid negative feminine stereotypes, there are costs to working in nontraditional fields like corrections (Jurik, 1988). The ethic of professional reform is more compatible with women COs' presence, but professional visions of unfailing worker dedication and emotionless objectivity are still gender-laden (Connell, 1993). Culturally emphasized femininity in society and in modern professional corrections associates women with emotionalism and lack of objectivity. Women's sexuality is viewed as disruptive in the professional work environment, and when sexual problems arise in the prison, women are the usual suspects (Jurik, 1988).

Corrections administrators may not exhibit open hostility to affirmative action programs, but they do underfund them (Jurik & Musheno, 1986). The few mentoring programs that corrections organizations sponsor for women place the burden of change on women workers rather than on the organization (e.g., Arizona Department of Corrections, 1992). Women bear the burden of their differentness with regard to behavior and physical appearance (e.g., ill-fitting uniforms) (Jurik, 1985). Women COs of color face additional cultural biases regarding dress and appearance (Maghan & McLeish-Blackwell, 1991).

Professionalism continues to mean that the job comes before family commitments. These conflicts may be greatest for women of color, who are disproportionately single mothers (Maghan & McLeish-Blackwell, 1991).

Studies of CO work-related stress in men's prisons suggest that women's stress levels are higher than those of men (Cullen et al., 1985; Jurik, 1988; Zupan, 1986). Women COs who are sexually harassed experience significantly higher levels of stress, both work-related and non-work-related, than women who do not report sexual harassment (Gross, Larson, Urban, & Zupan, 1993). Some researchers (Crull, 1980; Gutek & Nakamura, 1982) argue that, due to sexual harassment, women's turnover rates in nontraditional fields are higher than those of men.

However, there is no consistent turnover trend across corrections settings. The Federal Bureau of Prisons reports higher turnover rates for women than for men COs, but notes that few women resign because of job demands or the work environment (Ingram, 1980). The New York City Department of Corrections reports that men COs resign from jails at higher rates than do women COs (Steier, 1989). Jurik and Winn (1987) find that COs of color are significantly more likely than white COs to resign or to be dismissed, but that there are no significant differences between men and women CO turnover rates. In this study, a small sample size prevented the computation of turnover rates for women of different racial groups.

ORGANIZATIONAL MOVEMENTS
FOR CHANGE

Thus far, discussion of responses and strategies has focused on the individual. Although the evidence is largely anecdotal, there are indications that some agencies have made organizational changes to create a better environment for women. Many have established sexual harassment and family leave policies. To varying degrees, agencies have developed training programs for correctional staff and administrators that address the contributions of women workers (Johnson, 1991).

A few agencies report more extensive organizational changes to accommodate women COs. Innovations include implementation of cross-gender officer supervision teams; assignment of different levels of physical strength, communication, or counseling skills to work troubled areas within the prison; provision of screens or other devices for inmate privacy; and changes in weapon size that increase the shooting accuracy of women COs (Johnson, 1991).

There is little information on any collective organizational change efforts by women COs. Some research suggests that supervisors and administrators discourage the formation of support groups by women COs, although some women establish groups informally (Jurik, 1985, 1988). In some cases, unions have worked for women's equal job assignments (Zimmer, 1986, pp. 65-66).

In 1973, the ACA formed women's caucuses to compile research and advocate policies supportive of women workers (Morton, 1992). By the late 1970s, these caucuses became a task force that met as a separate entity. In 1990, it became Women in Corrections (WIC), an ad hoc committee of the ACA with approximately 150 active members from 25 states (Ruhren, 1992). WIC has supported the nomination of women for offices in the ACA (Ruhren, 1992). Helen G. Corrothers, former member of the U.S. Parole Commission and retired director of the U.S. Sentencing Commission, was the president from 1990 to 1992; she is the first black woman to hold office in the ACA ("The Honorable Helen," 1992, p. 176). The national women's professional association movement also stimulated the development of women's task forces in local and state agencies (Morton, 1992).

Women in a few departments have formed mentoring groups to work for women's promotions to supervisory and administrative positions (Arizona Department of Corrections, 1992). Community corrections staff in some states have formed women's support groups and alliances to promote women's professional development ("The Honorable Helen," 1992).

Some women COs have filed class action lawsuits against their departments. A suit in the District of Columbia alleges that sexual harassment—demands for sex and threats of retaliation for refusal—is "standard operating procedure" at all levels in the District's Department of Corrections (Harriston, 1994).

Collective action by women COs is extremely limited. Collective avenues of resistance and change clearly need further development if women are to bring about significant organizational-level changes in corrections.

Summary

This chapter has discussed the gendered organizational logic of corrections and how it frames women COs' careers. It reveals how social structures and conditions in other institutions including the State, economy, labor market, and family interact with the gendered organizational logic and gender relations within corrections. These structural and institutional patterns shape, and are shaped by, the everyday interactions and identities in prisons. Gender is both a fundamental organizing feature and an outcome of corrections work.

Just as some societal and organizational conditions moved women into more spheres of corrections, others have encouraged informal and formal barriers to women COs. Women are still proportional minorities as COs and corrections administrators in men's prisons; they experience the increased visibility that accrues to numerical minorities in work organizations. Coupled with cultural ideologies that devalue women—especially those doing "a man's job"—this visibility is usually detrimental. Conflict between rehabilitation and security functions reinforces cultural definitions that associate masculinity with competence and femininity with incompetence.

Extraorganizational pressures, including government fiscal crises and determinate sentencing laws, have increased overcrowding and danger in prisons. Combined with corrections administrators' ambivalence toward reform and affirmative action programs, these factors have hindered the implementation of reform policies. Safety concerns have bolstered the position of old guard staff who favor security over program functions and fear women's alleged physical weaknesses. Men inmates' privacy suits have provided a legal justification for restricting work assignments of women COs in men's prisons. Staff cutbacks have increased competition for promotions and fueled the resistance to women COs.

These societal and organizational conditions have impeded women COs' career paths by limiting formal on-the-job training and restricting work assignments. Images of feminine incompetence shape women COs' evaluations by men superiors. Contributions that are more likely to characterize the job performance of women COs are seldom reflected in performance evaluations. Thus, women COs continue to be assessed according to how well they meet standards based upon men's performance. Moreover, the rigidities of work schedules for correctional jobs, together with the absence or inadequate implementation of maternity and family leave policies, hurt women COs who have family responsibilities.

Pressures to conform to old guard images of masculine competence weigh heavily on women COs. They have higher levels of work-related stress than men COs. However, comparisons suggest that women and men COs share many work-related views.

Women rely on a range of strategies that emphasize ostensibly gender-neutral professional styles in the CO job. Although the professional model may effectively challenge old guard, working-class masculine images of CO competence, it may simply replace them with a modern, middle-class version of bureaucratic, rational masculinity.

Women COs may bring unique communication and conflict management skills to men's prisons, but women's performance is not monolithic. Women rely on diverse styles and strategies to cope with job-related problems. Some women accept men's protection, and some rely on sympathetic inmates. Women and men COs also use innovative or grassroots reform strategies to challenge their organizational climates. Despite the power of the traditional corrections' organizational milieu, some women COs do bring innovation and change to their jobs. They manage to strike a balance, negotiating the many obstacles and negative stereotypes that confront them in men's prisons.

Women corrections administrators and COs have begun some collective organizing. Women COs have joined unions and formed support and activist groups. Women COs and administrators have worked for improved policies to address sexual harassment and maternity leave, training programs to reduce hostilities toward women, and mentoring programs to facilitate women's advancement into administrative positions. However, national-level organizations for women are dominated by women corrections administrators, and the involvement of women COs in movements beyond a single prison facility or corrections agency has been limited. There are many miles to travel before women achieve true parity in the men-dominated world of corrections.

9

◻

Doing Justice, Doing Gender, Today and Tomorrow

Occupations, Organizations, and Change

In the preceding chapters, we have explored the social production of a gendered workforce in the justice system. Women began work in the criminal justice system (CJS) as specialists supervising women and children. The few women lawyers before 1970 were limited to specialties that focused on family issues. Over the past two decades, women's work opportunities in the justice system have greatly expanded. We have focused on the formerly all-men's fields of police patrol and correctional security in men's prisons, and more broadly on legal practice. In each field, growing numbers of women have entered positions formerly closed to them and gained a degree of acceptance on the job. However, women continue to confront overt hostility and more subtle forms of resistance that are deeply embedded in daily interactions, work cultures, and organizational rules. The gendered division of labor in these occupations continues to be contested terrain.

In this chapter, we begin with a brief review of our theoretical approach. We next compare the opportunities and barriers that women confront in these occupations and then assess the justice system's effects on women workers and women's impact on justice fields. In particular, we consider the social control implications of women's inclusion in justice occupations. The chapter concludes with a discussion of the contribution of our analysis toward a theory of workplace gender segregation and toward policies that promote gender equality.

Our Theoretical Approach:
A Recap

We began this volume by identifying workplace gender differentiation as part of a general cultural tendency to divide our world and people in it into opposing categories, with one category dominating the other. We tend to value the traits of the dominant group as good and devalue the other as different (Young, 1990). Socially constructed relations of dominance and subordination differentiate according to race-ethnicity and sexual orientation, as well as according to gender. Hierarchies of social relations are constructed in routine interactions and located within a larger structural context of divisions of labor, power, and culture. These structured actions reinforce beliefs that dominant and subordinate groups differ in essential ways and that such differences are "natural" (West & Zimmerman, 1987).

Our analysis of the social construction of a gendered labor force in justice occupations identifies four institutional sites of struggle over gendered divisions of labor, power, and culture (Messerschmidt, 1993). These sites are the family, State, labor market, and work organization. Within work organizations, interactions reference and shape organizational cultures, rules, and procedures, as well as other social institutions (Acker, 1992). Through these structured actions, workers do their jobs and "do gender" (West & Zimmerman, 1987).

Comparison of Opportunities,
Barriers, and Women's Responses

SIMILARITIES IN WOMEN'S
OPPORTUNITIES AND BARRIERS

In the past three decades, sociopolitical and legal changes have challenged traditional constructions of femininity, especially those related to women's work. These changes also challenged the close association between worker competence and masculinity in justice fields (Messerschmidt, 1993). The adoption of equal educational and employment opportunity laws facilitated women's paid labor force participation. The social upheaval and reform movements of the 1960s and 1970s altered CJS organizations and increased the employment opportunities for women. Economic recession and demographic shortages of white men workers, together with occupational growth and explicit Equal Employment Opportunity (EEO) mandates to hire women and minorities, not only increased the number of women in CJS fields but also expanded their work assignments to police patrol and supervision of men prison inmates. Similarly, expansion of the demand for lawyers led to the opening of new law schools, which, combined with antidiscrimination legislation, provided new opportunities for women attorneys.

Although professionalization and reform movements expanded justice work opportunities for white women and men and women of color, they have not greatly improved the environments and working conditions in these fields. Professionalization and reforms have not given line police and correctional officers (COs) a greater voice in formulating policy. Rather, these changes have meant growing concern with client rights of due process and increasingly vigilant supervision by professional managers. Workers have experienced a net loss of autonomy, discretion, and power.

Changes in the organization of legal practice also have diminished the autonomy and control of individual lawyers and the entire legal profession. Law is subject to the same economic pressures as other fields. The proportion of lawyers in small firms has declined relative to those who work in large firms, corporations, and government agencies. Lawyers must work longer days and produce more billable hours.

As women enter these changing justice fields, they also encounter considerable resistance to their presence. The opposition to women workers is associated not only with men's fears that women will compete with them for jobs and promotions, but also with concerns that women will change the nature and organization of the work itself. Justice occupations focus on exercising formal social control through making, interpreting, and enforcing society's rules. Men's resistance to women in justice occupations is related to their reluctance to share control over the definitions of illegal behavior and imposition of social order, in particular, the exercise of authority over men's wrongdoings. The issue of "equal access to control of social control" reflects a "deeper concern about who has a right to manage law and order" (Heidensohn, 1992, p. 215). Furthermore, policing, corrections, and law traditionally have been so closely associated with men that the jobs have offered a resource for doing masculinity. Women's presence in these fields threatens this close association between work and manhood.

Men's resistance, framed by gendered work cultures and gendered organizational logics, produces forms of gender bias common to all three justice occupations. The resulting gendered dynamics undermine women's efforts to gain acceptance, training, experience, favorable evaluations, and promotions. Women often receive differential treatment during the training process, including a lack of mentors and informal help in "learning the ropes." Women face discriminatory treatment including sexual harassment and other effects of being represented in token numbers such as heightened visibility, performance pressure, and subordinating feminine images. There often are double standards of both greater and reduced expectations for women.

Although men have resisted women's presence as coworkers, they are not abandoning justice occupations as they have in the case of several other occupations that large numbers of women have entered (Reskin & Roos, 1990). None of the three fields show signs of resegregating as "women's work," nor do such trends seem likely because the work centers on exercising responsibility for making society's rules, enforcing its laws, and controlling men violators. A more likely prospect is the growing concentration of women in the less prestigious assignments and specialties within each occupation.

Finally, the constraints of the contemporary workplace converge with social institutional patterns of family life and state policy to produce conflicts between women's family and work commitments. Workers in any field are supposed to prioritize their work above other time commitments, including household and family responsibilities. The structure of workdays in all three justice occupations is problematic for women with families. Full-time working women experience a double workday, as they perform paid work for 8 or more hours each day and unpaid household and child care labor "after work." Problems loom large with the expectation of 80- to 100-hour workweeks for lawyers, and the frequent special details, shift changes, and unpredictable overtime demands for police and COs.

DIFFERENCES IN OPPORTUNITIES, BARRIERS, AND RESPONSES

Despite common patterns, there are important differences in justice occupations that affect women's work opportunities. The job and labor queues of these occupations vary because of differences in hiring requirements, the nature of the work, working conditions, and job rewards. Historically, all three fields have been closely associated with masculinity, but the exact nature of this link varies across occupations. Differences are greatest between law and the two CJS occupations, but police and corrections also differ from each other in several ways.

Because the work of both police and corrections involves the physical control of "dangerous" lower-class men, officers traditionally were selected for brawn rather than for interpersonal or intellectual skills. Because neither occupation required extensive training or offered high salaries, policing and corrections were fields for white working-class men.

Competence among police and COs has typically been equated with dominant cultural images of traditional, working-class masculinity. Highly valued traits included physical aggressiveness, emotional reserve, and trustworthiness (Hunt, 1990). Accordingly, men's resistance to women colleagues was justified by claims that women were too physically or emotionally weak to withstand the demands and danger of the work. Women were viewed as unreliable partners, and their job performances were devalued as indicative of natural feminine incompetence or unnatural, unwomanly conduct.

Both policing and corrections adopted military-style, hierarchical organizational structures to prevent corruption and control line staff behavior. Despite such controls, police and COs continued to hold considerable degrees of discretion and were divided by numerous divisions and cliques (Hunt, 1990, p. 8).

The discretion and danger of work in these fields gave opponents ample opportunities to expose women to dangers not typically experienced by men staff. Women's vulnerability was then attributed to their allegedly natural physical weaknesses. However, any additional danger that women faced was less likely to be the manifestation of physical differences from men than to arise from systematic discriminatory practices that denied women adequate training and backup and placed them in situations designed to frighten, humiliate, and endanger them (Martin, 1980).

The sexualization of the workplace, including "locker-room" language, facilitated solidarity among men in police and corrections work. With women's entry into these occupations, such language is heightened, and women are treated as sex objects. At the same time that they are sexually harassed, women are socially isolated and resegregated into newly defined "women's job assignments." Complaints of reverse discrimination often accompany the entry and advancement of women. The consequences of environmental pressures include unique stressors, and in some cases, higher turnover rates, as women enter and depart from these occupations.

Increasing efforts to rationalize and otherwise reform policing and corrections have challenged the discourse of working-class masculinity, seeking to replace it with a middle-class version of masculinity as rational, professional, and rule oriented. Professionalization, reform, and affirmative action programs have threatened "old-line" occupational cultures in these occupations. By rationalizing hiring and promotion standards, these changes challenged the often arbitrary practices of prereform eras and facilitated the entry and advancement of white women and men and women of color. By mandating equal employment opportunity, due process rights of clients, and a human service approach, reforms encouraged pockets of men staff, supervisors, and administrators to support new definitions of competence on the job and women colleagues' place in it (Johnson, 1991; Jurik, 1985). But these organizational changes also brought resentment and active resistance in police and corrections agencies. New entrants represented outsiders, who, like many reform agency policies and administrators, were viewed as oppositional to the "real work" of line staff. To many line staff, resulting regulations and paperwork symbolize a loss of control over offenders, job satisfaction, and advancement opportunities.

Jennifer Hunt (1990) has argued that women symbolize outsiders in the worldview of many men police officers because "sex, violence, and corruption are seen as masculine, and therefore, as opposed to service work, nonviolence, and noncorrupt behavior that are feminine" (p. 10). Community policing programs are seen as more feminine and service oriented, whereas crime control programs accentuate the more masculine aspects of the job. Similarly, in corrections, "old guard" COs associate women with unwanted reforms and human service (read: feminine) dimensions of the work (Jurik, 1985).

In many agencies, such symbolic associations have crystallized into differential work assignment patterns that delegate the so-called feminine aspects of the jobs to women. Women police are often relegated to station house, dispatcher, or juvenile assignments, and women COs are assigned to supply room, inmate grievance procedure, or communication room duties. Men are then left to the "real" work of crime fighting in the streets or control of inmates in the cell blocks.

Although reforms have challenged these old-line views, CJS resources for implementing and enforcing them have been grossly inadequate. Prison crowding, tension in the streets, and a general decline in support for affirmative action goals among governmental authorities have attenuated the implementation of reform and affirmative action programs in many agencies. These problems have reinvigorated the old-line discourse that emphasizes force and weaves together physical strength, masculinity, and competence (Britton, 1995).

Because it emphasized communication and mediation over forceful coercion, the professionalization-reform ethic has been embraced by many women justice workers and their supporters as a discourse that is supportive of women, or that is at least gender-neutral (Jurik, 1988). However, professionalism and bureaucratic rationality are not gender-neutral; they are closely associated with culturally dominant views of elite white masculinity as the apex of rationality, objectivity, and emotionless affect. This association is well-demonstrated in the field of law.

In contrast to the working-class occupations of police and corrections, lawyers historically have exemplified a culture of elite white masculinity; law has been an occupation reserved for the sons of the aristocracy. Lawyers have been responsible for making the rules of society through rational debate and the assertion of universalistic principles, while simultaneously working to preserve the power of those in authority.

The limitations of the professional ethic become most apparent when examining resistance to women lawyers. The legal profession seldom poses the physical perils of police and corrections work, so objections to women in law could not center on their physical weaknesses. Instead, the legal fraternity has focused on women's ostensible lack of mental agility and "toughness" in the face of "coarse" public life. Because of their supposedly emotional natures and "lower" level of moral reasoning, women are considered insufficiently rational and objective for legal work. Resistance tactics in the legal profession have focused on withholding sponsorship and important cases, tracking into less prestigious specialties, excluding women from key referral networks, and engaging in verbal and nonverbal displays of disrespect that discourage potential clients and threaten the livelihood of women attorneys. The professional ethic of law is gendered, and legal work is a resource for doing masculinity.

Do Women Make a Difference?

In the introduction to this book, we asked if the addition of women to new fields within justice-related occupations prompts any significant changes in those occupations, the organizations in which they work, or in the quality of services delivered to clients. Assessment of women's effects on an occupation is closely linked to the debates within the feminist movement regarding whether women are essentially different from or essentially similar to men.

Early advocates of policewomen on patrol suggested that women would diffuse violence, be less threatening, and thereby reassure citizens and improve police-community relations (Milton, 1972; President's Commission, 1972). Supporters of women COs have suggested that they have calming and normalizing effects in men's prisons (Kissel & Katsampes, 1980).

Scholars have also debated whether women might behave differently enough from men to change the legal profession. Feminist legal scholar Carrie Menkel-Meadow (1985, 1986) argues that women's experiences and values differ from those of men and that their presence in sufficient numbers could transform the organization and practice of law. Although her argument focuses on law, it is relevant to the three justice occupations covered here. She suggests that with greater numbers and more power, women may increase an emphasis on "feminine values" that include less litigation, more mediation, greater empathy for subordinate groups, and more concern about how law can promote the general good. In all three occupations, women may inspire work structures that are less hierarchical, more consensual, and more accommodating to the family.

In contrast to difference feminists, others suggest that organizational norms, expectations, and job constraints severely restrict individuals' ability to change work organizations (Haney et al., 1973; Sykes, 1958). Kanter (1977) argues that it is more likely true that jobs make workers than that workers make jobs. She suggests that, given similar organizational conditions, women and men workers will behave similarly. Without assuming that women and men would behave exactly the same, others argue that the difference approach gives women too much ability to change legal practice; they agree that work organizations restrict options (Anleu, 1992).

The difference model views femininity as a more or less fixed aspect of individual identity. Historically, assigning certain attributes to women, particularly caring and nurturing, has resulted in disadvantage, regardless of whether these attributes are viewed as biological or social (MacKinnon, 1989). So-called feminine traits are deceptive distinctions that rest on a paradigm specifying a set of essential differences between men and women. This paradigm diverts attention from the similarities between men and women and the differences among women. For example, assertions that women lawyers are more interested in conflict resolution than in adversarial courtroom combat magnify small gender differences and create double binds for women who prefer the adversarial approach (Epstein, 1988).

For some radical feminist scholars, feminine attributes are neither natural nor constitutive of a "woman's voice;" they are the by-products of masculine dominance (MacKinnon, 1989). Masculine dominance structures and controls behavior and produces different access to resources and power in social institutions. This dominance perspective suggests that law and the CJS are so imbued with masculine values of objectivity and abstract equality that there is little room for women to make a difference.

A social construction of gender approach suggests that none of these competing theories offers an accurate description of the effect of women workers on the justice system. These dichotomies reify the behavior of a few women and men into opposing images of a fixed, unified masculinity and its opposite, femininity. Patricia Hill Collins (1991) seeks to avoid dichotomous thinking by adopting a both/and approach. Women may be *both* similar to *and* different from men, and they may be *both* similar to *and* different from each other. At all times, the actions of men and women shape and are shaped by larger social divisions of labor, power, and culture.

WOMEN'S RESPONSES TO BARRIERS

Women actively respond to barriers through a variety of strategies that vary over time and across occupations, individuals, and situations. Several response patterns characterize women in justice occupations. Although some have adhered to one pattern almost entirely, most women alternate among patterns depending on the circumstances.

Sometimes women have accepted constructions of femininity that require men's protection. Such paternalistic constructions of femininity usually have not been available to women of color or to lesbians in the justice workplace. Cultural images of women of color as "mules of the white man" or as sexually promiscuous, and images of lesbians as "tough" and sexually deviant rarely elicit masculine protectionism.

In other cases, women have adapted to the standards of the gendered organization and demonstrated competence by doing masculinity on the job, that is, by emulating styles of reasoning, speech, and demeanor thought to characterize men. This strategy in all three occupations illustrates the extensive power of the organization to mold its workers. Even women who have avoided this adaptation have felt pressured to act like men.

Women in policing and corrections also have developed conscious strategies for constructing femininity in ways that make it more compatible with images of competent job performance. They have presented themselves as professionals. Nonetheless, even seemingly gender-neutral professional images accentuate characteristics historically associated with elite white masculinity, namely rationality, objective impartiality, and organizational loyalty; they leave little room for emotions and concerns with personal relationships or social locations.

Some women have challenged the work structures in justice occupations. Women lawyers in private firms have been more successful in carving out career paths that are sensitive to childbearing and childrearing responsibilities than women in the other occupations, but flexible career paths continue to impose costs of lower incomes and decreased advancement opportunities.

Adaptation and resistance are always framed by situational and organizational contingencies. Moreover, these contingencies are inextricably bound with race-ethnicity, age, sexual orientation, seniority, and other dimensions of social relations.

GENDER, JOB PERSPECTIVES, AND PERFORMANCE IN JUSTICE OCCUPATIONS

Evidence comparing the work attitudes and behavior of men and women in our three occupations refutes any notion of strict gender dichotomies of performance quality or style. It reveals both similarities and differences in men's and women's job perspectives and performance and also significant differences in viewpoints and performance *within* gender categories.

Two studies suggest that men and women police officers have similar attitudes toward their departments, citizens, and their work (Worden, 1993) and that their primary sources of stress are comparable (Morash & Haarr, 1995). Both studies found some gendered patterns, but there were also significant race-ethnic differences that cut across sex categories.

Early evaluations of gender differences in police job-related behavior found that relative to men, women on patrol made slightly fewer arrests and received fewer citizen complaints and disciplinary reprimands. Few other significant differences were found (see Chapter 5 for details). Anecdotal evidence reported by men and women officers suggests that women handle situations differently from men: they are more willing to reason and less willing to use force or threat (Belknap & Shelley, 1992; Heidensohn, 1992; Hunt, 1984; Martin, 1980).

Women COs do not hold any more positive or lenient attitudes toward inmates than do men COs. With increasing organizational socialization, women's and men's work attitudes and behavior converge. Research reveals the power of police and corrections work organizations to shape employees regardless of gender, but the performance styles of women and men are still gendered (Jurik & Halemba, 1984; Worden, 1993).

Either because they behave less aggressively, or because citizens perceive that they do so, women police officers are less likely to provoke the escalation of police-citizen hostilities than are men officers (Martin, 1980). In men's prisons, reports indicate that women COs help to diffuse tensions and mediate conflict among men inmates and between men COs and inmates. Men inmates perceive that women's presence normalizes and humanizes the prison environment (Kissel & Katsampes, 1980).

Observers of the legal profession disagree about women's ability to change the profession. A survey of federal judges appointed by President Carter found that the women tended to be more feminist-identified, although there was some overlap of attitudes across sex categories (E. Martin, 1990). Similar overlaps in attitudes emerged from a number of the gender-bias task force surveys. Data on judicial decision making are inconclusive. Several studies have sought to link background characteristics such as race-ethnicity and gender with court decisions at trial and appellate levels, but these findings are also inconsistent (Gruhl, Spohn, & Welch, 1981; Gryski & Main, 1986; Kritzer & Uhlman, 1977; Spohn, 1990). Some research has suggested that women judges might be more attentive and resistant to gender bias (E. Martin, 1990). In the courtroom, they are less likely to undermine women lawyers with sexist and demeaning remarks and less likely to tolerate men's harassment. Their presence appears to improve men colleagues' attitudes toward women staff. They are supportive of efforts to expand employment and promotion opportunities for women courthouse personnel. However, the effects of women attorneys on clients or case outcomes have not yet been studied using actual cases.

Our analysis reveals the multiplicity of differences in work-related attitudes and job performance *within* gender categories. Simply put, all women do not perform the job in the same way. Just as there are wide variations among men in their job performances and, therefore, no "men's style" of policing, litigating a case, or guarding inmates, there is diversity among the women's experiences, attitudes, and performance.

Variations in performance style and in their work relationships cut across race-ethnicity, sexual orientation, ability, age, and length-of-service differences within both gender groups. In some cases, women of color are less likely than white women to perceive and report men's behavior as sexually harassing (Belknap, 1991). They tend to experience harassment as both sexually and racially motivated (Stambaugh, 1995). Women of color often perceive men of their race as more supportive of them than their white women coworkers. Lesbians often feel ostracized by both men and women coworkers.

In all three occupations, women and men experience many common problems. Men and women students experience law school as alienating. After law school, both experience difficulty in finding jobs during this period of declining job prospects in most occupations. Men and women lawyers are losing power and autonomy as they assume positions in large bureaucracies. The declining proportion of lawyers who become partners affects the job security of men as well as women. Moreover, growing numbers of women and men are unwilling to make the extreme personal and family life sacrifices required to attain a partnership.

In corrections and policing, both men and women officers are concerned about declining resources, bureaucratization, heavier workloads, increased client rights, and their inability to affect organizational policy. Both police and COs have turned to unions for support, but not always with beneficial effects.

WOMEN'S COLLECTIVE RESPONSES

In addition to individual-level responses, women lawyers, and, to a lesser extent, women in police and corrections have organized and initiated legal actions to challenge discriminatory environments. The success of women workers and their collective organization provide powerful challenges to perceived natural links between these occupations and masculinity. However, many forces undermine women's collective action in justice fields.

In all three occupations, women have formed professional associations for women in their fields. For women in policing and
corrections, these efforts have typically been more successful at the
national than at local levels. Many department-based organizations
have floundered because of lack of interest, fear of reprisals by the
men for involvement, or tensions among women from different
race-ethnic groups. Statewide organizations are weak and virtually
invisible. National organizations of women in policing and corrections primarily serve those in, or aspiring to, administrative positions. Because mobility across agencies is rare, the benefits that
national networks provide are limited.

Class-based differences among men in justice-related occupations are also found among women. Like men, women in law tend
to come from middle-class and elite backgrounds. By virtue of their
status and profession, many women lawyers have assumed leadership positions in the women's movement. They have been active
in shaping the legal challenges to gender discrimination throughout
society and in questioning the premises and processes of law. Their
activities have extended beyond the concerns of women clients to
question the bases of social relationships and the allocation of
power in society.

Local women's bar associations have provided more support and
contacts than has the National Association of Women Lawyers,
which has very limited membership and visibility. In the past
decade, women have slowly gained positions of responsibility in
state bar associations and the American Bar Association (ABA)
and have used such positions to bolster women's power in the
profession.

Although women in law have substantially higher average incomes than women in police and corrections, the income differences between men and women in law are much greater than are
the gender income gaps in corrections and policing. Women lawyers
are relatively advantaged and disadvantaged, depending on the
group with which they are compared. Their additional skill, status,
and income have given women lawyers greater resources with which
to demand organizational accommodations for childbearing and

child rearing (e.g., "mommy tracks"). They are better able to obtain and afford part-time, temporary, or other flexible work arrangements than women police officers and COs.

IDENTIFYING WOMEN'S CONTRIBUTION

We have argued that gender is a fundamental organizing feature of life in justice work organizations. Gender makes a difference in virtually every social context. Even when women prefer that they not be treated as women, their actions continue to be held accountable by others and by themselves as appropriately feminine or not. The sameness approach treats men and women as essentially the same; the difference approach treats all women as uniformly different from men but similar to each other (e.g., nurturing to clients); the dominance perspective views women as passive victims of masculine dominance. Sameness, difference, and dominance arguments all provide one-dimensional views of women: they ignore class, race-ethnic, cultural, and situational differences among women (as well as personality variations among individuals). None of these perspectives grasps how social structure and institutional arrangements simultaneously limit *and* permit variation, resistance, or innovation at work (Anleu, 1992).

Many feminists now argue that women themselves must determine when difference is relevant so that they can be *both* the same *and* different across situations and individuals. Cynthia Cockburn (1991) argues that the goal is not "equality but equivalence, not sameness for individual men and women but parity for women as a sex or for groups of women in their specificity" (p. 10). The goal is neither simple assimilation nor moral superiority, but to transform the nature and operation of work organizations and the political-economic system.

Our analysis of justice system changes that have increased work opportunities for women demonstrates the difficulty of isolating women's impact on the system or its clients. Increases in the range of jobs available to women are inextricably linked to society-level changes (e.g., the women's movement, equal opportunity struggles, increase in numbers of women workers, changing family roles), and justice system changes (e.g., CJS reform efforts, increasing numbers of CJS clients, and the shifting organization of legal work). Thus, assessing the effect of women's expanded presence on the CJS, its services, or clients is indeed a complicated matter.

Arguments that women's presence will facilitate the implementation of new human-service ethics in justice fields may overstate the benefits of such ethics to client groups. Bureaucratization, professionalization, reform policies, and women's entry may have affected client treatment, but in ways that mean more effective, not simply more humane, social control. The French social thinker, Michel Foucault (1979), noted that penal reforms in the 18th century—a shift from heavy reliance on capital punishment to prisons—were not designed to punish less, but to punish better. Foucault's characterization may be apt for the changes that we have described in the justice system. From the 1960s through today, new personnel and new regimes in the CJS may have intensified the State's control over client groups; management and human service techniques may be more effective than brute force (Cohen, 1985). Although some women staff may relate more humanely to clients on an individual basis, women's presence in these justice system jobs is not indicative of an overall feminine ethic, nor does it guarantee that all clients will receive improved treatment.

In a similar vein, we have noted that this reform ethos has been more overtly supportive of women working in the system, but it is neither profeminist nor even gender-neutral. Our analysis reaffirms the increasingly widespread recognition that gender distinctions (like so many other dichotomies), as well as the preoccupation with similarity versus difference, are indeed vestiges of a faulty cultural belief system.

Building Feminist Theory and Policy

Our analysis has implications both for developing theory and altering policy. The implications of women's work in the justice system as controllers have been largely ignored by feminist analyses. When women act as social-control agents, the social roles of victim and perpetrator no longer can be dichotomized along gender lines (Heidensohn, 1992). Instead, women's presence as controllers suggests that, in some way, they are "part of the problem," and share, however meagerly, in the system of oppression, hovering at the periphery of the power structure of gender (Connell, 1987).

Our analysis illustrates the usefulness of a gender constructionist approach to the study of occupational segregation. Earlier approaches have explained women's lower incomes and lesser occupational achievement as the result of differential socialization or their failure to make a sufficient investment in their "human capital." Theories also have emphasized the role of the organization in creating gender-neutral workers.

Instead, we have traced the social construction of a gendered workforce through four institutional sites of struggle over gender ratios and through interactional, organizational, and structural levels of social action. Our analysis has described the mechanisms whereby gendered divisions of labor are socially constructed but appear to be the natural outcome of individual characteristics (learned or innate). Our approach shows how gender, race-ethnic, sexual orientation, and class distinctions are generated simultaneously through categorization and differentiation in the family, State, labor market, work organization and at various levels of social action.

This model addresses both the complex and dynamic nature of doing gender while working in justice occupations. Not surprisingly, we view as oversimplifications others' demands for conclusions of either sameness or difference. Rather, as we have indicated, the differences *within* as well as across gender categories reveal the problems with such simplistic dichotomies.

Our analysis has numerous implications for social policy. The historical analysis of women's changing roles in the justice system reveals that federal requirements to promote affirmative action hiring policies can effectively increase the hiring of women. These pressures are probably most effective when attached to funding criteria.

We have discussed how and why men isolate, harass, and other-wise present visible, daily resistance to women. In the face of such opposition (despite official policies of assimilation), an important survival strategy is for the subordinated social group members to identify themselves as an interest group and as potential agents of organizational change.

However, collective organization is made more difficult by differ-ences within gender groups, including those of race-ethnicity, class, and sexual orientation. It is important that women's organizations recognize and appreciate the variations in situations, needs, and desires among women. Alliances across boundaries are essential, but they must be formed with sensitivity and must aim to promote work climates that will accept and appreciate difference (see Young, 1990, pp. 226-260).

In addition, much can be gained from emphasizing the common problems that women and men share in the work environment. Some CJS unions are beginning to recognize that many problems experienced by women (e.g., maternity leave issues) stem from larger organizational flaws that also pose problems for men workers (e.g., inflexible workdays and leave policies). All staff can benefit from safer work environments, more satisfied clients, and increased input into organizational policies and procedures. Women can begin by forming fluid alliances with each other and with supportive men. Then they must consider how they might make their case to hostile factions by identifying workers' common needs. In all efforts to form alliances, negotiations that recognize both difference and sameness will be key.

References

Abel, Richard L. (1986). The transformation of the American legal profession. *Law & Society Review, 20,* 7-17.

Abel, Richard L. (1989). *American lawyers.* New York: Oxford.

Abrahamson, Jill, & Franklin, Barbara. (1986). *Where they are now: The story of the women of Harvard Law 1974.* Garden City, NY: Doubleday.

Acker, Joan. (1989). The problem with patriarchy. *Sociology, 23,* 235-240.

Acker, Joan. (1990). Hierarchies, jobs, and bodies: A theory of gendered organizations. *Gender & Society, 4,* 139-158.

Acker, Joan. (1992). Gendered institutions: From sex roles to gendered institutions. *Contemporary Sociology, 21,* 565-569.

Alex, Nicholas. (1969). *Black in blue: A study of the Negro policeman.* New York: Appleton-Century-Crofts.

American Bar Association Commission on Women in the Profession. (1988). *Report to the House of Delegates* (mimeo). Chicago: Author.

American Bar Association Commission on Women in the Profession. (1993). Brochure. Chicago: Author.

Amott, Teresa L., & Matthaei, Julie A. (1991). *Race, gender, and work: A multicultural economic history of women in the United States*. Boston: South End.

Anderson, Karen. (1988). A history of women's work in the United States. In A. H. Stromberg & S. Harkness (Eds.), *Women working* (pp. 25-41). Mountain View, CA: Mayfield.

Angel, Marina. (1988). Women in legal education: What it's like to be part of a perpetual first wave or the case of the disappearing women. *Temple Law Review, 61,* 799-846.

Anleu, Sharyn Roach. (1992). Women in law: Theory, research, and practice. *Australian and New Zealand Journal of Sociology, 28,* 391-410.

Arizona Department of Corrections. (1992). *ADOC Women's Task Force proposal to the National Institute of Corrections*. Phoenix: Author.

Bartell Associates. (1978). *The study of police women competency in the performance of sector police work in the city of Philadelphia*. State College, PA: Author.

Bartlett, Harold W., & Rosenblum, Arthur. (1977). *Policewoman effectiveness*. Denver, CO: Civil Service Commission and Denver Police Department.

Bayley, David H., & Garofalo, James. (1989). The management of violence by police patrol officers. *Criminology, 27,* 1-26.

Belknap, Joanne. (1991). Women in conflict: An analysis of women correctional officers. *Women & Criminal Justice, 2,* 89-116.

Belknap, Joanne, & Shelley, Jill K. (1992). The new lone ranger: Policewomen on patrol. *American Journal of Police, 12,* 47-75.

Bell, Daniel J. (1982). Policewomen: Myths and reality. *Journal of Police Science and Administration, 10,* 112-120.

Bernat, Frances P. (1992). Women in the legal profession. In I. Moyer (Ed.), *The changing roles of women in the criminal justice system: Offenders, victims, and professionals* (2nd ed., pp. 307-322). Prospect Heights, IL: Waveland.

Bielby, William T., & Baron, James N. (1986). Men and women at work: Sex segregation and statistical discrimination. *American Journal of Sociology, 91,* 759-799.

Bird, Caroline, & Briller, Sara W. (1969). *Born female: The high cost of keeping women down*. New York: Basic Books.

Bittner, Egon. (1967). The police on skid row: A study in peacekeeping. *American Sociological Review, 32,* 699-715.

Bittner, Egon. (1970). *The functions of police in modern society.* Chevy Chase, MD: National Institute of Mental Health.

Bloch, Peter, & Anderson, Deborah. (1974). *Policewomen on patrol: Final report.* Washington, DC: Urban Institute.

Braverman, Harry. (1974). *Labor and monopoly capital.* New York: Monthly Review Press.

Britton, Dana M. (1995). *Controlling sex, controlling violence: Cross-gender supervision in men's and women's prisons.* Ph.D. dissertation, University of Texas at Austin.

Brown, Michael K. (1981). *Working the street: Police discretion and the dilemmas of reform.* New York: Russell Sage Foundation.

Brush, Candida. (1992, Summer). Research on women business owners: Past trends, a new perspective, and future directions. *Entrepreneurship Theory and Practice,* 5-30.

Burrell, Gibson, & Hearn, Jeff. (1989). The sexuality of organization. In J. Hearn, D. Sheppard, P. Tancred-Sheriff, & G. Burrell (Eds.), *The sexuality of organization* (pp. 1-28). Newbury Park, CA: Sage.

Byrne, Carol, & Oakes, Larry. (1986, November 9). Are female cops doing the job? *Minneapolis Star and Tribune,* pp. A1, A11-12.

California Highway Patrol. (1976). *Women traffic officer report: Final report.* Sacramento, CA: Author.

Chambers, David L. (1989). Accommodation and satisfaction: Women and men lawyers and the balance of work and family. *Law and Social Inquiry, 14,* 251-287.

Charles, Michael T. (1981). The performance and socialization of female recruits in the Michigan State Police Training Academy. *Journal of Police Science and Administration, 9,* 209-223.

Chodorow, Nancy. (1978). *The reproduction of mothering: Psychoanalysis and the sociology of gender.* Berkeley: University of California Press.

Chused, Richard H. (1988). The hiring and retention of minorities and women on American law school faculties. *University of Pennsylvania Law Review, 193,* 527-569.

Cixous, Helene. (1971). Sorties. In E. Marks & I. de Courtivron (Eds.), *New French feminisms* (pp. 90-98). New York: Schocken.

Cockburn, Cynthia. (1991). *In the way of women: Men's resistance to sex equality in organizations.* Ithaca, NY: International Labor Relations Press.

Cohen, Stanley. (1985). *Visions of social control.* Cambridge, MA: Polity Press.

Cole, Lorah. (1992, August). Mississippi associate superintendent strives to balance career and family. *Corrections Today,* pp. 124-126.

Collins, Patricia H. (1991). *Black feminist thought: Knowledge, consciousness, and the politics of empowerment.* New York: Routledge.

Collins, William C. (1991). Legal issues and the employment of women. In J. B. Morton (Ed.), *Change, challenge, and choices: Women's role in modern corrections* (pp. 13-18). Laurel, MD: American Correctional Association.

Connell, Robert W. (1987). *Gender and power: Society, the person, and sexual politics.* Stanford, CA: Stanford University Press.

Connell, Robert W. (1993). The big picture: Masculinities in recent world history. *Theory and Society, 22,* 597-623.

Cook, Beverly B. (1984). Women judges: A preface to their history. *Golden Gate University Law Review, 14,* 573-607.

Cooper, Candy J. (1992, January 5). Women cops taking on harassment fight. *San Francisco Examiner,* pp. A1, 10.

Cott, Nancy. (1987). *The grounding of modern feminism.* New Haven, CT: Yale University Press.

Crenshaw, Kimberle. (1990). Demarginalizing the intersection of race and sex: A black feminist critique of antidiscrimination doctrine. In K. Bartlett & R. Kennedy (Eds.), *Feminist legal theory: Readings in law and gender* (pp. 51-80). Boulder, CO: Westview.

Crites, Laura. (1973). Women in law enforcement. *Management Information Service,* p. 5.

Crouch, Ben M., & Alpert, Geoffrey P. (1982). Sex and occupational socialization among prison guards. *Criminal Justice and Behavior, 9,* 159-176.

Crull, Peggy. (1980). The impact of sexual harassment on the job: A profile of the experiences of ninety-two women. In D. Neugarten & J. Shafritz (Eds.), *Sexuality in organizations* (pp. 67-71). Oak Park, IL: Moore.

Cullen, Francis T., Link, Bruce G., Wolfe, Nancy T., & Frank, James. (1985). The social dimensions of correctional officer stress. *Justice Quarterly, 2*, 505-533.

Curran, Barbara A. (1986). American lawyers in the 1980s: A profession in transition. *Law & Society Review, 20*, 19-52.

Curran, Barbara A., Rosich, K. J., Carson, C. N., & Puccetti, M. (1986). *Supplement to the lawyer statistical report: The U.S. legal profession in 1985*. Chicago: American Bar Association.

Daly, Kathleen, & Chesney-Lind, Meda. (1988). Feminism and criminology. *Justice Quarterly, 5*, 497-535.

Daly, Mary. (1984). *Pure lust: Elemental feminist philosophy*. Boston: Beacon.

David, Deborah, & Brannon, Robert (Eds.). (1976). *The forty-nine percent majority: The male sex role*. Reading, MA: Addison-Wesley.

Davis, Angela Y. (1981). *Women, race, and class*. New York: Random House.

de Beauvoir, Simone. (1974). *The second sex* (H. M. Parshley, Trans.). New York: Vintage.

Eck, John, & Spelman, William. (1987.) Who ya gonna call: The police as problem busters. *Crime & Delinquency, 33*, 31-52.

EEOC Guidelines on Discrimination Because of Sex. (1965). *Federal Register*, 14927.

Epstein, Cynthia F. (1983). *Women in law*. Garden City, NY: Anchor.

Epstein, Cynthia F. (1988). *Deceptive distinctions: Sex, gender, and the social order*. New York: Yale University Press and Russell Sage Foundation.

Epstein, Cynthia F. (1992). Tinkerbells and pinups: The construction and reconstruction of gender boundaries at work. In M. Lamont & M. Fournier (Eds.), *Cultivating differences: Symbolic boundaries and the making of inequality* (pp. 232-256). Chicago: University of Chicago Press.

Feinman, Clarice. (1986). *Women in the criminal justice system* (2nd ed.). New York: Praeger.

Feldberg, Rosalyn, & Glenn, Evelyn N. (1979). Male and female: Job versus gender models in the sociology of work. *Social Problems, 26,* 524-438.

Fisher, Richard L. (1984). The changing role of corporate counsel. *Journal of Law and Commerce, 4,* 45-64.

Fitzpatrick, John S. (1980). Adapting to danger: A participant observation study of an underground mine. *Sociology of Work and Occupations, 7,* 131-158.

Fletcher, Ben C. (1988). The epidemiology of occupational stress. In C. L. Cooper & R. Payne (Eds.), *Causes, coping, and consequences of stress at work* (pp. 12-57). Chichester, UK: John Wiley.

Florida Supreme Court Gender Bias Study Commission. (1990). Report. *Florida Law Review, 42,* 803-981.

Fossum, Donna. (1980). Women law professors. *American Bar Foundation Research Journal, 4,* 903-914.

Foucault, Michel. (1979). *Discipline and punish: The birth of the prison.* New York: Vintage.

Frankenberg, Ruth. (1993). *White women, race matters: The social construction of whiteness.* Minneapolis: University of Minnesota Press.

Freedman, Estelle. (1981). *Their sisters' keepers: Women's prison reform in America 1830-1930.* Ann Arbor: University of Michigan Press.

Freeman, Jo. (1989). Feminist organization and activities from suffrage to women's liberation. In J. Freeman (Ed.), *Women: A feminist perspective* (pp. 541-555). Mountain View, CA: Mayfield.

Friedan, Betty. (1963). *The feminine mystique.* New York: Norton.

Freidson, E. (1970). *Profession of medicine.* New York: Dodd, Mead.

Frug, Mary Jo. (1992). *Postmodern legal feminism.* New York: Routledge.

Fry, Lincoln. (1983). A preliminary examination of the factors related to turnover of women in law enforcement. *Journal of Police Science and Administration, 11,* 149-155.

Fyfe, James. (1987). *Police personnel practices, 1986* (Baseline Data Report Volume 18, Number 6). Washington, DC: International City Management Association.

Gellis, Ann J. (1991). Great expectations: Women in the legal profession, a commentary on state studies. *Indiana Law Journal, 66,* 941-976.

Giddens, Anthony. (1976). *New rules of sociological method.* New Haven, CT: Yale University Press.

Gilbert, Michael John. (1990). *Working the unit: An inquiry into the discretionary behavior of correctional officers.* Ph.D. dissertation, University of Arizona, Tempe.

Gilligan, Carol. (1982). *In a different voice: Psychological theory and women's development.* Cambridge, MA: Harvard University Press.

Glenn, Evelyn N. (1992). From servitude to service work: Historical continuities in the racial division of paid reproductive labor. *Signs, 18,* 1-43.

Goffman, Erving. (1961). *Encounters.* Indianapolis, IN: Bobbs-Merrill.

Goffman, Erving. (1976). Gender displays. *Studies in the Anthropology of Visual Communication, 3,* 69-77.

Goldhart, Jill D., & Macedonia, Annetta T. (1992, August). Organizing in Ohio: Community corrections workers form alliance to promote women's professional development. *Corrections Today,* pp. 96-100.

Gray, Thomas. (1975). Selecting for a police subculture. In J. Skolnick & T. Gray (Eds.), *Police in America* (pp. 46-56). Boston: Little, Brown.

Greene, Jack R. (1993). Civic accountability and the police: Lessons learned from police and community relations. In R. G. Dunham & G. P. Alpert (Eds.), *Critical issues in policing: Contemporary readings* (pp. 369-394). Prospect Heights, IL: Waveland.

Gross, George R., Larson, Susan J., Urban, Gloria D., & Zupan, Linda L. (1993, October). *Sexual harassment and occupational stress among female corrections officers.* Paper presented at the annual meeting of the American Society of Criminology, Phoenix, AZ.

Gruhl, John, Spohn, Cassia, & Welch, Susan. (1981). Women as policymakers: The case of trial judges. *American Journal of Political Science, 2,* 308-322.

Gryski, Gerald W., & Main, Eleanor C. (1986). Social backgrounds and predictors of votes on state courts of last resort: The case of sex discrimination. *Western Political Quarterly, 39,* 528-537.

Gutek, Barbara A., & Nakamura, Cy. (1982). Gender roles and sexuality in the world of work. In E. Allgeier & N. McCormisk (Eds.), *Gender roles and sexual behavior: Changing boundaries* (pp. 182-201). Palo Alto, CA: Mayfield.

Hagan, John. (1990). The gender stratification of income inequality among lawyers. *Social Forces, 68,* 835-855.

Hagan, John, Zatz, Marjorie, Arnold, Bruce, & Kay, Fiona. (1991). Cultural capital, gender, and the structural transformation of legal practice. *Law & Society Review, 25,* 239-262.

Hale, Donna C., & Menniti, Daniel J. (1993). Discrimination and harassment: Litigation by women in policing. In R. Muraskin & T. Alleman (Eds.), *It's a crime: Women and justice* (pp. 177-189). Englewood Cliffs, NJ: Regents/Prentice Hall.

Hall, Elaine J. (1993). Smiling, deferring, and flirting: Doing gender by giving "good service." *Work and Occupations, 20,* 452-471.

Hall, Richard H. (1994). *Sociology of work: Perspectives, analyses, and issues.* Thousand Oaks, CA: Pine Forge Press.

Haney, Craig, Banks, Curtis, & Zimbardo, Phillip. (1973). Interpersonal dynamics in a simulated prison. *International Journal of Criminology and Penology, 1,* 69-97.

Harris, Richard N. (1973). *The police academy: An inside view.* New York: John Wiley.

Harriston, Keith. (1994, January 7). D.C. agency accused of harassment: Suit says sexual demands are the rule in corrections. *Washington Post,* p. A1.

Hartmann, Heidi. (1979). Capitalism, patriarchy, and job segregation by sex. In Z. Eisenstein (Ed.), *Capitalist patriarchy and the case for socialist feminism* (pp. 206-247). New York: Monthly Review.

Hawkes, Mary G. (1991). Women's changing roles in corrections. In J. B. Morton (Ed.), *Change, challenge, and choices: Women's role in modern corrections* (pp.100-110). Laurel, MD: American Correctional Association.

Hawkins, Richard, & Alpert, Geoffrey P. (1989). *American prison systems: Punishment and justice.* Englewood Cliffs, NJ: Prentice Hall.

Heidensohn, Frances. (1992). *Women in control? The role of women in law enforcement.* New York: Oxford University Press.

Hepburn, John, & Knepper, Paul. (1993). Correctional officers as human service workers: The effect on job satisfaction. *Justice Quarterly, 10*, 315-335.

Hochschild, Arlene R. (1989). *The second shift: Working parents and the revolution at home.* New York: Viking.

Hodgson, Shari, & Pryor, Bert. (1984). Sex discrimination in the courtroom: Attorney's gender and credibility. *Psychological Reports, 55*, 483-486.

Holeman, Harriet, & Krepps-Hess, Beth J. (1982). *Women correctional officer study final report.* Sacramento: California Department of Corrections.

Homer, Suzanne, & Schwartz, Lois. (1990). Admitted but not accepted: Outsiders take an inside look at law school. *Berkeley Women's Law Journal Annual, 5*, 1-74.

The Honorable Helen G. Corrothers. (1992, August). *Corrections Today*, p. 176.

Horne, Peter. (1980). *Women in law enforcement.* Springfield, IL: Charles C Thomas.

Hossfeld, Karen. (1990). Their own logic against them: Contradictions in sex, race, and class in Silicon Valley. In K. Ward (Ed.), *Women workers and global restructuring* (pp. 149-178). Ithaca, NY: International Labor Relations Cornell University Press.

Hunt, Jennifer. (1984). The development of rapport through negotiation of gender in field work among police. *Human Organization, 43*, 283-296.

Hunt, Jennifer. (1990). The logic of sexism among police. *Women and Criminal Justice, 1*, 3-30.

Hunter, Susan M. (1992, August). Women in corrections: A look at the road ahead. *Corrections Today*, pp. 8-9.

Hurtado, Aida. (1989). Relating to privilege: Seduction and rejection in the subordination of white women and women of color. *Signs, 14*, 833-855.

Hutzel, Eleanor. (1933). *The policewoman's handbook.* New York: Columbia University Press.

Ingram, Jane. (1980). *Task force report on the status of the female employee.* Unpublished report, Federal Bureau of Prisons.

Irwin, John. (1980). *Prisons in turmoil.* Boston: Little, Brown.

Jacobs, James B. (1977). *Stateville: The penitentiary in mass society.* Chicago: University of Chicago Press.

Jacobs, James B. (1983). *New perspectives on prisons and imprisonment.* Ithaca, NY: Cornell University Press.

Jacobs, Jerry. (1989). *Revolving doors: Sex segregation and women's careers.* Stanford, CA: Stanford University Press.

Jennings, Veronica T. (1994, January 27). Gaithersburg police's chief of change. *Washington Post,* p. Md-5.

Johnson, Perry. (1991). Why employ women? In J. B. Morton (Ed.), *Change, challenge, and choices: Women's role in modern corrections* (pp. 6-12). Laurel, MD: American Correctional Association.

Johnson, Robert. (1987). *Hardtime: Understanding and reforming the prison.* Pacific Grove, CA: Brooks-Cole.

Jones, Sandra. (1986). *Policewomen and equality.* London: Macmillan.

Jones, Terry. (1978). Blacks in the American criminal justice system: A study of sanctioned deviance. *Journal of Sociology and Social Welfare, 5,* 356-373.

Jurik, Nancy C. (1985). An officer and a lady: Organizational barriers to women working as correctional officers in men's prisons. *Social Problems, 32,* 375-388.

Jurik, Nancy C. (1988). Striking a balance: Female correctional officers, gender role stereotypes, and male prisons. *Sociological Inquiry, 58,* 291-305.

Jurik, Nancy C., & Halemba, Gregory J. (1984). Gender, working conditions, and the job satisfaction of women in a nontraditional occupation: Female correctional officers in men's prisons. *The Sociological Quarterly, 25,* 551-566.

Jurik, Nancy C., Halemba, Gregory J., Musheno, Michael C., & Boyle, Bernard V. (1987). Educational attainment, job satisfaction, and the professionalization of correctional officers. *Work and Occupations, 14,* 106-125.

Jurik, Nancy C., & Musheno, Michael C. (1986). The internal crisis of corrections: Professionalization and the work environment. *Justice Quarterly, 3,* 457-480.

Jurik, Nancy C., & Winn, Russell. (1987). Describing correctional security dropouts and rejects: An individual or organizational profile? *Criminal Justice and Behavior, 14,* 5-25.

Kanter, Rosabeth M. (1977). *Men and women of the corporation.* New York: Basic Books.

Kelly, Rita Mae. (1991). *The gendered economy.* Newbury Park, CA: Sage.

Kessler, Suzanne J., & McKenna, Wendy. (1978). *Gender: An ethnomethodological approach.* New York: John Wiley.

Kinsell, Lynn W., & Sheldon, Randall G. (1981). A survey of correctional officers at a medium security prison. *Corrections Today, 43,* 40-51.

Kissel, Paul, & Katsampes, Peter. (1980). The impact of women corrections officers on the functioning of institutions housing male inmates. *Journal of Offender Counseling Services and Rehabilitation, 4,* 213-231.

Kizziah, Carol, & Morris, Mark. (1977). *Evaluation of women in policing program: Newton, Massachusetts.* Oakland, CA: Approach Associates.

Klockars, Carl. (1988). The rhetoric of community policing. In J. R. Greene & S. D. Mastrofski (Eds.), *Community policing: Rhetoric or reality* (pp. 239-258). New York: Praeger.

Klofas, John, & Toch, Hans. (1982). Guard subculture myth. *Journal of Research on Crime and Delinquency, 19,* 238-254.

Krause, Elliott A. (1971). *The sociology of occupations.* Boston: Little, Brown.

Kritzer, Herbert M., & Uhlman, Thomas M. (1977). Sisterhood in the courtroom: Sex of judge and defendant in criminal case disposition. *Social Science Journal, 14,* 77-88.

Leinen, Stephen. (1984). *Black police, white society.* New York: New York University Press.

Lock, Joan. (1979). *The British policewoman: Her story.* London: Hale.

Lombardo, Lucien X. (1981). *Guards imprisoned: Correctional officers at work.* New York: Elsevier.

Lorber, Judith, & Farrell, Susan A. (1991). Preface. In Judith Lorber & Susan A. Farrell (Eds.), *The social construction of gender* (pp. 1-5). London: Sage.

MacCorquodale, Patricia, & Jensen, Gary. (1993). Women in the law: Partners or tokens? *Gender & Society, 7,* 582-594.

MacKinnon, Catharine. (1978). *Sexual harassment of working women.* New Haven, CT: Yale University Press.

MacKinnon, Catherine. (1989). *Toward a feminist theory of the state.* Cambridge, MA: Harvard University Press.

Madek, Gerald A., & O'Brien, Christine N. (1990). Women denied partnerships: From Hishon to Price Waterhouse v. Hopkins. *Hofstra Labor Law Journal, 7,* 257-302.

Maghan, Jess, & McLeish-Blackwell, Leasa. (1991). Black women in correctional employment. In J. B. Morton (Ed.), *Change, challenge, and choices: Women's role in modern corrections* (pp. 82-99). Laurel, MD: American Correctional Association.

Maguire, Kathleen, Pastore, Ann L., & Flanagan, Timothy J. (Eds.). (1993). *Sourcebook of criminal justice statistics 1992* (U.S. Department of Justice, Bureau of Justice Statistics). Washington, DC: Government Printing Office.

Manning, Peter K. (1977). *Police work.* Cambridge: MIT Press.

Manning, Peter K. (1984). Community policing. *American Journal of Policing, 3,* 205-227.

Marks, Linda. (1990). Alternative work schedules in law: It's about time. *New York Law School Law Review, 35,* 361-367.

Marquart, James W., & Crouch, Ben M. (1985). Judicial reform and prisoner control: The impact of Ruiz v. Estelle on the Texas penitentiary. *Law & Society Review, 19,* 557-586.

Martin, Elaine. (1982). Women on the federal bench: A comparative profile. *Judicature, 65,* 306-313.

Martin, Elaine. (1990). Men and women on the bench: Vive la difference? *Judicature, 73,* 204-208.

Martin, Patricia Y. (1991). Gender, interaction, and inequality in organizations. In C. Ridgeway (Ed.), *Gender, interaction, and inequality* (pp. 208-231). New York: Springer-Verlag.

Martin, Susan E. (1978). Sexual politics in the workplace: The interactional world of policewomen. *Symbolic Interaction, 1,* 44-60.

Martin, Susan E. (1980). *"Breaking and entering": Policewomen on patrol.* Berkeley: University of California Press.

Martin, Susan E. (1990). *On the move: The status of women in policing.* Washington, DC: Police Foundation.

Martin, Susan E. (1991). The effectiveness of affirmative action: The case of women in policing. *Justice Quarterly, 8,* 489-504.

Martin, Susan E. (1994). "Outsider within" the station house: The impact of race and gender on black women police. *Social Problems, 41,* 383-400.

Maryland Special Joint Committee. (1989). *Gender bias in the courts.* Annapolis, MD: Author.

Menkel-Meadow, Carrie. (1985). Portia in a different voice: Speculations on a woman's lawyering process. *Berkeley Women's Journal, 1* 39-77.

Menkel-Meadow, Carrie. (1986). The comparative sociology of women lawyers: The "feminization" of the legal profession. *Osgood Hall Law Journal, 24,* 897-918.

Messerschmidt, James. (1993). The state and gender politics. In J. Messerschmidt (Ed.), *Masculinities and crime* (pp. 155-164). Lanham, MD: Rowman & Littlefield.

Messerschmidt, James. (1995). From patriarch to gender: Feminist theory, criminology, and the challenge of diversity. In N. Rafter & F. Heidensohn (Eds.), *International perspectives in criminology: Engendering a discipline* (pp. 167-188). Philadelphia: Open University Press.

Milkman, Ruth. (1976). Women's work and economic crisis: Some lessons of the great Depression. *Review of Radical Political Economics, 8,* 73-97.

Miller, Douglas T., & Nowak, Marion. (1977). *The fifties: The way we really were.* Garden City, NY: Doubleday.

Milton, Catherine. (1972). *Women in policing.* Washington, DC: Police Foundation.

Mincer, Jacob, & Polachek, Solomon. (1974). Family investments in human capital: Earnings of women. *Journal of Political Economy, 82,* s76-108.

Minow, Martha. (1988). Feminist reason: Getting it and losing it. In K. T. Bartlett & R. Kennedy (Eds.), *Feminist legal theory: Readings in law and gender* (pp. 357-369). Boulder, CO: Westview.

Morash, Merry, & Greene, Jack. (1986). Evaluating women on patrol: A critique of contemporary wisdom. *Evaluation Review, 10,* 230-255.

Morash, Merry, & Haarr, Robin. (1995). Gender, workplace problems, and stress in policing. *Justice Quarterly, 12,* 113-140.

Morello, Karen B. (1986). *The invisible bar: The woman lawyer in America, 1938 to the present.* New York: Random House.

Morton, Joann B. (1991a). Pregnancy and correctional employment. In J. B. Morton (Ed.), *Change, challenge, and choices: Women's role in modern corrections* (pp. 40-50). Laurel, MD: American Correctional Association.

Morton, Joann B. (1991b). Women correctional officers: A ten-year update. In J. B. Morton (Ed.), *Change, challenge, and choices: Women's role in modern corrections* (pp. 19-39). Laurel, MD: American Correctional Association.

Morton, Joann B. (1992, August). Women in corrections: Looking back on 200 years of valuable contributions. *Corrections Today,* pp. 76-77.

New Hampshire Bar Association Task Force on Women in the Bar. (1988). Report. *New Hampshire Bar Journal, 29,* 213-298.

Nielsen, Sheila. (1990). The balancing act: Practical suggestions for part-time attorneys. *New York Law School Law Review, 35,* 369-383.

Nieva, Virginia, & Gutek, Barbara. (1981). *Women and work: A psychological perspective.* New York: Praeger.

Odem, Mary, & Schlossman, Steven. (1991). Guardians of virtue: The juvenile court and female delinquency in early 20th-century Los Angeles. *Crime and Delinquency, 37,* 186-203.

Owen, Barbara A. (1988). *The reproduction of social control: A study of prison workers at San Quentin.* New York: Praeger.

Parsons, Talcott, & Bales, Robert. (1955). *Family, socialization, and interaction process.* Glencoe, IL: Free Press.

Pate, Antony, Skogan, Wesley G., Wycoff, Mary Ann, & Sherman, Lawrence W. (1986). *Reducing fear of crime in Houston and Newark: A summary report.* Washington, DC: Police Foundation.

Pearson, Richard, Moran, Theodore, Berger, James, Landon, Kenneth, McKenzie, Janice, & Bonita, Thomas, III. (1980). *Criminal justice education: The end of the beginning.* New York: John Jay.

Pennsylvania State Police. (1974). *Pennsylvania State Police female trooper study*. Harrisburg, PA: Author.

Pike, Diane L. (1992). Women in police academy training: Some aspects of organizational response. In I. Moyer (Ed.), *Changing roles of women in the criminal justice system: Offenders, victims, and professionals* (2nd ed., pp. 261-280). Prospect Heights, IL: Waveland.

Poole, Eric, & Regoli, Robert. (1981). Alienation in prison: An examination of the work relations of prison guards. *Criminology, 19,* 251-270.

Potts, L. W. (1983). Equal employment opportunity and female employment in police agencies. *Journal of Criminal Justice, 11,* 505-523.

President's Commission on Law Enforcement and the Administration of Justice. (1967). *The challenge of crime in a free society.* Washington, DC: Government Printing Office.

Price, Barbara R., & Gavin, Susan. (1982). A century of women in policing. In B. R. Price & N. J. Sokoloff (Eds.), *The criminal justice system and women* (pp. 399-412). New York: Clark Boardman.

Price, Barbara R., Sokoloff, Natalie J., & Kuleshnyka, Irka. (1992). A study of black and white police in an urban police department. *The Justice Professional, 6,* 68-85.

Rafter, Nicole Hahn. (1990). *Partial justice, women in state prisons: 1800-1935* (2nd ed.). New Brunswick, NJ: Transaction.

Reskin, Barbara F. (1988). Bringing the men back in: Sex differentiation and the devaluation of women's work. *Gender & Society, 2,* 58-81.

Reskin, Barbara F., & Hartmann, Heidi (Eds.). (1986). *Women's work, men's work: Sex segregation on the job.* Washington, DC: National Academy Press.

Reskin, Barbara F., & Roos, Patricia A. (1990). *Job queues and gender queues: Explaining women's inroads into male occupations.* Philadelphia: Temple University Press.

Reuss-Ianni, Elizabeth. (1983). *The two cultures of policing: Street cops and management cops.* New Brunswick, NJ: Transaction.

Rhode, Deborah L. (1988). Perspectives on professional women. *Stanford Law Review, 40,* 1164-1207.

Rhode, Deborah. (1989). *Justice and gender.* Cambridge, MA: Harvard University Press.

Rich, Adrienne. (1980). Compulsory heterosexuality and lesbian existence. *Signs, 5,* 631-660.

Roach, Sharyn L. (1990). Men and women lawyers in in-house legal departments: Recruitment and career patterns. *Gender & Society, 4,* 207-219.

Roos, Patricia A., & Jones, Katharine W. (1993). Shifting gender boundaries: Women's inroads into academic sociology. *Work and Occupations, 20,* 395-428.

Rosenberg, Janet, Perlstadt, Harry, & Phillips, William R. F. (1993). Now that we are here: Discrimination, disparagement, and harassment at work and the experience of women lawyers. *Gender & Society, 7,* 415-433.

Rothman, Robert A. (1984). Deprofessionalization: The case of law in America. *Work and Occupations, 11,* 183-206.

Ruhren, Karen Carlo. (1992, August). WIC committee's history dates back twenty years. *Corrections Today,* p. 135.

Ryan, Barbara. (1992). *Feminism and the women's movement: Dynamics of change in social movement ideology and activism.* New York: Routledge.

Schafran, Lynn H. (1987a). Documenting gender bias in the courts: The task force approach. *Judicature, 70,* 280-290.

Schafran, Lynn H. (1987b). Practicing law in a sexist society. In L. Crites & W. Hepperle (Eds.), *Women, the courts, and equality* (pp. 191-207). Newbury Park, CA; Sage.

Schafran, Lynn H. (1989). Lawyers' lives, clients' lives: Can women liberate the profession? *Villanova Law Review, 34,* 1105-1122.

Schneider, Beth. (1982). Consciousness about sexual harassment among heterosexual and lesbian women workers. *Journal of Social Issues, 38,* 75-97.

Schneider, Beth. (1991). Put up and shut up: Workplace sexual assaults. *Gender & Society, 5,* 533-548.

Schoonmaker, Meyressah, & Brooks, Jennifer S. (1975). Women in probation and parole, 1974. *Crime and Delinquency, 21,* 109-115.

Schultz, Vicki. (1991). Telling stories about women and work: Judicial interpretation of sex segregation in the workplace in Title VII cases raising the lack of interest argument. In K. T. Bartlett & R. Kennedy (Eds.), *Feminist legal theory: Readings in law and gender* (pp. 124-155). Boulder CO: Westview.

Schulz, Dorothy M. (1995). Invisible no more: A social history of women in U.S. policing. In B. J. Price & N. J. Sokoloff (Eds.), *The criminal justice system and women: Offenders, victims, and workers* (2nd ed., pp. 372-382). New York: McGraw-Hill.

Scott, Joan W. (1990). Deconstructing equality-versus-difference: Or, the uses of poststructuralist theory for feminism. In M. Hirsch & E. Fox (Eds.), *Conflicts in feminism* (pp. 134-148). New York: Routledge.

Seccombe, Wally. (1986). Patriarchy stabilized: The construction of the male breadwinner norm in nineteenth-century Britain. *Social History, 11*, 53-75.

Seron, Carroll, & Ferris, Kerry. (1995). Negotiating professionalism: The gendered social capital of flexible time. *Work and Occupations, 22*, 23-47.

Shawver, Lois, & Dickover, Robert. (1986, August). Research perspectives: Exploding a myth. *Corrections Today*, pp. 30-34.

Sherman, Lewis J. (1975). Evaluation of policewomen on patrol in a suburban police department. *Journal of Police Science and Administration, 3*, 434-438.

Sichel, Joyce L., Friedman, Lucy N., Quint, Janice C., & Smith, Michael E. (1977). *Women on patrol: A pilot study of police performance in New York City.* Washington, DC: National Institute of Law Enforcement and Criminal Justice.

Simpson, Sally, & Elis, Lori. (1995). Doing gender: Sorting out the caste and crime conundrum. *Criminology, 33*, 47-82.

Sirianni, C., & Welsh, A. (1991). Through the prism of time: Temporal structures in post-modern America. In A. Wolfe (Ed.), *America at century's end* (pp. 421-439). Berkeley: University of California Press.

Skolnick, Jerome. (1966). *Justice without trial.* New York: John Wiley.

Skolnick, Jerome, & Bayley, David. (1986). *The new blue line: Police innovation in six American cities.* New York: Free Press.

Slotnick, Elliott E. (1984). Gender, affirmative action, and recruitment to the federal bench. *Golden Gate University Law Review, 14,* 519-571.

Smith, Dorothy. (1979). A sociology for women. In J. Sherman & B. Beck (Eds.), *The prism of sex: Essays in the sociology of knowledge* (pp. 135-187). Madison: University of Wisconsin Press.

Sokoloff, Natalie J. (1988). Contributions of Marxism and feminism to the sociology of women and work. In A. H. Stromberg & S. Harkness (Eds.), *Women working* (pp. 116-131). Mountain View, CA: Mayfield.

Spohn, Cassia. (1990). Decision making in sexual assault cases: Do black and female judges make a difference? *Women & Criminal Justice, 2,* 83-105.

Stacey, Judith, & Thorne, Barrie. (1985). The missing feminist revolution in sociology. *Social Problems, 32,* 301-316.

Stambaugh, Phoebe Morgan. (1995). *The promise of law: Understanding the sexual harassment complaint careers of women.* Unpublished Ph.D. dissertation, Arizona State University, Tempe.

Stanford Project. (1982). Law firms and lawyers with children: An empirical analysis of family/work conflict. *Stanford Law Review, 34,* 1263-1307.

Steirer, Richard. (1989). Women flourishing in correction department. American Justice Association Newsletter. Winter: 1.

Sulton, Cynthia, & Townsey, Roi. (1981). *A progress report on women in policing.* Washington, DC: Police Foundation.

Sweet, Cheryl. (1995, January). Flirting with disaster. *Phoenix Magazine,* pp. 53-58.

Swerdlow, Marian. (1989). Men's accommodations to women entering a nontraditional occupation: A case of rapid transit operatives. *Gender & Society, 3,* 373-387.

Sykes, Gary. (1985). The functional nature of police reform: The "myth"' of controlling the police. *Justice Quarterly, 2,* 52-65.

Sykes, Gresham M. (1958). *The society of captives.* Princeton, NJ: Princeton University Press.

Task Force on Corrections. (1973). *Task force report: Corrections.* Washington, DC: Government Printing Office.

Toch, Hans. (1980). *Therapeutic communities in corrections*. New York: Praeger.

Trice, Harrison M. (1993). *Occupational subcultures in the workplace*. Ithaca, NY: International Labor Relations Press.

U.S. Department of Justice, Bureau of Justice Statistics. (1992a). *Justice expenditure and employment, 1990* (Bulletin NCJ-135777). Washington, DC: Author.

U.S. Department of Justice, Bureau of Justice Statistics. (1992b, February). *State and local police departments, 1990* (Bulletin NIC-133284). Washington, DC: Author.

U.S. Department of Justice, Federal Bureau of Investigation. (1981). *Uniform crime reports 1980*. Washington, DC: Government Printing Office.

U.S. Department of Justice, Federal Bureau of Investigation. (1986). *Uniform crime reports 1985*. Washington, DC: Government Printing Office.

U.S. Department of Justice, Federal Bureau of Investigation. (1991). *Uniform crime reports 1990*. Washington, DC: Government Printing Office.

U.S. Department of Justice, Federal Bureau of Investigation. (1994). *Uniform crime reports 1993*. Washington, DC: Government Printing Office.

U.S. Department of Labor. (1990). *Employment and earnings, 38*. Washington, DC: Government Printing Office.

Van Voorhis, Patricia, Cullen, Francis T., Link, Bruce G., & Wolfe, Nancy Travis. (1991). The impact of race and gender on correctional officers' orientation to the integrated environment. *Journal of Research in Crime and Delinquency, 28*, 472-500.

Vasu, Michael L., & Vasu, Ellen Storey. (1991). Gender stereotypes and discriminatory behaviors toward female attorneys: The North Carolina case. *Campbell Law Review, 13*, 183-207.

Walby, Sylvia. (1986). *Patriarchy at work*. Minneapolis: University of Minnesota Press.

Walker, Samuel. (1977). *A critical history of police reform*. Lexington: Lexington Books.

Walker, Samuel. (1983). *The police in America: An introduction*. New York: McGraw-Hill.

Walker, Samuel. (1985). Racial minority and female employment in policing: Implications of "glacial" change. *Crime and Delinquency, 31,* 555-572.

Walker, Samuel, & Martin, Susan E. (1994, November). *Women and minorities moving up the ranks.* Paper presented at the annual meeting of the American Society of Criminology, Miami, FL.

Waters, Malcolm. (1989). Patriarchy and viriarchy: An exploration and reconstruction of concepts of masculine domination. *Sociology, 23,* 193-211.

Weiss, Catherine, & Melling, Louis. (1988). The legal education of twenty women. *Stanford Law Review, 40,* 1297-1344.

Wells, Alice S. (1932). Twenty-two years a police woman. *The Western Woman, 7,* 15-16.

West, Candace, & Fenstermaker, Sarah. (1993). Power, inequality, and the accomplishment of gender: An ethnomethodological view. In P. England (Ed.), *Theory on gender/feminism on theory* (pp. 151-174). New York: Aldine.

West, Candace, & Fenstermaker, Sarah. (1995). Doing difference. *Gender & Society, 9,* 8-37.

West, Candace, & Zimmerman, Don H. (1987). Doing gender. *Gender & Society, 1,* 125-151.

Westley, William. (1970). *Violence and the police.* Cambridge: MIT Press.

Wexler, Judie G., & Logan, Deanna D. (1983). Sources of stress among women police officers. *Journal of Police Science and Administration, 13,* 98-105.

White, Sam E., & Marino, Kenneth E. (1983). Job attitudes and police stress: An exploratory study of causation. *Journal of Police Science and Administration, 11,* 264-274.

Williams, Christine L. (1989). *Gender differences at work: Women and men in nontraditional occupations.* Berkeley: University of California Press.

Williams, Joan. (1990). Sameness, feminism, and the work-family conflict: Faulty framework: Consequences of the difference model for women in the law. *New York Law School Law Review, 35,* 347-360.

Worden, Alissa P. (1993). The attitudes of women and men in policing: Testing conventional and contemporary wisdom. *Criminology, 31,* 203-242.

Wright, Kevin N., & Saylor, William G. (1991). Male and female employees' perceptions of prison work: Is there a difference? *Justice Quarterly, 8,* 505-524.

Young, Iris M. (1981). Beyond the unhappy marriage: A critique of dual systems theory. In L. Sargent (Ed.), *Women and revolution* (pp. 43-69). Boston: South End.

Young, Iris M. (1990). *Justice and the politics of difference.* Princeton, NJ: Princeton University Press.

Young, Malcolm. (1991). *An inside job: Policing and police culture in Britain.* Oxford: Clarendon.

Zaretsky, Eli. (1978). The effects of the economic crisis on the family. In Radical Political Economic Collective (Eds.) *U.S. capitalism in crisis* (pp. 209-218). New York: Union for Radical Political Economics.

Zimmer, Lynn E. (1986). *Women guarding men.* Chicago: University of Chicago Press.

Zimmer, Lynn E. (1987). How women reshape the prison guard role. *Gender & Society, 1,* 415-431.

Zimmer, Lynn E. (1989). Solving women's employment problems in corrections: Shifting the burden to administrators. *Women in Criminal Justice, 1,* 55-79.

Zupan, Linda L. (1986). Gender-related differences in correctional officers' perceptions and attitudes. *Journal of Criminal Justice, 14,* 349-361.

Zupan, Linda L. (1990, March). *The employment of women in local jails.* Paper presented at the annual meeting of the Academy of Criminal Justice Sciences, Denver, CO.

Zupan, Linda L. (1992). The progress of women correctional officers in all-male prisons. In I. Moyer (Ed.), *The changing role of women in the criminal justice system* (2nd ed., pp. 323-343). Prospect Heights, IL: Waveland.

Cases Cited

Bradwell v. Illinois, 83 U.S. 130 (1872).

Bundy v. Jackson, 641 F.2d 934 (D.C. Cir., 1981).

Dothard v. Rawlinson, 433 U.S. 321 (1977).

Geduldig v. Aiello, 417 U.S. 484 (1974).

General Electric Company v. Gilbert, 429 U.S. 125 (1976).

Motion to Admit Goodell, 39 Wis 232 (1875).

Griggs v. Duke Power Co., 401 U.S. 424 (1971).

Grummett v. Rushen, 779 F.2d 491 (9th Cir., 1985).

Hardin v. Stynchcomb, 691 F.2d 1364 (11th Cir., 1982).

Harris v. Forklift Systems, Slip Opinion 92-1168 (1993).

Hishon v. King & Spalding, 467 U.S. 69 (1984).

Kohn v. Royall, Koegel & Wells, 59 F.R.D. 515 (S.D.N.Y. 1973), appeal dismissed, 496 F.2d 1094 (2nd Cir. 1974).

Meritor Savings Bank FSB v. Vinson, 477 U.S. 57 (1986).

Price Waterhouse v. Hopkins, 109 S.Ct. 1775 (1989).

Reynolds v. Wise, 375 F.Supp. 145 (N.D. Texas, 1974).

Roe v. Wade, 410 U.S. 113 (1973).

Author Index

249

Subject Index

About the Authors

Susan Ehrlich Martin is a Health Scientist Administrator at the National Institute on Alcohol Abuse and Alcoholism and directs its research programs on alcohol and interpersonal violence, alcohol in the worksite, women's alcohol-related problems, and alcohol and injury. She was formerly a project director at the Police Foundation in Washington, D.C., where she conducted studies, including an examination of the status of women in policing. Her previous and continuing research interests focus on women's problems as workers, victims, and substance abusers. She holds a B.A. in history from Swarthmore College, an M.S. in education from the University of Rochester, and a Ph.D. in sociology from the American University.

Nancy Jurik is Associate Professor of Justice Studies at Arizona State University. She has published research in the areas of women and crime, women in corrections, and other gender and work issues. Her ongoing research focuses on women and men in home businesses and self-employment loan programs in the United States. She is especially interested in issues surrounding gender and enpowerment claims developing in contemporary employment-related social programs. She holds a B. A. and M. A. in sociology from Southern Methodist University, and a Ph. D. in sociology from the University of California, Santa Barbara.